War and the Transformation of Global Politics

Rethinking Peace and Conflict Studies

Series Editor: **Oliver Richmond**, Reader, School of International Relations, University of St. Andrews

Titles include:

Jason Franks
RETHINKING THE ROOTS OF TERRORISM

Vivienne Jabri
WAR AND THE TRANSFORMATION OF GLOBAL POLITICS

James Ker-Lindsay
EU ACCESSION AND UN PEACEKEEPING IN CYPRUS

Roger MacGinty
NO WAR, NO PEACE
The Rejuvenation of Stalled Peace Processes and Peace Accords

Carol McQueen
HUMANITARIAN INTERVENTION AND SAFETY ZONES
Iraq, Bosnia and Rwanda

Sergei Prozorov
UNDERSTANDING CONFLICT BETWEEN RUSSIA AND THE EU
The Limits of Integration

Oliver P. Richmond
THE TRANSFORMATION OF PEACE

Rethinking Peace and Conflict Studies
Series Standing Order ISBN 1–4039–9575–3 (hardback) & 1–4039–9576–1 (paperback)

You can receive future titles in this series as they are published by placing a standing order. Please contact your bookseller or, in case of difficulty, write to us at the address below with your name and address, the title of the series and the ISBN quoted above.

Customer Services Department, Macmillan Distribution Ltd, Houndmills, Basingstoke, Hampshire RG21 6XS, England

War and the Transformation of Global Politics

Vivienne Jabri
Department of War Studies
King's College London, UK

First published 2007 by
PALGRAVE MACMILLAN
Houndmills, Basingstoke, Hampshire RG21 6XS and
175 Fifth Avenue, New York, N. Y. 10010
Companies and representatives throughout the world

PALGRAVE MACMILLAN is the global academic imprint of the Palgrave Macmillan division of St. Martin's Press, LLC and of Palgrave Macmillan Ltd. Macmillan® is a registered trademark in the United States, United Kingdom and other countries. Palgrave is a registered trademark in the European Union and other countries.

ISBN-13: 978–0–230–00657–7   hardback
ISBN-10: 0–230–00657–4   hardback

This book is printed on paper suitable for recycling and made from fully managed and sustained forest sources.

A catalogue record for this book is available from the British Library.

Library of Congress Cataloging-in-Publication Data
Jabri, Vivienne, 1958-
    War and the transformation of global politics / Vivienne Jabri.
        p. cm.
    ISBN-13: 978–0–230–00657–7 (cloth)
    ISBN-10: 0–230–00657–4 (cloth)
    1. War. 2. Peace. 3. World politics–1989- I. Title.

JZ6385.J33 2007
355.02–dc22   2006051441

10   9   8   7   6   5   4   3   2   1
16   15   14   13   12   11   10   09   08   07

Printed and bound in Great Britain by
Antony Rowe Ltd, Chippenham and Eastbourne

For Mary Nankivell

Contents

Preface and Acknowledgements

The subject matter of this book started germinating a number of years ago when critical thought in International Relations began to question the primacy of the state as the location of politics, conceiving the political in other spaces, from the local to the transnational. Many, specifically within cosmopolitan discourses and ranging from feminism, to Frankfurt School critical theory, to poststructuralism, sought to conceive of a post-Westphalian global order that called for rethinking not just the formative texts of International Relations, but our understanding of borders, difference, and the shifting dynamics of inclusion and exclusion in a globalised arena. One major element that it seemed to me required particular attention within the critical genre of the discipline was the place of war and violence in such transformations. My aim in this book is precisely to address this question.

My previous book *Discourses on Violence* (1996), aimed to uncover the discursive and institutional continuities and practices that reproduce war and violent conflict. The aim here is to explore the place of war in the transformations that we witness in global politics. I highlight above the intellectual impetus for this project. However, the more immediate context that has in many ways functioned as the driving force behind this project are the wars and acts of violence that have so dominated global politics in the recent past, from the wars of intervention in the Gulf and the Balkans, to the violence of September 11th and its aftermath in the invasions of Afghanistan and Iraq, to the wider so-called 'war against terrorism', all having profound impact on our conceptions of politics and its locations, the international and its locations, the role of the state in relation to its citizens, the place of humanity as such and its tense relationship with the state and the international. My intellectual agenda was hence reinforced by the events of the world, events that were immediately global in their implications, not just in relation to institutional practices, but more significantly for the lived experience of individuals, communities, and populations, whose lives have been affected by a seemingly perpetual presence of violence in our late modern context.

The book is throughout inspired by the writings of Michel Foucault and his analytics of war and power. War in Foucault's work is never confined to the battlefield, but permeates deep into the social sphere and the practices of control that govern social relations. While Foucault himself confined his investigations to the domestic sphere, my aim here is to shift analysis to the global arena and hence to place the spotlight on the relationship between war and the transformations of the international as a distinct political space, one that is at the same time interlaced with social relations that transcend the domestic/international divide. The aim is hence to show how the wars of late modernity seek to reconstitute this global arena, so that war becomes a tool of control that is now globally manifest, problematising modern distinctions between the inside and outside, the sovereign state and the anarchic international, zones of peace and zones of violence, war and security, war and peace.

The book is hence as much about war as it is about peace, as much about modern continuities and their late modern manifestations. The aim throughout is not only to provide an understanding of the present, but to locate this in the context of a powerful past, a modern legacy that sought some element of certainty and a late modernity that reveals the apotheosis of modernity and its paradoxes, its critical ethos on the one hand and its violence and exclusions on the other.

There are a number of individuals who have been sources of inspiration, encouragement, and support, and without whom this book could not have been completed. I want to first of all thank Oliver Richmond, editor of the Palgrave Macmillan series, *Rethinking Peace and Conflict Studies*, for early comments on the project and his support. I also want to thank Rob Walker, who is a constant source of challenge and intellectual inspiration. Just as Oliver insists that I focus on peace as much as war, so too Rob insists that I be especially attentive to the international and its conceptualisation. I hope the book heeds both calls and provides some food for thought.

My gratitude also goes to King's College London for granting me with the sabbatical leave necessary for the completion of the book. I am also grateful to the European Commission Framework Six funded project, *Challenge: European Liberty and Security*, which has been a valuable source of funding for the dissemination of aspects of this work in workshops and conferences.

I am, in addition, indebted, to so many people for ongoing exchanges of ideas and conversations. I want to specifically thank Claudia Aradau, Didier Bigo, Jenny Edkins, Elspeth Guild, Jef Huysmans, Andrew Neal, and Raia Prokhovnik for their engagement and comments on various aspects of my work. All of the above have a generosity of spirit and an intellectual strength that is always sustaining and enabling. I am grateful to Christine Sylvester for her friendship and encouragement through the years that I have known her.

There are also a number of people in the Department of War Studies without whose support this book would not have been completed. I especially want to thank my Head of Department, Brian Holden Reid, for his support in seeking my sabbatical leave. I am also grateful to individuals who took on my duties while I was away. Primary among these are, once again Claudia Aradua, Didier Bigo, and Elspeth Guild, as well as Mervyn Frost, Cornelia Navari, Peter Busch and Mike Goodman.

At Palgrave, I am grateful especially to Alison Howson, Gemma d'Arcy Hughes and Shirley Tan.

I am, as always, dependent on my friends and family for the unconditional love which sustains me. Specifically, I want to mention Mary Nankivell, Diana Davies, Dorian Jabri, Chris Smith, and Jennie Wilson. All in their own ways show me that relationships are the ultimate source of beauty in life.

1
Introduction: Understanding War and Violence

The practice of violence, like all action, changes the world, but the most probable change is to a more violent world.

Hannah Arendt[1]

Practices of violence permeate the global arena. They take form in diverse locations, from the complex decision-making structures of governments to the most clandestine and informal processes associated with networks to the invisible private location of the individual planning a destructive act. Violence in late modernity has this wide span of operations, manifest at times in inter-state conflicts, but mostly involving practices that are transnational in their locations. Just as the spatial terrain of violence can be global in reach, so too the temporal element of political violence transcends the immediacy of the battlefield. The late modern condition, with its intensified social relations, renders proximate distant events so that practices of violence are almost immediately brought forth into the global space, rendering war in late modernity immediately accessible to the judgement of this arena in all its diverse manifestations, public and private. The use of violence as a form of political practice is situated in contests over interests, values and resources; however, its enabling conditions stem from discursive and institutional continuities that are deep-rooted in social relations.

The aim of this investigation is to contribute towards understanding the relationship between war and politics. In particular, as the title of the study suggests, it concentrates on war and its implications for contemporary international politics, suggesting that practices of political violence, including the wars conducted by states, constitute a global matrix of war that incorporates not just a diversity of agents, but a complex array of interactions that draw upon the globality of the contemporary era in seeking to affect change both locally and globally. War in late modernity is at one and the same time both transformative of global relations as well as being subject in turn to the globalising transformations associated with late modernity. Drawing primarily on Michel Foucault's understanding of war and relations of power, but steering a course from Kant's modern conception of peace through to Habermas's late modern rendition on cosmopolitan peace, the aim is to present an understanding of war as a practice situated in social relations, presenting a picture of the intimate and constitutive relationship between war and peace. While Foucault himself confined his analytics to the domestic sphere of the liberal democratic state, this investigation locates its analysis in the global arena, placing emphasis on the international as a political space that is nevertheless deeply interlaced with social relations that transcend the domestic and the international. Understanding war in these terms suggests from the outset that war, like other tools of power, is a mechanism implicated in practices of control encompassing spaces across the globe. As a technology of social control, when manifest globally, war is also transformative of such relations so that it is now always problematic to claim distinctions between the inside and outside, the domestic and the international, the zone of civic peace and the zone of war, the sovereign state and the anarchic outside. The violence of late modernity is implicated in the realisation of such indistinctions, so that the transformations of the global political space, including the inscription of this space in cosmopolitan terms, cannot be understood in the absence of an analysis that places the spotlight on the place of war in relation to global politics.

A critical understanding

Writing on war and violence in the present context of global politics the author is presented with a number of choices relating to the framing of the project; substantively in relation to history, epistemologically in relation to the construction of knowledge, and ontologically in relation to the elements seen as the driving forces behind war and its place in social and political life. It is tempting, historically, to start with the war that currently preoccupies the author, locating this in the context of the dynamics of present-day global politics, which in turn must be placed in the historical trajectory that superseded the present. It is also tempting to start with an epistemological framing, one that is immediately sceptical of the pretences of "scientific" approaches, preferring instead a hermeneutic approach more suited to the study of human action and human society. Not content with the recognition that meaning frames our understanding of the world, the author reflects on their own positionality with respect to the present and its wars, the present and its contests, so that interpretation is not objectified in turn, so that what the author states, how the author investigates, is itself always already of the world, of politics.

A core component of discourses on war centres on the idea that it can be subject to regulation, both moral and institutional. From St Augustine, to St Aquinas, to later and more contemporary "just war" thinkers, the predominant view is that humanity possesses the doctrines necessary for placing limits on war, both in terms of its availability as a choice in response to context and in terms of conduct once this choice is taken.[2] The regulation of war also forms a significant element in the writings of Vattel, Pufendorf and Grotius, wherein emphasis is placed on international law as the vehicle through which an international "society" of states could function as the limit superimposed upon the anarchical international system, a limit defining a set of normative constraints on state behaviour.[3] The trajectory of war's place in the discipline of International Relations again suggests a predominant interest in the regulation of war.[4] The initial interest, in the immediate aftermath of the First World War, was in the amelioration of the condition of war through a greater scholarly understanding of the conditions that made war and its devastations possible. We see here largely a historical and legal framing of war between states, with a concomitant interest in developing the international institutions that would render war undesirable or even irrational. There was here a predominantly liberal internationalist concern with establishing international capacities for the prevention of future war, capacities centred on ideas relating to collective security underpinned by international law and international institutions.[5] Even as the ideals of liberal internationalism came up against the realist challenge, it remains the case that the discipline's structuring ideas centre, as authors such as E.H. Carr and Hedley Bull showed all too clearly, around the dual notions of power and regulated order.[6] Later, as some in the field sought the application of the methods of the natural sciences, this interest in the amelioration of the condition of war as an aspect of the human condition gives way to concerns over method; a positivist ethos wherein the criteria of science could rely on a strict divide between the object world investigated and the realm of the epistemic subject. The focus of interest had shifted from one centred on the regulation of war to discovering causal explanations for war's occurrence.[7] However, while much of this scientific endeavour in International Relations sought to inductively discern regularity in the correlation of factors that led to war, the aspiration to achieve the ultimate prize in science, namely causation, appeared to remain beyond reach. Until that is, the "structure" of international relations came to be of significance in framing a distinct theory of international relations,[8] so that the causes of war could be located in the structure of the international system. The overriding assumption here was that just as the presence of particular elements in the atmosphere could cause a hurricane, so too the presence of particular dynamics in the international system could enable war.[9] Others, similarly causally inclined, sought understanding in terms of decision-makers; that interests defined by statespersons, identify the conditions wherein war may be seen as the continuation of policy, following Clausewitz, through other means.[10]

The "scientific" approach to the study of international relations generally and of war in global politics in particular seeks to establish rules by which the construction of theories and their testing could be prejudged. According to Habermas's interpretation of such criteria,

> Theories comprise hypothetico-deductive connections of propositions, which permit the deduction of lawlike hypotheses with empirical content. The latter can be interpreted as statements about the co-variance of observable events; given a set of initial conditions, they make predictions possible... However, the meaning of such predictions, that is, their technical exploitability, is established only by the rules according to which we apply theories to reality.[11]

These rules ground theory in empirical observational statements seen as "reliable in providing immediate evidence without the admixture of subjectivity."[12] This dualism between the object world observed and the subject world of the observer is crucial in any positivist approach to the philosophy of science built on a constitutive interest in "technical control of objectified processes".[13] What is crucial to understand in this framework of understanding is that the observational statements relied upon in establishing the validity of claims are seen as un-problematically corresponding to reality.

There is evidently much written in politics and international relations on the applicability or otherwise of the criteria used in the judgement of theories in the natural sciences to the social sciences and these will not be rehearsed once again in the context of this book.[14] A point that must, however, be reiterated in the present context is that the study of human action and human society raises a fundamental criterion of demarcation that differentiates this realm from natural systems, namely the human capacity to not simply utilise language, but to do so in the interpretation of the world. While some in the philosophy of the social sciences prefer a strict dividing line between the natural and social sciences, conferring to the former the capacity to provide "explanations" of phenomena and the latter hermeneutic "understandings" of human action,[15] what is important to draw from this debate is that, in the field of the social, that which in the study of nature may be thought of in terms of the subject/object dualism, is in the social sciences an inter-subjective interaction, a subject-subject relationship. In Habermas's terms, "Access to the facts is provided by the understanding of meaning, not observation." Hermeneutic knowledge is, as Habermas states, "mediated" through the interpreter's "pre-understanding" so that the "subject of understanding" is always implicated in what is essentially an inter-subjective space of understanding. This relocation of the subject in systems of knowledge is crucial in any critical understanding of the social and political sphere and directs attention, as we will see below to the linguistic framing of the world, in this context, of war and global politics. It is crucial to appreciate, however, that such a relocation of the subject in systems of knowledge by no means implies a wholesale rejection of a capacity to provide "nomological knowledge", law-like statements about social systems. An example here might relate to the workings of capitalism, those elements and relationships which define, and indeed constitute, a capitalist structure and the forms of outcomes that such a structure can produce. The materiality of the world produces consequences that are not simply a product of interpretation or even discursive construction. To suggest otherwise would in effect be to deny the possibility of a critical social science and its capacity to reveal the workings of power in socio-political and economic relations.

It is in this sense, the capacity to unravel claims to validity, that Habermas can suggest that any critical reflection seeks to go beyond the production of nomological knowledge: "It is concerned with going beyond this goal to determine when theoretical statements grasp invariant regularities of social action as such and when they express ideologically frozen relations of dependence that can in principle be transformed."[16] Habermas uses the concept of "self-reflection" to suggest a process whereby theoretical statements set in train a process of reflection on the mutability and/or transformability of their assumed law-like character. War may hence be seen as an invariant product of the anarchical international system; but any critical reflection unpacks the taken-for granted elements of this theoretical viewpoint, including the idea of anarchy as the immutable feature of the international system. Any critical understanding of war and its place in global politics relates it to structures of domination, including not just the material forces of social and political life, but the discourses surrounding war and its legitimisation. Writing in the aftermath of the September 11th 2001 attacks in the United States, James Der Derian states: "I believe the best the academician can do is to thickly describe, robustly interrogate, and directly challenge the authorized truths and official actions of all parties who posited a world view of absolute differences in need of final solutions."[17]

In presenting a distinctly critical reading of the place of war in the transformation of global politics, this investigation appreciates Habermas's understanding of what constitutes a critical social science, but seeks to go further in its emphasis throughout on the relationship between knowledge and power, a relationship that is core to Michel Foucault's corpus. To this relationship, Foucault adds a third, namely subjectivity, so that this triptych, power, knowledge, and subjectivity frames the current investigation into war and its various articulations in contemporary global politics. Foucault's analytic of truth inquires into the constitution of knowledge; what comes to be taken as said at a particular time in history, just as his analytic of power reveals that the problem of knowledge is not one of epistemology but of politics, and hence relations of struggle and contestation. In this sense, the subject of knowledge is not the transcendent Cartesian self, but a subject constituted in relation to as well as being implicated in systems of knowledge and relations of power. Crucially, this does not imply the "relativisation" of the subject, "a subject that evolves through the course of history", but rather providing an account of the "constitution of knowledges, discourses, domains of objects...without having to make reference to a subject which is either transcendental in relation to the field of events or runs in its empty sameness throughout the course of history."[18] The idea of critique, therefore, of critical reflection, does not inhabit a space that is exterior to the world and its events; it is rather of the world and hence of politics. The aim of critical thought in Foucault is not only to provide what Deleuze, writing of Foucault, refers as a "diagnostic" of our present, but includes "analysing and reflecting upon limits" coupled with "an experiment with the possibility of going beyond them."[19]

This book draws on critical social and political theory to develop an understanding of the ways in which political violence and war are, in the late modern age, redefining politics and the sphere of the international. In highlighting the domination of contemporary politics by discourses and practices that reinforce a politics of antagonism and existential threat, the book provides inroads into a critical reading of the present, pointing to the dangers that lie at the heart of such practices, dangers that have manifest implications not only for the liberal democratic state, but for the emergence of a global sphere of interaction based on mutual recognition. The book suggests that any critical reading of international politics must at once incorporate both critique and a transformative agenda based on an alternative reading of politics, one that, in late modernity, must recognise the complexity of political agency and its location, not just in relation to the continuities of power, but also in the interactive sphere of public discourse and contestation.

When Andrew Linklater wrote in *The Transformation of Political Community*[20] of the potential emergence of what he called a "dialogical community" as the basis of a post-Westphalian international politics, his emphasis was on the transformative potential of dialogue and the recognition of difference as the basis of interaction in international relations. What we witness today is the prevalence of war and the politics of antagonism.

In recognising the historic significance of the complex interplay between state-building, war, and capitalism, Linklater points to the paradoxes of modern political communities, paradoxes that have witnessed the intensification of control and exclusion on the one hand, and the expansion of what he calls a "moral community" based on inclusion on the other. The challenge that emerges from Linklater's account, a challenge salient for any critical theorist in International Relations, is precisely faced in the present context of international politics. For, the paradoxes that Linklater highlights are, in late modernity, emergent from the extreme intensification of the institutions of modernity, specifically the state as the location of constraint and enablement, war as a global sphere of operations, and a neoliberal order implicated in such operations. Understanding the place of war and political violence in the present context thus demands that they be located in relation to the institutional backdrop that defines late modern political life.

Much of critical thought, from Michel Foucault's analytics of the relationship between war and the social sphere to Michael Mann's rendition on war and social power, reveal war's presence as a continuity in modern society.[21] These readings provide the starting assumptions of the analysis the book provides, for it seeks to reveal the transformative impact of recent wars, including Afghanistan, Iraq, and the more widely defined so-called "war against terrorism". What we see in the late modern context of boundless and limitless warfare is the dismantling of traditional conceptions of state boundaries and their associated rules and the emergence of a global sovereign subjectivity that regards the global within its sphere of operations. As we have seen in relation to recent cases of incarceration without due process, practices interpreted by many as constituting, following Agamben, the politics of exception,[22] this raises fundamental questions for the liberal democratic state and emergent global discourses on rights. Of crucial significance in understanding these wars, as will be shown later in this investigation, is that they are not only conducted by modern liberal states, but are deemed to be "liberal wars", aimed at the transformation of the international from a location subject to the restrictions of sovereignty to one that is primarily defined in terms of humanity as a whole.

The book will therefore address the question of how we might understand the current "global matrix of war"[23] and its implications for the international as a distinct juridico-political space that, in an era of globalised social, economic, and political relations, is no longer solely defined in terms of sovereign states, but in terms that invoke cosmopolitan conceptions of political community, rights, and humanity at large. The aim of Chapter Two will be to unravel the complex interconnections that constitute what I am referring to as the global matrix of war. While the study acknowledges that there are a plethora of different types of conflicts, past and present, that might be drawn upon in understanding the dynamics of antagonism and war, what is of particular interest in the present context are wars that have a global remit; in other words, wars the agents of which consider the global space as an arena for their operations. Such wars have profound implications, not in the sense that they diminish the significance of the state, but in their potential capacity to redefine the sphere of the international and its social, political, and juridical articulation. The cosmopolitan rendering of such rearticulation is taken up in Chapter Three, where I consider Immanuel Kant's treatise on "perpetual peace", its conditions of possibility and the contemporary interpretation of the Kantian project through Jurgen Habermas's conception of "cosmopolitan peace." Both are formative voices in liberal conceptions of the international and the universalising imperative that constitutes the project of modernity. This discussion provides a background to an analysis, in Chapter Four, of the close and intricate relationship between the liberal reordering of the world and the global matrix of war. Concentrating on wars constructed in terms of the rescue and protection of populations, the chapter explores the global remit of these wars, their location in relation to the ongoing project of modernity, and their constitutive role in re-defining the sphere of the international. The chapter highlights the dangers and contradictions implicated in these interventionist wars, dangers that become apparent in the ways in which boundaries are redrawn, exclusions reestablished. Such exclusions become apparent in Chapter Five, where the global matrix of war is shown to be imbricated with racial and cultural signification, where the project of modernity comes face to face with its postcolonial other. As will be shown through this interrogation of the consequences of the so-called liberal wars of the present, wars that, in the post-September 11th context, with the invasions of Afghanistan and Iraq and the wider global war against terrorism, now include those defined in terms of security, any cosmopolitan rearticulation of the international must at the same time subject itself to imminent critique, recognising thereby its own particularity in political discourse. This theme is taken up in the final concluding chapter to this investigation, Chapter Six, which seeks an alternative reading of a distinctly political form of cosmopolitanism, one that is not constitutively reliant on a global matrix of war, but one, nevertheless that recognises the political significance of global solidarities and the contests implicated in political mobilisation around questions relating to war and peace and their location in relation to continuing transformations in the global polity at large.

The meaning of war

Any critical investigation must start with reflection upon its own terms, the language within which a project is framed. Initially, it is always a challenge to use both terms, "war" and "violence", in one sentence. To do so suggests a distinction between the two, perhaps alluding to the formal nature of war, involving legal entities called states, and the non-formality of violence, suggesting illegality and hence criminality, associated with non-state actors. There are many different types of war, from the inter-state to the civil, to wars of independence, usually involving guerrilla organisations. There are also wars of attrition, genocidal wars, network warfare and so on; classifications that inform more on the nature of the behaviour involved and the parties implicated than war *per se*, its complexities and its location in relation to other forms of human interaction, including the socio-political. War as a term also suggests the involvement of distinct entities, possessing defined grievances brought forth into an arena that is distinguished from the norm. Where violence can take place in the everyday and the routine of social encounters, war is seen as an extraordinary occurrence, a situation of crisis and existential danger. However, war constitutively involves direct violence, though the use of the term in recent times has expanded to cover policies aimed at the combat of undesirable social problems, such as the so-called "war on drugs" or the "war on obesity". The more recent coinage, "war on terrorism" is perhaps of the same genre and suggests the aspiration to defeat terrorism and those associated with terrorism. In framing the issues thus, terrorism becomes another social problem to be defeated and its perpetrators vanquished.

The politics of representation, how language is used to represent the reality of war and the use of violence, is central to any rendition on war and violence. To separate these two concepts is in many ways to sanitise war of its constitutive violence; that war's aim is direct injury against those deemed the enemy. The violence associated with war must hence be understood in terms that highlight discursive distinctions between war and violence; that there is a politics involved in using the two terms separately and in highlighting the association between them. In considering instances of violence in the twenty-first century we might highlight racist violence in the inner cities of Europe as well as the violence of what are deemed to be "humanitarian" wars of intervention. Both instances involve injurious acts aimed at the very corporeality of the other targeted. Both emerge from a particular political position which, while articulated differently, is nevertheless based on some notion of enmity. Both are based on the view, held by the perpetrators, that violence as such, violence as instrumentality, has the capacity to turn word into deed, to convert aim into achievement. While agreeing with Hans Joas when he states "there is not just an analytical need, but also a moral one, to create or increase our sensitivity to the distinctions between different kinds of acts of violence, instead of applying a global formula that reduces them all to the same level",[24] it is also important to highlight that which links different forms of what I prefer to understand as distinctly "political" modes of violence. Hence, the difference between the stabbing in a school yard associated with petty theft and the stabbing in a school yard associated with racial hatred. There is both an analytical and a moral need to understand the distinctly political bases of the latter and its historical link with other politically motivated articulations of violence. As Hannah Arendt points out specifically in relation to racist violence, "Violence in interracial struggle is always murderous, but it is not 'irrational'; it is the logical and rational consequence of racism, by which I do not mean some rather vague prejudice on either side, but an explicit ideological system."[25] It is in this sense that a distinctly political form of violence is articulated, but the relationship between violence and politics is itself subject to inquiry, just as representations of violence in discourse are in themselves contested and such contestation is nowhere more apparent than in acknowledging the place of injury in violent practices.

War is the perpetration of deliberate violence and is hence constitutively meaningful in terms of injury, or to be more precise, the affliction of injury upon the bodies and property of the enemy targeted. As Elaine Scarry points out, "war belongs to two larger categories of human experience...First, it is a form of violence; it is a member of a class of occurrences whose activity is 'injuring'. Second, it is a member of a class of occurrences that are contests."[26] The perpetration of violence against the enemy is then instrumental to the core, involving the making of decisions that perceive the injury of the other as the direct means through which socio-political objectives may be achieved. In this conception of war, Clausewitz's formulation appears loud and clear; that war is the continuation of policy through other means; the means are those of injurious coercion. And yet, the fact of injury is often, as Scarry points out, absent from renditions on war.[27] This distinctly human behaviour, built up and transformed through the centuries of human history, calls for sacrifice, importantly not just of the enemy and its population, but of self. The latter is highly significant, for unlike previous eras in the history of warfare, late modern war seeks to ameliorate the need for self-sacrifice; that war and hence the infliction of injury may take place in the near absence of harm to those perpetrating the act. We will return to this point later. Suffice it to point out at this stage that this aspiration for war in the absence of injury to the self is, in the context of the present juncture of history, one that dominates strategic thinking in the West, and hence has a particular cultural signification.[28]

War is injurious, it is corporeal, and it is societal. It is societal in that it inevitably involves populations and can transcend the boundaries of states, involving individuals and communities as well as organised units in the form of states. It is constitutively built upon antagonism and therefore enmity. It assumes the presence of threat and demands sacrifice, primarily of the other, but also of self, in the name of a greater good. War is hence also a manifestation of contest wherein an "other" is conceived and constructed as enemy, the target of violent acts. War in this sense constitutes violent conflict which in turn must be understood in social terms, implying not just the practices of situated agents, but deeply-rooted institutional forms that constitute the enabling conditions for violence, both materially and discursively. It is therefore not adequate to simply conceive of war's meaning in terms of its injurious acts, nor is it sufficient to locate war in instrumental rationality as a superficial reading of Clausewitz might suggest. For even in Clausewitz there emerge ontological commitments that see war as constitutive of individuality and political community conceived in this case as the nation.[29] Even in its most instrumental articulation, therefore, violence has a constitutive manifestation and is hence seen as being formative of the subject. This ontological commitment is also reflected in Sorel, whose understanding of the emergence of the subjectivity of a self-emancipating working class is also brought forth, enabled, through violence, an understanding that is clearly present in Walter Benjamin, as it is in Frantz Fanon's reading of the struggle of the colonised subject.[30] We might normatively wish to confine violence to instrumentality, for such confinement renders it somehow manageable and short term, but a failure to understand, and more importantly reveal, the constitutive role of violence in terms of subjectivity is itself normatively short term, for it limits our full understanding of how political violence relates to subjectivity and the social sphere.

The social sphere in itself contains deep-rooted discursive and institutional forms that provide the enabling conditions for war. The discourses of war draw upon deep-rooted articulations of affiliation and identity based on exclusionist social boundaries that are themselves reconstituted in the perpetration of violence against a constructed enemy.[31] There might be attempts at the separation of leaders and populations, as is evident in, for example, the recent wars in Afghanistan and Iraq, nevertheless populations are always involved, and not just as unintended targets, for they are at once both the inevitable target as well as being the source of collective identity and therefore political subjectivity. Existing social boundaries become sharpened in time of war, resulting in strategies that have, in the recent past, included the extremes of violence, as seen in the Rwandan genocide or the ethnic cleansing that was the defining feature of the Balkans, ongoing violence and exclusion, as seen in the Israeli-Palestinian conflict, and the communal profiling now associated with practices constituting the "war against terrorism". While these constitute historically different cases, they nevertheless are comparable in the discourses and practices of exclusion that enable the enactment of violence against the enemy other, and that come to sharply contrast the insiders from the outsiders, the affirmation of self as against an "other". As we will see later, in a late modern context of globalised social relations, uncertainty, and fragmentation, such constructions of self and other come to be manifest in increasingly transnational terms.

The enabling conditions that also constitute the discourses of war centre on practices of legitimisation. In a statement that has resonance throughout this investigation, Arendt points out,

> Violence is by nature instrumental; like all means, it always stands in need of guidance and justification through the end it pursues. And what needs justification by something else cannot be the essence of anything. The end of war – end taken in its twofold meaning – is peace or victory; but to the question And what is the end of peace? There is no answer...[32]

I will return to the question "what is the end of peace" later in this study. What is important to highlight in this introduction to the understanding of war is that war always stands in need of justification and such justification forms the language of war as much as this language itself relies on matrices of inclusion and exclusion. Such justification is framed by a language of strategy and morality, both of which are mutually dependent in the two formative categories of the just war doctrine, namely *jus ad bellum*, or justified cause, and *jus in bello*, or justice in the conduct of war. From St Augustine's *City of God* to Michael Walzer's *Just and Unjust War*, the formative assumption in this language of war is that some notion of "justice", or some notion of "good", must override considerations of peace defined as the absence of war. The discourse of just war is structured around inclusion and exclusion. It assumes that the use of force is claimed by a legitimate authority, taken in recent times as the sovereign state, though as we will see later, the attribution of sovereignty in late modernity is itself subject to contestation. Force is directed against a defined enemy, and the location of this enemy is itself of interest in conditions wherein enemies may be internal and external, located increasingly in indeterminate transnational spaces just as much as they can still be other states, and other collective categories. That moral concepts rely on strategic concepts in this enabling doctrine of war is especially evident in *jus in bello* criteria that seek to differentiate combatant from non-combatant or that seek to define "proportionality". In a late modern context of high technology warfare, punishment is collective, even as the civilian casualties of war are often deemed to be "unintended" or the "collateral damage" of high-precision targeting. That strategic and normative (just war) discourses on war constitute together the "structuring language of war" is dealt with in another study and will not be repeated here.[33] What is important to highlight is that elements of the just war doctrine, though contested, are nevertheless formative of the regulative aspects of established rules of war where moral expectations associated with the conduct of war are a defining, and many would argue, a settled aspect of the international law of war, though this is now increasingly contested. The regulation of behaviour in war is expressed in a number of international conventions, including the Hague and Geneva Conventions, both constituting important elements in humanity's attempts to regulate war, to confer it rules that might be drawn upon in our judgement of violent acts committed in the name of some greater cause. The need for justification must be understood in the context of judgement, and such judgement may be made on strategic instrumental grounds just as it may be made on moral grounds. Both, however, are always contested and hence always political.

How a war is justified and which judgements reach the public sphere are intricately related to existing structures of domination, including dominant discursive practices. These too constitute the enabling conditions for war. As indicated above, wars share discursive repertoires framed around justification and rationalisation. The linguistic constructs that frame such repertoires draw upon existing social boundaries just as they are implicated in the sharpening of such boundaries of inclusion and exclusion in time of violence. The inside and outside, the self and other, the included and the excluded submerge individuality and international division in the name of cohesion, consensus, and solidarity internally and the monolithic and hence predictable representation of the enemy externally. The boundary between the internal and the external, the self and other, is however, increasingly in flux and how such boundaries are drawn becomes, as will be shown later, of central interest in contemporary practices associated with war. Suffice it to point out at this stage that the discourses of war, both in the form of the distinctions drawn between self and other and in the legitimisation of war, rely on some conception of bounded political community, and in the modern era, the political community centrally implicated in war is the modern state as a social formation. As we will see later, a crucial element of transformation in the late modern era relates to the transformations associated with the state in globalised social, economic, and political relations. Such transformations have implications not only for the state as the source of legitimacy in the enactment of violence, but for the ability of the modern state to contain and therefore to control political violence. How the state as a form of social organisation and as administrative unity relates to war in late modernity becomes a salient question when states cannot be conceptualised as like units in possession of sovereignty as the linchpin of autonomous action in a system of states. Weber's definition of the modern state could never apply equally to all proclaimed sovereign states in the modern international system: "A compulsory political organisation with continuous operations will be called a 'state' in so far as its administrative staff successfully upholds the claim to the *monopoly* of the *legitimate* use of physical force in the enforcement of its order."[34] The operative word here is "successfully", for the dominant mode of distinction in contemporary discourses utilised in the legitimisation of wars of intervention is that which distinguishes the "failed" state from all others.

However, even prior to such distinctions, the sovereign state is historically associated with violence. The transformations of one come to be of significance in the transformations of the other. The dominance of realism and neorealism in International Relations has in many ways disabled the discipline from making significant contributions to our understanding of how such transformations are historically inter-related, for the trajectory of thought, from Hobbes to present-day realist interpretations of the international system take the state as a given unit and see war as a product of the international system of states.[35] Other than the capabilities of the state in comparison with other states, the variability of the state as a coherent administrative unity is not taken into account. The significance of such variability comes to the forefront of analysis when we take into account sociological discourses on the state. With the Weberian understanding of the modern state being central, authors such as Michael Mann, Charles Tilly and Anthony Giddens, see a central importance in the relationship between internal control and the state's capacities in organised physical violence used internally to consolidate power and externally against the state's enemies. Internal consolidation in the emergence of the modern state involved not just the development of organised armed forces, but a greater specialisation and rationalisation of administrative institutions. State power over territorially bound populations is established, according to Michael Mann, through an interaction between increasingly sophisticated methods of administrative rule, in combination with the emergence of the "nation-state" which came to represent the citizen's sense of belonging within a specified political community.[36] Historically, the consolidation of power in the modern state as well as the emergence and use of nationalism as the basis of political community have involved, and indeed continue to involve, violence. Charles Tilly perhaps provides the strongest statement on the historical links between "war-making" and "state-making" in the modern era. Drawing an analogy with "protection rackets", Tilly reminds the reader that governments have historically created threats and then extracted resources for protection. The monopolisation of violence, according to Tilly came to serve four activities; war-making directed at outsiders; state-making directed at internal rivals; and the protection of clients, which Tilly interprets as the entrepreneurial class; and finally, extraction aimed to gather the resources requisite of these activities.[37] Giddens, in turn, draws upon these ideas as well as Michel Foucault's writings on surveillance and control to suggest a definition of the modern state as "the pre-eminent power container...a territorially bounded, administrative unity."[38] This definition, as will become clear is highly significant when thinking about the variability of states and contemporary transformations in the context of globalisation. Suffice it to say at this stage, that Giddens's conception of the modern state – borrowing heavily from Michel Foucault's understanding of disciplinary power – and its relation to violence highlights "surveillance" as a key attribute of the modern state, enabling the "pacification" of internal society and the relocation of violence externally. The "success", for want of a better term, of the modern state comes historically to rely on key developments in military organisation, innovations that can be exploited in military technology, and effectiveness in techniques of surveillance of internal societies, all of which contribute to the near marginalisation of violence within them, so that the military comes historically to be replaced by the police in maintaining civic order.

A number of elements emerge in the above sociological discourses on the historical trajectory of the modern state that are of vital significance in thinking about the relationship between violence, politics, and their transformations in the contemporary era. The first relates to state sovereignty and its transformations. Historically, as the above short review of the sociological literature indicates, sovereignty as the outward manifestation of statehood comes to be reliant on internal control. Secondly, the breakdown of such control, in administrative and coercive terms, comes to represent the breakdown of the state and hence, potentially, the loss of its sovereignty. In terms of responses to such breakdown, state-building comes to form a central concern, affirming what Giddens sees as the "norm of monopolistic state authority."[39] However, in the context of late modernity, where the transformation of spatiotemporal processes means, as Rob Walker highlights, that "simple distinctions between inside and outside may still provide a basis for rhetorics and chauvinisms but the hope that temporality may be tamed within the territorial spaces of sovereign states alone is visibly evaporating."[40] Sovereign power is in this sense relocated elsewhere and seeks to extend beyond the territorial boundaries of the state.[41] All three elements have violence as a constitutive force in such transformations.

In highlighting the discursive and institutional backdrop to war, the aim is to stress at the outset of this investigation that when agents make decisions relating to violence, they draw upon and are therefore enabled by existing social continuities. It is also to stress that just as violence and the form it takes impacts upon these continuities so too any discursive and institutional transformations feed into changes in the ways in which violence is enacted, its locations, and its modes of legitimisation. While it is important to recognise that war is, as Elaine Scarry points out above, about contest, it is indeed violent conflict, it is also important to recognise war's location in relation to the discursive and institutional context that enables and surrounds the use of violence in political confrontation. Such confrontation in turn suggests the existence of grievance articulated by distinct parties to a conflict, grievances which are themselves attributed to distinct enemies. However the limits of this conception of grievance are themselves highlighted by Johan Galtung's insistence on the notion of "structural violence";[42] that injury cannot be confined to manifest physical violence, but may derive from structural continuities that so unequally impact upon life chances, that their impact can be as devastating as manifest violence. While this particular study concentrates on the use of physical violence in situations of conflict, it nevertheless takes seriously the view that injury results from structural inequalities, including those that stem from discourse or speech,[43] a point that I will raise again later in this study.

As I state above, war is corporeal just as it is societal. In inflicting death, injury and destruction and in demanding sacrifice, it is constitutively a social phenomenon and being so is immediately transformative of social relations and social interactions. This "fact" of war, that it has transformative effects, has as we see above, been highlighted by other authors, those sociologically oriented, from Charles Tilly to Michael Mann to Anthony Giddens, to name but a few. What is important to highlight at this early stage is that the fact of war as a social phenomenon renders it constitutively associated with the condition of peace; that but for war peace would not be a possibility, could not form an aspect of the human imagination, could not, indeed be a meaningful concept. If war is considered to be transformative of social relations, then the peace of the latter is somehow historically dependent on the violence of the former. Once again, while this problematic association of war and peace will be returned to later in this study, it is nevertheless important at this early stage to simply highlight the historical, discursive, as well as ontological relationship between these very human conditions.

Narratives of war

Any reflection on war and its place in global politics must by necessity be influenced by the events of the world. At the present juncture of history, any discourse on war and violence has, within its sights, particular instances of war and violence that are assumed to be significant, politically and globally. The assumption of significance is, in itself, a matter not just of judgement by the social scientist as detached being, nor is it a matter of which conflicts gain greater coverage in a global media. Rather, significance accrues from the contingencies surrounding a particular event, the agents involved, the controversies surrounding decisions made, the wider impact of those decisions, as well as the discursive construction of particular events as significant. An immediate comparison of the discourses surrounding the Israeli-Palestinian conflict or the wars in the Balkans with conflicts in sub-Saharan Africa, such as the civil war in Sudan or that in Uganda provides certain clues as to the ways in which even those of us in the social sciences can be influenced by these wider discourses and the certainties that they generate. In terms of which events we select as formative of our analyses and renditions on war, which have had most influence, far better to acknowledge the author's situatedness within the wider social discourse than attempt any "scientific" measure of significance. Even this context is however uncertain in its effects on the rendition given, or the analysis provided. We might perhaps think, being located in London in 2005 and thereafter, that our starting point can be the events of July 7th 2005 and the bombings of London's public transport system. These events, as they unravelled, suggested at first some connection with Afghanistan, Pakistan, and the movement now known as Al Qaeda.[44] We might delve into the causes and find articulations that point to the invasion of Iraq, the conflict over Kashmir, or the Israeli-Palestinian conflict. These outward narratives, available in the public sphere, cannot however form the full story of why it is that individuals seemingly leading ordinary lives constitute themselves as sacrificial entities in the name of some affiliation, some identity. Another rendition might begin with the attacks of September 11th 2001 on New York and Washington, but once explanations are sought they tend to traverse other locations, other regions of the globe, other lives, other violent practices.

The historical trajectory of any conflict, any war, is but a collection of memories held and shared in the context of collectivities, in the public sphere. Memories are, however, but traces and fragments, holding some in the grip of history while totally evading others. It is then all too simple to extract from history the war and violence associated with particular instances of conflict, render these in terms of legality or even justice, forcing their dynamics into some formulaic discourse on the rational or even the moral. However, when relocated in the past, the events of the present come to regain their complexity so that understanding becomes possible, the hegemonic discourses of the day come to be subject to challenge, and the place of violence and its relationship to politics comes to acquire primacy as a question in our explorations of how war is implicated in the sphere of politics and in the sphere of the social. The blatant presence of history in the present brings forth the subject of politics, the subject of identity, the subject of memory, and reveals thereby how violence is implicated in the construction of subjectivity. The telling of the tale on the part of the author is never easy, for there is always the risk, especially in a high stakes context of global antagonism; for example the Cold War or the current global context constructed as a "war against terrorism", that the explanations of the author, the distinct historical consciousness that underpins these explanations, may be taken, as Judith Butler points out, as exonerations.[45]

Writing on war brings forth particular responsibilities, not least of which is the responsibility to recognise the impact of the writing in the construction of narratives that come to form the certainties surrounding particular situations of violent conflict. Such reflexivity is however often absent in renditions that aspire to scientific status or the formulaic application of the just war doctrine. What connects both over and above what differentiates them is the element of instrumentality: where word is unproblematically converted to action, intent to prosecution.[46] While the normative discourse of just war theory sees itself as self-consciously distant from the empiricism that underpins scientific approaches to the explanation of war, its various elements are totally dependent on a certain reading of violent conflict that assumes certainty in relation to motivation and the consequences of violent action. What links both scientific and normative approaches to war is, furthermore, the assumption of the objective separation of the author from the social and political context of the war in question.

There is, however, another option in the writing of war. This is to see war in its historical and sociological context, a context that implicates not just those participating in war, but the author engaged in war's representations. Such an understanding comes closer to conveying the experience of war, its impact on lived experience, and the different ways in which war and the various practices associated with war are implicated in the formation of the subject, in articulations of identity, and in the locations wherein the different renditions of war find voice. Any critical approach to war seeks to not only make sense of war, reflect on it as a seeming continuity in the human condition, but to move beyond the confines of disciplinary boundaries to reveal the complicities of the discourses of war in its enactment and continuity. Any discourse on war, including that which claims a critical voice, is implicated, somehow situated in what Michel Foucault refers to as the "games of truth"[47] surrounding any writing on the social sphere and especially, in the present context, the place of war in this sphere, in politics, in economic relations, and in the formation of subjectivity and political agency. There is then, despite positivist protestations to the contrary, no possibility of standing outside these games of truth and the various interpretative schema that constitute them.

In any critical discourse on war and our attempts at the understanding of the politics of war and violence; war's place in the constitution of the sphere of the political, the games of truth constituted by and constitutive of the discourses of war are in themselves the subject of scrutiny, specifically in the ways in which these games of truth produce the complicitous as well as the dissident in the context surrounding the narratives of war and the certainties proclaimed and pronounced as a war takes place or is brought forth in historical memory. The period immediately preceding the invasion of Iraq, for example, saw a number of authors responding to the impending crisis, some simply taking for granted the veracity of the discourses of the two major governments involved in the war, the United States and the United Kingdom, others looking to the UN and its resolutions to argue the case for and against war, while others still looking to the consequences of war in the wider Middle East and the global contexts.[48] At no other time has David Campbell's depiction of the complicities of academic discourse in relation to war been so apt. While Campbell's notion of "epistemic realism", where "the world comprises material objects whose existence is independent of ideas or beliefs about them; it favours a narrativizing historiography in which things have a self-evident quality that allows them to speak for themselves...",[49] was pertinent in his analysis of the First Gulf War, that which followed Iraq's invasion of Kuwait, it can be said to apply to the discourses surrounding the March 2003 invasion of Iraq. There was here and in the run-up to the earlier invasion of Afghanistan, a multiplicity of academic voices articulating the "moral certitude" that stems from the epistemic realism formative of stories that simply reflect hegemonic renditions on a particular situation. Given the controversies surrounding the war in Iraq, any academic voice engaged in its legitimisation contributed to the legitimising tools available to those seeking to prosecute this particular war. So deep-rooted is the assumption that the disciplines stand outside of the practices they form as their subjects of inquiry that their complicity in the appropriation of the right of judgement upon she/he who may be killed in time of war is not a matter of reflection.

The account of any war must, by necessity, involve a number of narratives, some mutually conflicting, others mutually complementary, all told from some specific perspective on causation and consequence. It is tempting to start with the causes of war, move towards its dynamics in the form of war's manifestations on the ground, and arrive at an analysis of its end-point if there is such. Such a linear rendition of war has its attractions. We are tempted to ask the "why" questions in the hope that we might move on to analysing the effects, in this case, the transformative effects we hypothesise as accruing to war. In seeking to formulate our answers, we are driven to provide explanations of how it is that the decision for war was taken, what mechanisms were implicated in the enabling of such a decision, who the personalities were that formulated the decision and brought it to fruition. If individuals and their groups can make decisions, we discern that they must do so in conditions that render such decision possible. The narrative might reasonably either begin with the individual decision-makers or with the enabling conditions. Given the remits of any account of the human and social, the choice is perhaps one of emphasis, but it could be one of prejudice. The inclinations of the author might lie with the agent of history, the individual decision-maker or group of decision-makers construed as having the capacity to make a difference. On the other hand, the author might be inclined towards the structural conditions that enable, and compel, agents into particular courses of action. In considering war's causes, the author is somehow forced into what might be called a back-and-forth movement between decisions and mechanisms, agents and structural conditions.

The story's telling is ultimately the responsibility of the story-teller, its reading ultimately the responsibility of the reader. Some might argue that the responsibility of the social scientist is to provide a scientific explanation of war, any war, so that such explanation might be transferable to other wars. Others, of the more historical persuasion, might stress the particularity of the specific war under scrutiny. Once again we are in the realm of prejudice and inclination. We might argue that these are matters for epistemology and the status of our claims about the world. On the other hand, we could argue the case for a recognition of the inherently political aspect of how we tell the story, how we interpret the world. The discourses of war are perhaps as potent politically as war itself. The manifold responsibilities of the author are here blatantly present, if not always acknowledged. That account which proclaims to be "scientific" is itself a product of choices made in the telling of the account and has consequences in the realm of the discourses that surround any war. It is tempting here to argue that all ultimately comes down to interpretation and that the social sciences must be content with the limits of our enterprise, limits set in place by our interpretative capacity. We might "understand" a war, we might accrue the reasons that agents themselves give, but we cannot hope to provide causal explanations, those that suggest necessity.

The author might, despite the above choices, be so interested in the particular war that any epistemological debates about causes and reasons, agents and structures, become secondary to the telling of the story; a telling that acknowledges the choices made and the ultimate political locations of those choices. As I state above, the narrative of the war in Iraq, for example, could indeed start with the causes of the war, its beginnings, thereby recounting the initial stages in the run-up to the war. What I want to suggest here, however, is that the story can also be told in the latter stages of the war, namely the story of the occupation, for it is here that we see hints, or indications, of how this war is related to the transformations we see in global politics and the place of war therein. These hints are not easily unravelled, however, and the narrative must take its course, moving back and forth between causation and consequence, the agents implicated and the enabling conditions surrounding them, and indeed constituting them as agents. The themes that can be highlighted at this early stage centre on the mechanisms of power, its material basis, the implications of discourse and linguistic construction, the significance of cultural difference, the significance of race and racism, the implications of a twenty-first century form of colonialism, and the discourses of peace surrounding the war.

The meaning we accrue to war is hence imbued with epistemological and ontological controversies, controversies that see their parallels in considerations of how war relates to the realm of politics. Any meaning that is given to war in any particular rendition on war is itself steeped in the politics of the present and all elements that tend to be taken as given. In this particular study, war is, as far as possible, understood in distinctly social terms, suggesting war's location in society and its constitution. War is hence not some extra-social element that takes place outside society, but is rather both its product and implicated in its formation and transformation. War, in other words, has a recursive relationship to society. The temporality and spatiality of war is significant and how these boundaries are drawn immediately focuses attention on the political implications of such epistemological decisions. As we have argued above, war is constitutively injurious, corporeal, and societal. Each element points to war's location in relation to social and political transformations. However, prior to the consideration of war's transformative potential, how war relates to the societal is important and must be highlighted. What can immediately be stated is that war draws immediate social meaning and such meaning is itself steeped in the historical trajectory of those involved. The breakdown of Yugoslavia and the wars subsequent to these monumental events in European history carried with them historical discourses that not only located the meanings of these wars in relation to the so-called "ancient hatreds" between the various nations involved, but in relation to European history more widely conceived, a history replete with the extremes of violence. Any imagery stemming from the Balkan wars carried such resonance that Europe's historical memories of violence

were awaked and indeed impacted upon wider responses to the conflicts. Images of camps in Bosnia brought forth memories of concentration camps and the Holocaust; images of inter-ethnic massacres
brought forth memories of the mutual violence perpetrated by Serb
and Croat during the Second World War. That war has social meaning
is hence not just a matter that is applicable or confined to those immediately involved, but goes further into the wider social and political
context of the conflict. It is in this sense that Campbell can write about
the complicities of third parties in the reconstruction of exclusionist
discourses that took the ancient hatred thesis for granted.[50]

The temporal reach of a war is hence not confined to the crisis
moment wherein the decision for war is made. The immediate present
of any war in itself is a temporal locale that contains its past and its
future. There is here no linearity, but a framework of time that contains the present and the past, while holding some element of the
moment to come, the anticipated moment of future memories fore-
told. Hence the significance of any image of war, a moment captured
to represent the present containing within it the traces of history
and memory just as it portends the future to come. In this sense, the
temporality of war is never determined by those responsible for its
prosecution, the few involved in the making of decisions for war. Nor
can such temporality be replicated in any discourse that seeks an
understanding of war and its location in relation to society. For the
temporal boundaries of any war are in themselves a product of
the societal matrices surrounding the war, the historical trajectories
that are drawn upon, consciously and unconsciously, in the construction
of certainties surrounding the war and the meanings accrued to its violence. While the meaning of the war over Iraq may, for those engaged
in its prosecution be confined to immediate interests, its meaning for
populations on the receiving end go far beyond into a past replete with
colonial incursion and an even further past associated with the glories
that historical memory can accrue. What is crucial to understand is that
the temporality of war is never confined to its immediate ramifications.

Just as war's temporality cannot be confined to war's immediate
manifestations, so too its spatiality cannot be confined to the battlefield,
if such a battlefield exists. The consequences of war involve the armed
as well as the unarmed. With technological innovation, war's ramifications are also never confined to the immediacy of populations targeted.
The live reporting of war renders distant happenings proximate, so
that the witnessing of war's effects comes to form a crucial social
element of war, wherein the social in the present juncture of history is

at the same time global. War is in this manner rendered a spectacle, whether it comes in the form of the attacks on the World Trade Centre or the so-called "shock and awe" tactics of the bombardment of Baghdad.[51] The "message" of war goes far and wide and the implications in terms of the meaning of war and our understanding of it are crucial, as we will see later. Suffice it to say for the present that any responses to war, both official and non-official, are influenced by the presence of the media, to an extent that in recent times, especially in the wars in Afghanistan and Iraq, certain sectors of the media, those not immediately under the control of those prosecuting the wars, have in themselves becomes targets.[52]

War permeates the everyday and the routine. While its temporality is associated with the extraordinary, as we saw above, its present manifestation carries history and portends the moment to come. However, there is a location that persists in its continuity outside the violence of war, in many ways resists the totalising effects of war. The everyday and the routine, the mundane order of things, of life lived even in the midst of war, carries on despite the disruptive and destructive manifestations of war. The existence of conventions governing behaviour in war; the Geneva and Hague conventions, for example, suggest another social meaning of war; that it, like society, has its formative rules, that there are forms of behaviour that society at large condemns. In witnessing the extremes of violence in time of war, the bombardment of major cities, the systematic use of rape, the torture of prisoners of war, the incarceration of and collective punishment of communities, we might conclude that anything goes in time of war; that war represents the breakdown of the social realm and suggests a reversion to a Hobbesian state of nature. However, in the wider spatiality of war, the expanding social arena within which war takes place, conduct in time of war is itself subject to wider judgement, both ethical and political.

In suggesting that war is constitutively societal I therefore argue that the meaning of war has a wider content than the immediate battlefield sense. I have suggested ways in which the social meaning of war is manifest in the various articulations and social matrixes surrounding war. However, the societal element of war in late modernity must go even further, for it is the case that while conventionally we might seek to differentiate the peace of the social arena from the violence of the battlefield, the social arena is itself subject to the discourses of war and their institutional manifestations. Those elements that render war meaningful, antagonism, enmity, the construction of the other, the removal and subjection of the other, are all continuities that permeate the "peace" of the social order and suggest the "structuration" of war into the social arena.[53] This calls, as we will see in Chapter 2, for a conception of war that recognises war's excess, an excess that permeates spaces not immediately associated with the devastations of war. If we consider the social arena to cover a terrain far wider than the immediate domestic space, the impact of war and its associated practices go far wider.

War and the late-modern

The idea of "transformation" suggests discernable change, a substantial movement from one temporal locale to another and the idea of the distinctly "late" modern suggests the transformation of modernity itself. As many social theorists have pointed out, the modern is associated with progress, science, advances in technology, all brought forth through the efforts of human agency, an agency capable of autonomous rational judgement and reflection on the world. Modernity implies a break from the past, a past replete with tradition and dogma, constraining of the capacity of the individual self to be the subject of knowledge and hence the self determining entity the primary force of which was progress and human emancipation. The institutions of modernity, the state and the capitalist mode of production and exchange, formed the linchpin of human creativity in the capacity to rationalise the world around them, ensuring what Howard Caygill calls the "management of doubt"[54] and some semblance of certainty underpinned by calculative rationality. The institutions of modern societies reflect this calculating imperative whereby significant aspects of lived experience come to be subject to monitoring mechanisms that render human complexity readable and hence governable. As Stephen Toulmin's *Cosmopolis* highlights, modernity itself emerged from the debris of conflict and religious warfare, instantiating the transformation not just of the institutions of political authority from the religious to the secular – marking the gradual emergence of the territorial state – but of an ethos that sought certainty contained in timeless and universal concepts relating to knowledge, systems of ethics, as well as political thought. For Toulmin, "in the bloody theological deadlock of the Thirty Years' War, philosophical scepticism became *less*, and certainty, *more* attractive."[55]

Drawing on the sociological literature on war and the state, Andrew Linklater agrees that "State-building, geopolitical rivalry and war, and capitalist industrialisation are three forces which have interacted to lend modern political communities their peculiar identities..."[56] While these accounts, as we have seen above, place emphasis on the complex interactions that have historically been formative of modern societies, incorporating the surveillance and pacification of internal rivalries, capitalist production, and industrialisation, and the consolidation of power through the monopolisation of violence, each location of power has, as Giddens points out, historically produced modes of resistance aimed at countering such power, including the emergence of social movements focusing on civil liberties, trade unions, the peace movement, the feminist movement, and struggles for national self-determination. What Giddens refers to as the "dialectic of control" is significant for Linklater, for it suggests certain "ambiguities of modernity" which "reveal themselves in the strange paradox of the modern state: on the one hand, it is the site on which radical intensifications of social control have been established but, on the other hand, it has been the setting for unprecedented efforts to eradicate the tyranny of unjust exclusion."[57] This ambiguity is important for it suggests that the modern state is not simply a location of exclusionary practices but has historically contributed as a site wherein movement towards the "widening" of political community into the international sphere could take place. The complex interaction between war, state-building, and capitalist industrialisation is core to the transformations formative of modern societies, but accounts of such transformation must incorporate within them emphasis on the "legal and moral dimensions of international relations" which suggest the widening of political community into the international sphere as another element of modernity.[58]

The transformations associated with modernity are therefore centred on the dynamic intersection between state-building, war, capitalist industrialisation, and the widening of political community through dialogue and consent across state boundaries. In Linklater's reading of modern transformations, this last stems from the ambiguities of modernity, ambiguities emergent from the dialectical nature of control wherein, on the one hand, we see the increasing success of the modern state in the consolidation of its power coupled with the expansion and deepening of capitalism as a mode of production and exchange, while on the other, we see the development of social movements seeking to consolidate the rights of citizens, demands for accountability, and struggles against inequality. In addition to drawing on the sociological literature on the modern state, Linklater seeks to supplement their analyses with conceptions of a wider community of discourse that recognises the dynamics of modernity internationally conceived. This in turn relies on traversing Hegel's conception of historical subjectivity, Marxist critiques of Hegel's reifications of the state, E.H. Carr's efforts at transcending the dualism between utopianism and realism, and finally Kantian inspired Habermasian conceptions of dialogue and cosmopolitan citizenship. Without interrogating the details of the intellectual routes through which Linklater suggests the gradual transformation of political community towards ever-expanding communities of discourse, from the "pluralist", to the "solidarist", to the "post-Westphalian", what is crucial to highlight is that each such step is a move to a higher moral order that is gradually binding the universal community of humankind. For Linklater, "States which block these developments are not as enlightened as they may claim to be since they fail to contribute to the unfinished project of modernity."[59]

While Linklater places emphasis, following Habermas, on moral-practical learning as the core dynamic of an expanding dialogical community, what is significantly underplayed is the extent to which violence and modes of exclusion emergent from a globalised social, economic, and political arena are implicated in global transformations that see the reframing of both political community and political authority beyond the state.

Any understanding of the implications of the project of modernity cannot be complete without some reflection on the fact that a significant or indeed formative moment of that project was colonialism and its ramifications in the postcolonial era. For this defining moment of modernity was itself an expression of, not just a desire to expand into and exploit the resources of non-European societies, but of a sense that the "European", or the "Western", as such were the civilisational locus the imperative of which was to civilise others, bringing them forth into modernity and enlightenment. David Slater identifies three constituent elements of what he calls "Euro-Americanism", discourses and practices that have their legacy in the colonial era and that still underpin the West's relations with other societies. The first stresses the "civilisational role of the West"[60] where the Weberian premise that Europe was the "distinctive seat of economic rationalism"[61] is also reflected, as Slater highlights, in contemporary thought which sees the West as "the haven of human rights, enlightened thought, reason and democracy."[62] The second element associated with Euro-American primacy is the perception that attributes possessed by the West are somehow "intrinsic" to European and American development and not a product of interactions with the non-western other. For Slater, "This sense of self-affirmation is often associated with a posited superiority which has permeated many discourses, from progress and civilisation through to modernisation and neoliberal development, and has helped fuel the drive to expand and colonize other cultures."[63] As we will see later in this study, such discourses of "self-affirmation" have had lasting implications in relation to intervention and the use of violence in interactions with the non-western other.

The association of the West with modernity, progress, and civilisation has implications in the construction of the non-West as the "recalcitrant recipient"[64] of knowledge systems, institutions, policy-frameworks that emanate from the West. Such discourses and the practices associated with them inevitably define the non-West in terms of negation; a form of negative identification that signifies other societies as perpetually lacking in agency and hence the capacity for self-definition and even self-determination. The discourses and policy frameworks associated with post-conflict reconstruction or even "peacebuilding" are similarly imbued with constructions that frame recipient societies as lacking, not just in capacities but in history, in memory, in local knowledge systems. The universalising imperative of modern rationality is historically associated with the violent subjugation of the non-West, persists to the present in practices of intervention in the name of humanity at large, and determines the conditions of possibility wherein such practices penetrate the arena of "peace" and its "building" in societies believed to be beyond the zone of peace. The background to the universal, the reasoning, the democratic, the modern is, according to many authors writing from the non-West, war, violence, and conquest.[65]

Modernity is hence associated with an unequal spatial distribution that has implications for our understanding of how war and violence are implicated in the project of modernity and its transformation. Understanding the place of war in the late modern and specifically in relation to late modern global politics requires, therefore, an understanding or exposition of how power operates at the present juncture of history. This forms a core theme to this investigation and its exposition draws from the early Frankfurt School, to later critical theory, poststructuralist thought, and the postcolonial literature. The point that must be emphasised at this early stage of the study is that power as such underpins discourses and practices surrounding both war and peace and presents particular challenges to conceptions of the discourses and practices we might seek to develop in normative and praxiological frameworks surrounding the latter; what might be called the condition of peace. Any understanding of how power operates in the present is hence also an understanding of the spatial and temporal articulation of power, its workings in geo-political space and in the minutiae of socio-political relations. Once again, as high-lighted earlier in this chapter, just as questions relating to war bring forth questions relating to agency and structural continuity, so too the question of power and its differential locations through time and space.

A triptych, namely war, knowledge, and power runs through this investigation. The transformative potential of war in late modern global politics I associate with particular workings of power that span the modern through to the late modern era that best describes the present. This triptych places emphasis not just on discourses but also on practices, suggesting that war is sustained through knowledge systems and frameworks of understanding that are not merely drawn upon in the legitimising discourses of war, but also in the knowledge systems and frameworks of understanding that provide the conditions of possibility for war as a transformative vehicle in late modern poli-tics. In this latter context, the paradigm moment of the realisation of practices that I see as constituting the late modern matrix of war/power is contained in invocations of "humanity" and "rescue" where late modern war comes face to face with a politics of representation steeped in knowledge systems that have a territorial base and a framework of understanding that dissociates the colonialism of the past with its present-day articulations. That we are indeed involved in an analysis of a triptych, war, knowledge, power, where no element is far removed from the other, is strongly reflected in concepts such as humanity, rescue, and reconstruction, for here lies not just a reliving of a long-forgotten colonial past, but at once the construction of a break from this past. A war that enables colonisation in the name of humanity – an example being the war in Iraq – is at once a declaration to this humanity that the right of war in one location is also and at the same time a mode of regulation and domination in another. Thinking of the operations of power in the present calls for a conceptualisation of the relationship between violence and domination, the matrix of war and the matrix of power. As we will see later, and framing the analysis in Foucaultian terms, while war and power are related in the suggested triptych, they are nevertheless subtly different in relation to their subjectivisations, the subject positions they produce. For, where the violence of war seeks the obliteration of the subject, the "other", rela-tions of power assume the capacity of the other to act, to resist. As we will see, it is this nexus between war and power and its differential impact on differently positioned subjects in relation to these matrices that is core to understanding the present.

The institutional clusterings of modernity and their transformations in late modernity are then mutually constitutive and mutually implicating. War has formed a central element of the formations and transformations of these institutional clusterings, as will become clear in the course of this investigation. However, institutions and the subject positions they generate have a recursive capacity, one that in a sense modifies, so that just as war is centrally implicated, so too are social interactions that might be deemed to form the basis for peace and a mode of interaction based on dialogue and mutual recognition. Both are possibilities, and being so, defy any formulaic representation that simply associates the modern with war or its transformation with uncertainty. The final chapter of this investigation will therefore concentrate on a distinct form of "political cosmopolitanism" that might inform practices of resistance against violence in political transformation.

The next chapter provides an understanding of the global matrix of war in the context of late modernity. No longer is it the case that we can spatially and temporally confine our investigations of war and the political violence that is war to inter-state conflict and antagonism. For if there is a predominant defining feature of the global matrix of war it is that its manifestations are distinctly transnational, involving state as well as non-state agents, possessing the capacities to transcend the domestic/international divide, so that the global terrain is rendered the remit of their operations. The implications of the global matrix of war are profound, for they point immediately not just to the very modern conception of our abilities to regulate the sphere of the international, but to the reframing of the international, from one based on the equally modern Westphalian order, defined and confined in terms of bounded territoriality, to one that, in the late modern context, seeks the transcendence of such boundaries and their redrawing in the name of a global terrain conceived in terms of humanity at large.

2
The Politics of Global War

> *So they left no stone unturned,*
> *Put fingers in every pie,*
> *Left no darkness unwormed,*
> *Let no sleeping dogs lie.*

Simon Armitage[1]

The violence that preoccupies as I write this covers so wide a span of the global arena that it is difficult to imagine peaceful spaces, though these exist and define, in some incalculable sense, the vast array of human interactions. Nevertheless violent conflict preoccupies precisely because of its seeming persistence irrespective of the very modern idea that we have the capacity to eradicate it. The defining certainties of modernity – the state, citizenship, democratic space, scientific and technological advancement, rationality over tradition – have, in the late modern era come face to face with uncertainty, unpredictability and the reemergence of the parochial and the particular. There is both a disenchantment, a loss of faith, in rationality's capacity to "legislate for peace" as well as a resilience borne of the project of modernity itself, a resilience that has temporal and spatial expression, universalising in its remit to contain the unpredictable and the particular.

Rationality's capacity to legislate for peace assumes, as I will indicate in the next chapter, and as I will further explore in the rest of this book, a universal remit, a spatial domain that spans the global arena, moving into locales wherein conflicts emerge, seeking to implement practices where those involved might somehow move towards relationships that are by and large devoid of violence. Yet the very assumption of a universal remit suggests an acquisitive ethos, one that assumes unproblematic entry into spatial domains that are locally defined, even as such local articulations have, throughout history, and across regions, negotiated a presence in relation to others, in relation to spaces wider than the merely local.

The universal remit is, however, implicated in violence and somehow the legislation for peace that it seeks can come to constitute the moment of violence. The war in Iraq, its invasion and occupation, can be interpreted in precisely such terms, where the nuance of different explanations ultimately comes to rest in the universalising moment that is the acquisitive. The operational remit of the war is tendered in universal terms and constructs the war itself as a global war, one where humanity at large, somehow or other, has a stake. Perhaps this universalising remit saw its global legitimisation in the United Nations Security Council Resolution that confirmed the occupation and the continued presence of foreign troops, and, more significantly, allowed the transfer of Iraqi resources into the control of the occupying powers.[2] However, it is important to remember that the global reach of this war was not simply due to the reasons proffered for its enactment. That the United States, as a hegemonic power, was involved is clearly one explanation for the globality of this war. That a military machine equivalent in expenditure to half the total world military expenditure again rendered this particular war global in its significance. That the war was one aimed at both an Arab and Islamic population again rendered this particular war global in its transnational, affiliational, significance. That the war and its method of enactment was brought forth into a global arena by a global media, rendering the war's violent manifestations open to a global public gaze again raised the global stakes in this particular war.

However, not all wars invite a global gaze, and indeed not all wars invite a universal remit. There is then a hierarchy of conflicts, some more global than others, some more high-stakes than others, inviting a hierarchy of response mechanisms and at times none. Yet, some of these persistent conflicts have the greatest human costs. We can but look to the African region to immediately discern the costs of the most extreme articulations of violence; local conflicts that know no bounds in terms of their penetration into the lived experience of individuals and communities alike. Rwanda, Sierra Leone, Somalia, Liberia, the Democratic Republic of the Congo, Sudan and the Darfur region, Uganda, Ethiopia and Eritrea, are but a few regional conflicts that have generated often reluctant interventions by other states and international organisations. Others emerge and simply add to Africa's violent crises, the Algerian civil war, the Zimbabwean situation not yet labelled a conflict, the conflict over the western Sahara, conflicts that come and go so to speak, that have a stop-start character, as factions regroup and as external others come to be involved variously as regional allies, peace-keepers, and so on. This catalogue of violent conflicts, claiming hundreds of thousands of lives,[3] perhaps can be seen to represent Africa's own "extreme emergency", to borrow from Michael Walzer.[4] Yet there is a reluctance to intervene and the impetus to legislate for peace in the name of universality is here rather limited in its aspirations.[5]

The imperative to legislate for peace, then, has global reach, is universal in its aspirations, and yet produces in its wake a hierarchy of conflicts, a hierarchy associated with the stakes involved, stakes that transcend the simple fact of human suffering. Wars might be said to possess transformative capacity, but some are more transformative than others, some have a greater reach than others. Yet, despite such differences, in the aftermath of the Cold War, when global and regional rivalries between the United States and the Soviet Union could no longer function as obstacles to international intervention in local conflict situations, the discursive framing of such conflicts witnessed a shift from the Cold War's proxy wars to humanitarian crises emergent from the wholesale breakdown of societies. This was a period in global politics when the United Nations came to acquire a significant role in conflict situations beyond its traditional peacekeeping remit, as witnessed in the aftermath of the resolution of conflict in Namibia in 1988, in El Salvador from 1991, and in Cambodia in 1992. With the UN Security Council backing the use of force to reverse Iraq's invasion of Kuwait in 1991, came what seemed to be an affirmation of the international institution's role in the governance of global order. Just as "international peace and security" could no longer be defined simply in inter-state terms, so state sovereignty could no longer function as a barrier, as Michael Barnett highlights, against intervention in the name of "cosmopolitan" peace and "human" security.[6] Responses to local conflicts involving humanitarian emergencies could no longer, in turn, be confined to diplomatic practices or limited and "neutral" peace-keeping operations, but required the active protection of populations variously against the tyranny of their own governments or the widespread and dispersed violence perpetrated by armed factions. As the UN and its institutions had long recognised, and as international conventions around the protection of civilians had institutionalised, the state as such could not be assumed to protect the welfare and rights of its citizens. The universality of human rights called for global measures in the name of their protection. While such measures were, in the past, confined to regimes of sanctions, such as those imposed against Apartheid South Africa, they could, from henceforth, involve UN-sanctioned enforcement measures potentially incorporating armed intervention.

A distinctly liberal agenda appeared to be the driving force behind such transformations; that the promotion of the rule of law internationally was requisite upon the establishment of the rule of law and democratic institutions domestically. The "universal" as a normative construct in ethical discourse was to be recognised as the actuality of emerging global relations and global order. The discourses and practices of dominant states and international institutions seemed to vindicate liberal international claims as to the relationship between domestic structures of governance and international order. Concepts such as "peacebuilding" and conflict "transformation" were no longer confined to locations in the world of non-governmental organisations and academic conflict and peace research, but entered the discourses of an international public policy driven by UN institutions and certain dominant states, specifically the United States.[7] The basic tenets of liberal international thought, human rights, representative government, and the rule of law, were from henceforth to be the driving principals upon which a "new" global order could emerge, one that was rule-governed and "domesticated." In a context of increasing globalisation, such domestication would emerge from the gradual institutionalisation of regulatory practices that covered not just economic and financial transactions, but matters relating to conflict and security. The triumphalism of liberal discourses apart,[8] these discourses seemed to imply a relocation of political authority, a relocation that assumes a universal remit of operations.

How then can we claim that this "agenda for peace",[9] could be interpreted in terms that see war at the heart of its operations, as an operative tool in its realisation? Posing this question is not based on the assumption that war is an ever-present condition in global politics. The politics that shape global interactions are clearly not based on perpetual war. Rather, the Foucaultian reversion of the Clausewitzian formula: that (global) politics is a continuation of war through *other* means, comes to form a compelling point of departure in an exploration that seeks to place the spotlight on practices of violence and how these impact on global political relations. The point of Foucault's reversal is located in the italicised word I highlight in the above statement, namely the word "other", for as we will see below, what I am calling the "global matrix of war" that permeates relations of power globally is manifest in a diversity of practices – including war in its traditional sense, but certainly not confined to this sense – and involves a diversity of agencies in a complex web of relations transcendent of state boundaries and hence the political and normative significance that such boundaries have held since the inauguration of modernity itself.

The aim of this chapter is to provide an understanding of the complex relationships that constitute what I am describing as a global matrix of war. In particular, it provides an analysis of the place of war in late modern politics and specifically in the constitution of relations of power globally. The chapter is divided into three sections. The first provides a picture of the late modern transformations that constitute the backdrop to global articulations of war. This section highlights in particular the mutually reinforcing relationship between a global neoliberal order and a war that has global reach. The second section provides an understanding of the global matrix of war, highlighting the intricate relationship between war and the social sphere, a relationship that impacts upon our conception of the juridico-political ordering of the world. The third section returns to the global matrix of war and its implications in contemporary global politics, implications that form the subject matter for the remaining chapters of the book.

A global social and political sphere

The subject of "globalisation" is vast and has, not surprisingly, produced its own specialist literature. What can be drawn from the literature is some degree of consensus on the complex interrelationship between economic, political and cultural aspects of globalisation, the differential ways in which such transformations are manifest globally,[10] and the significant debate in the literature on the relationship between economic globalisation, the location of political authority, and patterns of global governance.[11] While there are fundamental epistemological and ontological disagreements between positivist and constructivist accounts – the measurable "reality" of globalisation and its effects versus the social construction of globalisation and the impact of discourse on practices – what is important to draw from these debates is that globalisation may be understood in both "realist" and constructivist terms; that the ontological materiality of globalised social, economic and political relations, is intricately related to signifying practices situated in discourse. The distinctly "global" as a socio-political sphere is then brought forth into experience in the interactions of both material and discursive terms. The global matrix of war is in turn manifest in material and discursive terms.

As I stated in Chapter 1, transformations imply both continuity and change, suggesting the co-presence of past and present. However, the very term transformation raises questions relating to the instantiation of a break from the past, questions centred on the contingency of events as opposed to their significance in structural terms. While the temptation is to discern causal directionality between the activities of situated agents and structural change, no such causal relationship can be discerned beyond the attribution of significance discursive practices bring forth into the realm of meaning. Such discursive practices are in themselves situated in relation to structures of domination, so that not all constructions of the social realm come to occupy hegemonic status. Hence when Hirst and Thompson suggest, in their discussion of economic globalisation, "that we should be cautious in a wider sense of ascribing structural significance to what may be conjunctural and temporary changes, dramatic though some of them have been",[12] their aim is to empirically substantiate significance. However, what I am arguing is that the attribution of significance is itself a practice situated in relations of power. The question is not so much that events take place and have consequences; rather, it is that distinct events have different potentials in their capacity to enter, become the object of, discursive formations that then come to constitute systems of knowledge.[13] Particular readings of the past are always brought forth into the service of the present so that such categories as social solidarity, a community of belief, the right to sovereignty, the human, come to form the conceptual frames through which representations of the present are articulated. When Foucault states that events differ in their "capacity to produce effects" he is precisely pointing to their location in discursive practices steeped in relations of power.[14]

Transformations imply continuity and change at one and the same time. The present is variously described in terms that include such elements as individuation, dispersion, fragmentation, uncertainty, all of which seem to point to the breakdown of the order of things, portraying an image of an age having gone through and continuing to undergo monumental transformation from the assumed certainties of the past. These are seen as global transformations, impacting upon lived experience everywhere. However, it is important to recognise that this impact is unequally distributed, so that the experience of globalisation is, as Zygmunt Bauman highlights, differently felt across the populations of the globe. This is especially the case in relation to the technological manifestations of globalised social relations: "rather than homogenising the human condition, the technological annulment of temporal/spatial distances tends to polarize it."[15] Late modern transformations are seen to have both institutional and experiential manifestations. These in turn have their impact on the conduct of war and violent conflict. Importantly, such transformations have their ramifications in the state, sovereignty, and the location of political authority.

The intersection of the social and the political is brought into sharp focus when we consider the implications of social change – manifest globally – for the defining feature of modern political life, namely the location of political authority and its relationship to practices of government. For it is the case that the increasing compression of social life, its developing density of interconnectedness, is at the same time accompanied by the greater institutionalisation of governmental practices that transcend the boundaries of the state. Where social theorists from Castells, to Giddens, to Beck place emphasis on these social transformations,[16] political theorists such as Hardt and Negri or Walker raise fundamental questions relating to how the rearticulation of the social has fundamental implications for the rearticulation of the political, or more precisely, the juridico-political framing of an emergent global arena. As Rob Walker points out:

> The line between the international and the imperial is very difficult to identify with any clarity, though it is also a line that expresses a limit condition of the regulative ambitions of modern political life. To cross this line is to shift from legitimacy to illegitimacy, from the acceptable to the unacceptable, from the normal to the exceptional.[17]

The emergence of the global as a distinct arena of politics does not imply the diminution of sovereignty as such; it suggests its possible relocation. The social and political theorists I highlight above differ in their interpretations of how power operates in the present; however, they all place emphasis on transnational relations, networks and flows, structurated globally through the workings of the capitalist global order sustained and even transformed through information technology. The dialectics of late modern social life, as I have indicated elsewhere, come to be defined in terms of a globalised and rampant neoliberalism on the one hand, and the reassertion of locality on the other.[18] This relationship becomes crucial, as will be seen later, for the emergence of conflict that reaches global scale, conflict that pits the terms of grievance precisely in the oppositional terms of the global versus the local, the universal versus the particular. Nevertheless, the emergence of the global as a social and political sphere suggests the interpenetration of the local and the global, so that in the context of violence, just as the latter brings with it both enablement and constraint, so the former can have global ramifications. It is these ramifications – expressed in terms of global response mechanisms – that are of interest to the present investigation, for it is these that ultimately reveal the workings of power in the present. To understand the place of war and political violence in this context is to unravel at the same time the congealment of hegemonic institutionalised practices that determine the legitimate, the acceptable, and the remits of authority and hence politics. For it is precisely the hegemonic structure of present relations of power that in many ways control entry into the space of the political – that space which enables the articulation of grievance, of identity, of the right not only to claim agency, but to possess the right to politics and political expression.

Understanding relations of power in the present juncture of history, and in particular, understanding the place of war in these relations, calls for an appreciation of the mutually constitutive relationship between social forces and their emergent subjectivities, structures of domination and their differential implications in terms of lived experience. What is clear from the above social and political renditions is the intricate relationship between different articulations of power, from the economic, to the societal, to the political, to the military, so that it is tempting to agree with Hardt and Negri when they suggest that the hegemony of neoliberal capitalism renders possible the integration of different forms of power, specifically the economic and the political, so that a "new inscription of authority" emerges that has the capacity to view the world within its remit of operations.[19] At the same time, and despite the temptations proffered in Hardt and Negri's analysis, the act of inscription is itself derivative from the capacity to inscribe, the capacity to draw upon technologies of control that view the global as the terrain for their applications. Suffice it to state at this stage that relations of power are manifest in different modes from the power to kill, to the power to regulate and thereby govern socio-political relations. Such government may involve war, it may involve discourses aimed at the manufacture of threat or those that seek to define friend and enemy, just as it may involve the rebuilding of societies, the resolution of conflict, and the establishment and implementation of codes of conduct relating to all aspects of social life, from the economic to the environmental. In the context of late modernity, such practices of government occur at local, national, regional, as well as global levels, involving a complexity of interactions where the "inside" and "outside" are no longer necessarily delimited by the boundaries of the state, but involve the intersection of states, international institutions, networks of intelligence, as well as domestic and international jurisdictions. In amongst these different modalities of government, political authority, the capacity to intervene, the capacity to inscribe, differs from agent to agent, suggesting differential modes of enablement and constraint.

There is a tendency in the literature to write of different violent conflicts as if each had an objective essence irrespective of the frameworks of understanding that relocate the reality of their interactions into discourse, that bring them forth into language. How a conflict is described, the associations of concepts and statements drawn upon, the locations wherein utterances relating to specific conflicts are articulated, how certain discourses come to be naturalised and taken for granted, are all related to practices taking place in contingent social and political relations wherein inscriptions of grievance, legitimacy, acceptability, the capacity to have voice, are already subject to matrices of regulation and control. In this sense descriptive practice becomes politically significant, for any such practice is imbued with relations of power. Political knowledge, therefore, is itself situated in and constitutive of such relations and is not external to them. Any critical understanding of war and its relationship to politics acknowledges Foucault when he states:

> One would try to show whether the political behaviour of a society, a group, or a class is not shot through with a particular, describable discursive practice. This positivity would obviously not coincide either with the political theories of the period or with economic determinations: it would define the element in politics that can become an object of enunciation, the forms that this enunciation may take, the concepts that are employed in it, and the strategic choices that are made in it. Instead of analysing this knowledge – which is always possible – in the direction of the episteme that it can give rise to, one would analyse it in the direction of behaviour, struggles, conflicts, decisions, and tactics.[20]

Discursive practices introduce the object into the field of knowledge, an introduction that has profound ramifications in terms of both the interpretations that we draw upon to make sense of present warfare and the practices associated with war and its uses in contemporary global politics. The interpretation of events, the conceptual frameworks within which we place them, has profound impact on their location within the sphere of politics and hence on the ways in which individuals, groups, organisations, and governments respond. As Foucault shows in his later analytics of power, the episteme is itself implicated in the directionality of behaviours, conflicts and struggles that constitute relations of power in specific historical contexts.[21]

If we look to the episteme, the frameworks of knowledge that reveal interpretations of the present, we find a range of descriptions, some of which tend towards the spatial, "imperial war" for example, others specify the temporal, reflected in constructs such as "postmodern wars", "new wars" or "protracted" wars, while others still seem to imply both, such as "network wars". However, in the present juncture of history, it is the intersection between the spatial and the temporal that is of significance when thinking about the *politics* of global war, for while the temporal provides an indication of the transformation of the contingent event into the norm, the spatial reveals the conditions wherein the local moment of crisis and emergency is transposed into the global arena and how such transposition impacts upon the juridico-political framing of the international system and emerging relations of power. I want to suggest that it is precisely this framing of the international system coupled with conceptions of changing relations of power that provides a basis for understanding the implications of the types of wars highlighted above and the response mechanisms designed to variously shape, regulate, or control their outcomes.

Traditionally in political and international thought, the juridico-political framing of the international system has been based on the sovereignty of states, defined internally in relation to a specified population within a given territory, and externally in relation to other like units, namely other states. So powerful is this distinctly modern Westphalian conception of the state that it has historically governed not just relations between states, but the design of international institutions aimed at the government of such relations.[22] While the historical sociology of the state, as we saw in the last chapter, reveals the struggles and confrontations implicated in the gradual emergence of the modern state as a coherent "power-container", to quote Giddens, nevertheless the form of power that the state represents came to be so deeply rooted in social and political life, first in the European context and then internationally, that to conceive of the government of societies or their external relations in ways that transcend the state form could be represented in political thought in terms that suggest either a form of cosmopolitanism or a mode of imperialism. Any reconception of political space, any distancing move away from the sovereign state was in itself defined in terms of the state and its remit of social control. With increasingly sophisticated and rationalised systems of control, with the consolidation of power internally, the directionality of violence came to be expressed ever outwards in relations with other states.[23] It is precisely this framing of the history of the modern state that enables a conception of the international system in realist, neorealist, as well as liberal internationalist terms, where the assumption at the very outset is that this system is constituted by relations between units whose independence is encompassed by a juridico-political concept, namely sovereignty.[24] Even liberal internationalist constructions of international law continue to be defined in terms of the state and inter-state relations, even as the behaviour of the state and its institutions comes increasingly within the remit of such law.

The question that emerges from these renditions on the modern state returns us to the state's historical sociology, for the challenge in contemporary global politics emerges primarily from the failure, in the late twentieth and early twenty-first centuries, of particular states to consolidate power internally, through both technologies of control and frameworks of legitimacy. As we will see below, while certain interpretations of late modern wars tend to understand such failure in essentialising terms, we might also argue that "failure" is only meaningful as such if the terms of reference are taken for granted; namely the terms of reference that construct the realm of the international in terms of sovereign states. The implications are profound and have consequences that ultimately connect the absence of the consolidation of power internally with the juridico-political ordering of the international system. What are the dynamics wherein the breakdown of states can contribute towards a monumental effect, such as the reordering of the international system and its regulative practices as we have known them in the modern era? I want to argue that practices of war, in their different manifestations, are centrally implicated in the ways in which both relations of power and their framing in juridico-political terms, are constituted in late modern social and political life. I also want to show that the implications do not simply impact on states considered failed or broken, but touch the very definition of the liberal democratic state, the apotheosis of the modern state as we have known it from the Enlightenment to the present.

While many may express a nostalgia for modernity's certainties, the two foremost challenges one might substantively make in response to modern conceptions of the inter-state system relate firstly to the changing nature of the terrain we understand as the global, and secondly the significance of the "types" of state constituting relationships in global politics. Where modernity sought uniformity and predictability, wherein states are simply units engaged in calculative responses to other states or to the imperatives of the system, the globalised arena is one of uncertainty and unpredictability, where states vie for position, often in competition not with each other but with non-state agencies, from international corporations to non-governmental organisations to a diverse range of networks. What is most problematic is that some of these agencies compete with the state in fields that, for the modern nation state, were in the Weberian sense conceived as belonging within its monopoly, namely security and the means of violence.[25] The transformations of the late modern era are, therefore, not simply transformations that relate to the global level; but they crucially impact on the nature of the modern state itself and how the distinctly late modern state responds to what is seen to constitute a threat to its traditional remit of operations. The governmental and social element of the state becomes crucial in this age of global transformations, for the state can no longer be conceived as a closed unit, mechanically engaged in the calculation of its distinct interests as it competes with similar units in the equally mechanical workings of an international system of states.

When the internal make-up of the state is taken into account, the elements that constitute the mode of governance, the bureaucratic machinery of the state, as well as the "social sphere" acquire significance in our considerations of issues relating to war and peace in a globalised era. Each of these elements in turn has its transnational manifestations; in other words, each is somehow linked in a complex array of relationships that render the internal/external divide highly problematic. The spatiality of practices of government as well as relationships traditionally associated with civil society (what I am here referring to as the social sphere) cannot be conceived in terms of the insularity of a civic order maintained through technologies of control and legitimised through discourses of identity and affiliation. The "intensification"[26] of time and space relations that characterises an era of globalisation not only describes an era of increasing connection and mutual vulnerability, but changes our understanding of the dynamics of war and peace in the late modern era. In doing so, such changes render the social sphere as such highly significant when considering not just the origins and causes of conflict, but its dynamics and the options we might have in response to conflict. The distinctly global spatiality of the social sphere renders proximate distant events, so that grievances traditionally associated with local conflicts come to acquire global resonance, global affiliations, and hence global responses. While such responses might be institutional in some instances, coming forth in the form of the United Nations or coalitions of states, they may, in addition, involve actors within the global social sphere finding their own distinct expressions and articulations of grievance, so that what were local issues come to have global manifestations, global rearticulations. The emergence of the challenges associated with the violence of globally dispersed, and often clandestine, organisations is precisely the manifestation of what I am referring to as the global spatiality of the social sphere.

Late modern manifestations of war, from those associated with state breakdown to those associated with so-called clandestine network organisations to interventionist wars, have certain features that suggest continuity rather than differentiation, even as it is tempting to draw distinctions based on the agents involved. Elements of continuity relate to the role that violence plays in the constitution of subjectivity and the reconstitution of juridico-political space. The violence enacted in conditions of social breakdown, in transnational networks, and in interventionist wars comes to acquire an existential rather than an instrumental character, implicated at once in the formation of identities as well as political spaces. The project of modernity sought to establish the conditions wherein constitutive violence could be subject to temporal as well as spatial regulation. The late modern period is once again challenged by constitutive violence, one that seeks to reformulate the temporal and spatial limits brought forth by modernity itself. It is in this sense that late modern manifestations of war acquire an existential character; they are about the project of modernity itself, the modern subject, and modernity's institutional achievements.

The aim of the following section is to provide an understanding of how war comes to be articulated in global terms. What I am referring to as the matrix of war is intricately related to the transformations of the contemporary era, and specifically those relating to relations of power. The section draws heavily on Michel Foucault's analytics of war and power, but moves beyond Foucault in seeking to unravel the distinctly *global* aspect of war and its implications in relation to the socio-political transformations of the late modern context. While Foucault concentrates his analytics to the West, the challenge of this investigation is to rethink the dynamics of war and politics in global terms. Doing so raises questions relating to the "international" as a distinct juridico-political arena wherein any conception of the politics of war and peace must be located.

A global matrix of war

It is important to distinguish first of all between wars that draw from a globalised arena and those that view the global as the arena for their operations. One manifestation of the global spatiality of the social sphere emerges from the proximity of distant events. That civilian populations are by and large the targets of factional conflict and sheer criminality, that such activities are often sustained by global networks of finance and ethnic loyalty, present distinct human rights challenges in what is seen as an increasingly cosmopolitan global arena. That a number of such situations, Sierra Leone, Bosnia, Kosovo, Somalia, to name but a few, have resulted in external armed intervention suggests for authors such as Mary Kaldor and Jurgen Habermas,[27] the emergence of a "new" form of war, namely the "humanitarian war" where human rights and their protection become paramount. That local events can no longer be insulated from a global gaze is at the heart of debates around the global responsibilities emergent from the global spatiality of the social sphere.

The transformations of war in late modernity are a crucial component in understanding relations of power and discourses that seek the reordering of the juridico-political framing of the international system beyond the nation-state. Wars that dominated the immediate post-Cold War era, the Balkans, Central Asia, Africa, and elsewhere, and that continue to take place, are indeed transnational, but they are not global in their remit. While they draw upon the resources of a globalised arena and are brought forth into this arena through late modern transformations in information and communications technology – transformations that in a sense globalised local wars – those immediately involved do not view the global arena as being within the purview of their control. Rather, what these local practices of violence centre on is a transformation of their immediate polity, a reversal of processes that had historically led to the establishment of their modern states. The remaking of the state, and hence its breakdown, are the driving force behind the local wars that dominated the global agenda in the 1990s and, though enacted locally, have had transforming effects on the global arena, primarily through military intervention in the name of "rescue". The Cold War had largely, though not totally, confined such conflicts to a relatively limited geographic space; the post-Cold War era witnessed their permeation into the wider global arena.

That these so called "new wars" are associated with the "failure" of statehood is highly significant in considering the response mechanisms aimed at their amelioration. What is important to highlight is the unravelling of the modern state as well as a whole array of consequences that stem from such unravelling, primary amongst which relate to the dissolution of the distinction between private and public, internal and external, civilian and military, war and criminality. The break-up or unravelling of such distinctions renders the state permeable, beyond control by government and its institutions. War comes to be used as a form of political mobilisation and is therefore not just about the defeat of an enemy, but often includes the targeting of civilian populations: "The point of the violence is not so much directed against the enemy; rather the aim is to expand the networks of extremism...battles are rare, and violence is directed against civilians...Violations of humanitarian and human rights law are not the side effect of war but the central methodology of new wars."[28] Violence in itself can no longer be thought of in terms simply of defeating an enemy. Violence becomes constitutive, formative not just of identity, though this too is important, but of the reconstruction of entire social formations. More than this, however, when violence is constitutive, it comes to form the expression of political subjectivity. Violence becomes existential rather than simply instrumental, generating in its wake "cultures of violence" wherein violence is seen in terms of heroism, as in the past, or in terms of martyrdom, as in the present context of Jihadi violence.[29] Political space is in this sense obliterated, rendered an impossibility, opening up a socio-political void that is then occupied by those who seek the reconstruction of social space in their own exclusionist vision. These situations of war are a salutary reminder of the primacy of the modern state form and its remit in the government of social relations. It is indeed also a reminder of the social consequences emergent from the breakdown of such modalities of modern government and of the dangers involved when the distinctions that sustain the social divide between the private and the public are broken down.

What is important to highlight is that the very discourses surrounding such wars; that they are "new", that they involve the "unravelling" of the modern state, that they obliterate the distinction between public and private, war and criminality, that they draw upon violence and the generation of hate in the constitution of new social frameworks based on exclusionist identities, are all features that point towards a rethinking of political space and the global as well as domestic implications of the largely transnational working of such wars. More importantly, the ramifications of the unravelling of the states implicated appear to have both temporal and spatial consequences; in relation to the former, transforming the very basis of social identity and social solidarity in many ways back into a premodern phase wherein ethnic and religious communal affiliation and exclusion become primary forces for mobilisation, and in relation to the latter, the unravelling of the state suggests at once both the breakup of the state and its vulnerability to other states or network organisations functioning transnationally. While the practices associated with such wars appear to hark back to some pre-modern era of warlordism or religious medievalism, these could also be described as distinctly *late* modern wars, suggesting at once the fragmentation of the certainties of modern life, certainties that variously relied on the capacity of the modern state to govern and to forge a baseline of social solidarity centred on the nation-state, bounded, and hence subject to control.[30] Any possibility of a reversal of such fragmentation can either emerge from the victory of one faction over all others so that a renewed monopoly over the means of violence is established, or through forms of external intervention that aim variously to control territories and populations, to ensure victory for one side, to put in place mechanisms for the protection of civilian populations, and ultimately to rebuild the institutional basis of government in shapes that concur with a neoliberal global order.

Late modern war is situated in a social sphere that is global in its reach. Our conception of the "international" shifts from one defined in terms of the international system of states and towards a globalised terrain of interactions, a terrain that stresses not just the complex interconnections between various agencies and networks, but the very idea of "humanity" as encompassed in our understanding of human rights. Kaldor's description provides us with an understanding of how the dynamics of new wars not only draw upon the global arena, but have the potential to reconstitute the global as a socio-political space. James Der Derian's description of "network wars" provides us with some indications of how these modes of warfare connect to global relations of power and the generation of meaning around practices of violence in the late modern era. Writing in the aftermath of the events of September 11th 2001 and the outset of invasion of Afghanistan, Der Derian states,

> new and old forms of representation and violence synergised on 9/11. The neomedieval rhetoric of holy war reverberated from the minaret to the television to the Internet. A hypermodern war of simulation and surveillance was played out at flight schools, airports and in practically every nook, cranny and cave of Afghanistan. A remote aerial war was directed from Central Command in Tampa, Florida, 7,750 miles away from targets that were surveyed by drone aircraft like the Predator and Global Hawk, and destroyed by smart GPS-guided JDAM's (Joint Direct Attack Munitions with a circular error probably of about 10 feet), CBU-87 and CBU-103 'cluster bombs' (Combined Effects Munitions containing more than 200 bomblets that have antitank, antipersonnel, as well as an incendiary capability), and dumb bombs, topped by the 15,000 pound 'Daisy Cutters' (BLU-82) that explode three feet above the ground and incinerate anything within 600 yards. Special Operations forces led an anti-Taliban coalition in a limited yet highly successful land campaign.[31]

Leading the way in the "revolution in military affairs", the United States conducts this "virtuous" war in the name of the "holy trinity of international politics – global free markets, democratic sovereign states, and limited humanitarian interventions."[32] Technical capability and ethical imperative are, according to Der Derian, at the heart of the transformation inaugurating what he calls the virtuous war. War in this situation is as much about the targeting of enemies as it is about the production of meaning. Where Kaldor's new wars draw upon a globalised social and economic arena and impact upon the global arena in their ramifications, Der Derian's network wars indeed draw upon a globalised arena and impact upon the reconstitution of this space. However, his antagonists do more in that they view the global as the purview of their operations. This is reflected in statements made by Bush at the outset of the war in Afghanistan and by Bin Laden in response to the air strikes. The all-encompassing global compass of the "war against terror" is reflected when Bush states that "every nation has a choice to make. In this conflict there is no neutral ground." Similarly, Bin Laden, claiming that "These events have divided the world into two camps, the camp of the faithful and the camp of infidels." This was then a "mimetic war of images" and words, a "battle of imitation and representation" that permeates every aspect of lived experience and "sanctions just about every kind of violence".[33]

The perspectives covered above place emphasis on the spatial and temporal manifestations of a form of confrontation that is not only global in scope but covering the routine and the most extraordinary time of crisis. While the global aspect of these wars reveals the dissolution of boundaries in the enactment of war, nevertheless boundary is articulated in the construction of enemy others. The network wars that Der Derian describes must also be understood in terms of the dispersed violence which particular network organisations and cells engage in as their distinct articulation of a global war. The bombings of New York, Madrid, London, Bali, Istanbul, Casablanca, and elsewhere are indicative of a form of war whose recruits are transnational in their workings and in affiliation, connected more to an idea of a community of believers rather than a territorial entity related to a nation. This particular aspect of network war must be juxtaposed with the distinctly global aspect of what has come to be known as the "war on terrorism", for the agencies involved and those who confront them view the global space as their remit of operations, transforming what used to be understood as local issues into distinctly global concerns not just in terms of international actors' diplomatic or other involvement in these conflicts, but as an arena of violent confrontation.[34]

As we see from the above, practices of violence, their manifestations in what are described as "new wars" and "network wars", involving local factions whose violence is expressed in injury and the perpetuation of fear directed against civilian populations, through to network organisations and urban cells whose violence is transnational in its orientation, to the violence of a hypermodern war machine, constitute the dynamics that point to the ways in which late modern practices of violence not only draw upon a global social and political arena, but are implicated in the potential reconstitution of relations of power globally. Some authors in International Relations and in social and political thought read these relations of power in terms of the overwhelming military and economic capacities of the United States, suggesting that any understanding of relations of power must consider the exceptionality of the United States. Others seek to concentrate on the transformations of the juridico-political framing of the international system, suggesting the emergence of new forms of political authority that transcend the state.

In the remaining part of this chapter I seek to bring forth into our understanding of the present a picture that unravels the intricate connections between the practices of violence and technologies of control (the government or regulation of social relations) that view the global as the terrain of their operations. As we will see, there are three modes of power operative in what I am describing as the global matrix of war and, drawing upon Michel Foucault's analytics of war and power, I see these as encompassing: a) the direct use of violence and hence the power to kill, b) disciplinary power directed at individuals and communities, and c) biopower directed at the life and welfare of populations. As we will see further still, the matrix of war in this sense does not just involve war in its traditional battlefield sense, but incorporates practices from torture and incarceration to the reframing of social relations. We might, in anticipation of the next chapter, refer to a matrix of peace interlaced with that of war. But I stray ahead too much at this juncture in the analysis, and return to the two perspectives that describe relations of power in the present: those that read these relations of power in terms of the exceptionality of the United States and those that suggest the emergence of new forms of political authority that transcend the state and with it the international system as such.

Traditionally, in the discipline of International Relations, conflict, and specifically war, is located in the anarchical system that neorealist thought envisages as determining relations between states. Kenneth Waltz's "third image" is hence systemic in its conception of the causality of war, rejecting any modes of understanding that place emphasis on the innate characteristics of the individual self or the type of governmental structure internal to states; the "first" and "second" images respectively.[35] Given Waltz's predilections for systemic explanations of war, explanations that make distinct assumptions relating to the workings of the international system as well as the nature of the state as the basic unit of this system, it is not surprising that this particular neorealist's reaction to recent manifestations of war and conflict have been highly critical in their condemnation of, for example, the so-called "war on terrorism" and the invasion of Afghanistan.[36]

Within the discourses of International Relations, the neorealist conception of power and its relationship to the anarchical international system have been subject to much methodological, epistemological and ontological debate which will not be repeated here. However, the core premise that derives from Waltz's interpretation of the contemporary era is that where a state holds hegemonic power, possesses the overwhelming panoply of military and economic resources to conduct a global war, there are no constraints remaining in the system that can impede its desire for global domination. As indicated by Michael Barnett and Raymond Duvall, the logic of this discourse dominates recent interpretations of the United States' involvement in Afghanistan, Iraq and the wider so-called war against terrorism: "Much of the conversation triggered by the U.S. invasion of Iraq, for instance, has focused on unipolarity, the ability of the United States to use its military and economic resources to overcome resistance by states and non-state actors, and whether other states will balance against or bandwagon with U.S. power."[37] The unilateralism of the United States is seen to define its exceptionalism; in this case, this is an exceptionalism that is structural, having a definition in other words, that is global in reach, both in terms of capacity and in terms of its location in the global arena, its system-defining potential.

In the post-September 11th 2001 era, in the aftermath of the invasions of Afghanistan and Iraq, talk of "US Empire" is now common coinage. How is "American Empire" understood and how does this concept help in our understanding of war in the present juncture of history? One dominant approach suggests, as we have seen above, that the United States derives its status from its military capacity and its intentions to use them in compelling other states and in combating non-state actors. The fact of "empire" does not simply rely on military means, however, but can incorporate other capacities, including the capacity to generate "social effects". These social effects may be local as well as global, the latter being manifest in what Barnett and Duvall refer to as "institutional power": "institutions can mobilize bias to serve U.S. purposes and eliminate points of potential opposition to serve U.S. concerns. Moreover, global institutions created an asymmetrical distribution of benefits, and the United States has been a primary beneficiary".[38] It is important however to locate such actor-specific attributes within wider social relations and structural continuities, related both to the discursive attribution of the United States as the ultimate power in the international system of states and to the hierarchical positioning of the United States within global economic and wider social relations. The United States in this sense possesses global reach and its involvement in any confrontation renders that conflict global in its manifestations. As we have seen in conflicts past and present, any local actor, located in distant lands or indeed within the United States itself, wishing to "globalise" their conflict, seeks active intervention by the United States.[39] As we will see below, those suggesting the emergence of "new" forms of political authority globally still invoke the power of the United States as a foremost driving force in the manifestations of a distinctly *global* conception of war.

The idea of a global war suggests a global remit of operations, a global spatiality wherein modern distinctions between the external and the internal, the zone of war and the zone of peace can no longer hold. According to Hardt and Negri,

> The world is at war again, but things are different this time. Traditionally war has been conceived as the armed conflict between sovereign political entities, that is, during the modern period, between nation-states. To the extent that the sovereign authority of nation-states, even the most dominant nation-states, is declining and there is instead emerging a new supranational form of sovereignty, a global Empire, the conditions and nature of war and political violence are necessarily changing. War is becoming a general phenomenon, global and interminable.[40]

The many different conflicts, from Colombia, to Sierra Leone, to Afghanistan, to the Israeli-Palestinian conflict, to the conflict in Aceh, represent, for these authors, not wars distinct from each-other, but "civil war", in the singular, or even "imperial civil wars", forms of civil war conceived not in its traditional meaning of a conflict taking place within one single sovereign territory, but one that sees its articulation in terms of the global terrain as a distinct juridical and political space. According to Hardt and Negri, "This does not mean that any of these conflicts mobilizes all of Empire – indeed each of these conflicts is local and specific – but rather that they exist within, are conditioned by, and in turn affect the global imperial system",[41] which, as indicated above, constitutes a new inscription of political authority that is manifest in global terms. There is also a temporal aspect to the manifestation of this global civil war. Where modernity was defined in terms of the relegation of war to the external relations of states, so that politics could take place within the civic peace of the internal order, the postmodern era relocates the exceptionality of war to the internal arena which is now globally defined, constituting a generalised "state of exception".[42] The primary agent of this generalised state of exception is the United States which, as the only remaining superpower, can constitute itself as "the exception from the rule", exempting itself from international rules and obligations. It is then the intersection between the generalised state of exception and the exceptionalism of the United States that "provide a glimpse into how war has changed in today's world."[43]

In these conditions of "imperial war", the generalised state of exception, war comes to be reconstituted so that there are no longer enemies as such; rather, war is fought against "concepts" or sets of practices as is the case in the so-called "war against terrorism". In this context, it is no longer possible to distinguish war from policing activity conducted in the name of humanity as a whole and legitimised in the name of human rights. The "renewed" concept of just war brings with it "the allied concept of evil": "Posing the enemy as evil serves to make the enemy and the struggle against it absolute and thus outside of politics – evil is the enemy of all humanity...these resurrected discourses of justice and evil are symptoms of the ways in which war has changed and lost the limitations that modernity had tried to impose on it"[44] enabling the emergence of pre-emptive wars legitimised in the name of the security of populations. This shift from defence to security is part of the "logic" of the state of exception transforming global war into a regulative tool the agent of which is "imperial sovereignty"[45] and the object of which is social life as a whole. In this context of war as the articulation of "biopower",[46] war in the service of life, international law as the modern attempt to place limits on war gives way to war as constitutive of a new form of authority that has within its purview of operations such technologies, as we will also see in later chapters, as the rebuilding or even the redesign of nations in the name of peace. According to Hardt and Negri,

> The political program of 'nation building' in countries like Afghanistan and Iraq is one central example of the productive project of biopower and war. Nothing could be more postmodernist and antiessentialist than this notion of nation building. It reveals, on the one hand, that the nation has become something purely contingent, fortuitous, or, as philosophers would say, accidental. That is why nations can be destroyed and fabricated or invented as part of a political program. On the other hand, nations are absolutely necessary as elements of global order and security...The contemporary projects of nation building are...imposed by force through a process that now goes by the name of 'regime change'.[47]

The picture Hardt and Negri present is at first sight appealing in many respects not least of which is the idea of one singular system of power encompassed in a global juridico-political framework. Where international law constituted modernity's effort at the regulation of war between sovereign states, no such limitation exists in the age of

Empire, where the formative antagonism is that between the network forces of Empire and the networks of all others. Global war in this sense is a generalised state of exception where war constitutes a perpetual presence. Every action and reaction, every confrontation is in a sense related in some way to the imperatives of Empire, though the only distinction (interpreted as conflict) they acknowledge as significant is the system transforming one that relates to the reinforcement or resistance to imperial power. The global state of war is also a "postmodern" condition wherein the old institutions of modernity are undermined; the sovereignty of the nation-state, the nation as a coherence self-determining mobilising mode of identification, international legal frameworks constraining the actions of states; the shift in the definition of the legitimate violence; the dissolution of the distinction between inside and outside, war and peace, war and criminality, defence and security. In this generalised condition of indistinctions, a condition that Giorgio Agamben refers to as the state of exception, the enemy is no-where and everywhere and the responses rely upon the paramount military machine, the exceptionalism that is the United States itself, whose capacity to confront the enemies of humanity extends to a "full spectrum dominance" that acts in the name of humanity and in the minutiae of humanity's interactions, transforming itself from a sovereign nation-state into a network power that draws upon not just its own vast and monumental resources but those of the vassals of empire, so to speak, other states and non-state actors. In this general global state of war, violent conflicts that do not threaten the imperial order are left to fester, while those that do threaten this order are dealt with using a panoply of techniques, from nation-building, to full scale warfare, to the use of communications technologies, to welfare programmes and other social mechanisms aimed at the production of populations as "docile bodies". The global terrain is hence a terrain of perpetual war where the very boundary between peace and war is diminished. The postmodern war is a war that is indeterminate and general at one and same time. Gone is modernity's aspiration to manage doubt and uncertainty.

Hardt and Negri's rendition on what they call global war is at the same time highly problematic. The dissolution of the distinctions they suggest are taken as given and their workings remain undefined. The generalised state of exception they describe is, more fundamentally, not so generalised but is rather very particular in its manifestation. More significantly in our present context, the modern attempt to limit war, to regulate relations between states, is not diminished, but might be said to be rendered more complex, more in acknowledgement of the always already permeable boundary between the inside and the outside, the ever dependent relationship between wars directed against the "other" and the government of social relations in the modern liberal polity. Furthermore, to conceive of global relations of power and their reframing in a "new" juridico-political structuring of the world through the supremacy of the United States is itself to draw attention away from the minutiae of practices that constitute the governmentalities of the present and the complex ways in which war comes to be a constitutive element in these governmentalities.

As I state above, in seeking to define a late modern matrix of war, I will draw upon each of the above perspectives. However, I want to draw out the intricate connections between the practices of violence and technologies of control (the government or regulation of social relations) that view the global as the terrain of their operations.[48] As I indicated earlier, there are three modes of power operative in what I am describing as the global matrix of war and, drawing upon Michel Foucault's analytics of war and power, I see these as encompassing: a) the direct use of violence and hence the power to kill, b) disciplinary power directed at individuals and communities, and c) biopower directed at the life and welfare of populations. The matrix of war in this sense does not just involve war in its traditional battlefield sense, but incorporates practices from torture and incarceration to the reframing of social relations. I also suggested that we might, in anticipation of the next chapter, refer to a matrix of peace interlaced with that of war; in other words, the capacity to "legislate for peace" is itself dependent on the capacity to wage war in the name of humanity. The remainder of this section draws on Michel Foucault to give definition to what I am referring to as a global matrix of war and its manifestation in the late modern context.

Foucault's lecture series, *Society Must Be Defended*, is of crucial significance in our conceptions of contemporary manifestations of war in the global arena. Foucault's understanding enables a conceptualisation of war that exceeds its traditional battlefield sense. The term "war" in Foucault has an excess that blurs the boundary between the spaces of war and peace, the battlefield and the social realm. To suggest that war may provide the basis for the analysis of the social realm is hence to suggest that this realm has running through it antagonism and confrontation, strategies and tactics aimed at enemy others, and political and social institutions the very structuring of which enables such relations to run, either silently or not so silently, through the social sphere.

Practices relating to war are in this sense spatially located both inside and outside the modern sovereign state and, in the late modern period, have a distinct transnational manifestation. While Foucault's analytics provide us with a picture of how the social sphere is interlaced with practices that suggest the continuation of relations of war, enabling, as we will see below, a conception of war precisely as a mode of control, his insistence on a shift away from the state as a location of law, and hence the absence of a conception of the international as a distinct social and political arena, present particular problems in extending Foucault's analytics precisely to the sphere of the international.

In distinguishing between the "historico-political discourse of war" and the "philosophico-juridical" discourse of law and sovereignty, Foucault wishes to shift analysis of relations of power away from law as the pacifying third force that arbitrates between conflicting forces in society and towards historical practices, the actuality of relations of force.[49] This shift is highly significant in the present context, for it immediately points critically to the determining assumption of liberal thought, namely the primacy of law in the establishment of a peaceful civic order, suggesting instead the possibility that underpinning this order are all the struggles and confrontations, partisan rivalries that permeate not just social institutions but claims to truth. That Foucault appears to question the modern conception of the internal civic order as a zone of peace (read in terms of an internal order codified in law) is highly significant in contemporary renditions on global war, for it suggests at first sight that war has a presence both at the level of practices and at the level of representation. This presence is articulated in a diversity of ways, some involving confrontation and struggle, others engaging in a discourse of fear and the ever-present condition of existential threat, while others still involving disciplining practices that seek the production of "docile bodies" defined within the architectonics of disciplined social formation and the removal of those deemed to constitute a threat to the success of such practices.[50] In the matrix of war, there is hence the level of discourse and the level of institutional practices; both are mutually implicating and mutually enabling. There is also the level of bodies and the level of population.

Developing his analytic of war and using war as the matrix through which relations of domination are analysed enable Foucault to shift the focus of his historical investigations to another level, to the human population as species, humanity at large, an emergent form of power from the late eighteenth century to the present that targets populations, specifically the *life* of populations. As Foucault states: "Unlike discipline, which is addressed to bodies, the new nondisciplinary power is applied not to man-as-body but to the living man, to man-as-living-being; ultimately, if you like, to man-as-species."[51] Where discipline seeks the division of the multiplicity into individual bodies "that can be kept under surveillance, trained, used, and, if need be, punished", this other technology addresses a "global mass". This latter mode of power constitutes for Foucault a "biopolitics" of the "human race".[52] The question that therefore emerges relates to how this shift from disciplinary power to biopower informs Foucault's analytic of war and how this analytic helps in understanding the practices that I have described as constituting a matrix of war.

Biopower intervenes in a diversity of mundane social relations; it enables the "government" of social relations in all their complexity. Where this form of power becomes relevant in the context of the analytic of war is in Foucault's suggestion that an additional domain concerning this technology of power is that of relations between human beings "in so far as they are living beings"[53] and their environment; the latter including what might be referred to as the inter-human environment, relations between human beings sharing spaces. We might construe such spaces in terms of the "urban problem" as Foucault does, or expand this yet further to include neighbourhoods, communities, and populations linked across state boundaries. Any phenomenon that involves human beings as "mass" or as population can come to constitute a domain of intervention for a biopolitical technology of power. Crucially, such intervention takes place not at the level of the individuals concerned, but at the level of "general phenomena", the collective. We can immediately discern Foucault's contributions here to our analysis of war and the emergence of war as a distinctly global phenomenon. His conception of disciplinary power focuses attention on the production of docile bodies, shaped variously into a fighting machine, a working machine, or indeed a consumer machine. His conception of biopower is conceived as aimed at the protection of the "security of the whole from internal dangers".[54] If the life of the population becomes paramount, wars fought are fought in the name of populations, in the name of life. War happens in order to regulate life, just as other modes of intervention seek precisely such regulation. As Foucault states,

> Wars are no longer waged in the name of a sovereign who must be defended; they are waged on behalf of the existence of everyone;

entire populations are mobilised for the purpose of wholesale slaughter in the name of life necessity: massacres have become vital. It is as managers of life and survival, of bodies and the race, that so many regimes have been able to wage so many wars, causing so many men to be killed. And through a turn that closes the circle, as the technology of wars has caused them to tend increasingly toward all-out destruction, the decision that initiates them and the one that terminates them are in fact increasingly informed by the naked question of survival.[55]

The population in whose name war is fought is, however, a distinct population, one that is racialised as the predominant race. As Stuart Elden points out, Foucault "has shown that politics is saturated with relations of war and racial conflict", a presence that is enabled by the "mathematicizing of the political."[56] Such mathematicisation ensures that a form of power that has life as its purpose is also one that kills through the division of life and hence the division of categories of population. The critical moment in Foucault's analytic of war emerges when practices of government are revealed through the prism of war, revelations that immediately point to the control of bodies and populations, and above all the ways in which discourses of war are generative of particular subjectivities.

Foucault's analytics seek to move discourse away from sovereignty and towards the microcosmic working of power in the interstices of social and political life. A question that haunts his work, however, is the extent to which it takes into account the sphere of the international as a space of operations that is intricately linked to the workings of societies and their internal state institutions. The paradox here is that while war clearly forms a central element in Foucault's corpus, this is a war of society against itself rather than war directed against other societies. Nevertheless, Foucault's analytics of biopower at first sight provide an indication of how it relates to the wars of the present, wars that are represented in discourses of legitimisation, as those fought in the name of humanity. The spatial reappears, it is international, but it remains juxtaposed with a generalised terrain that links colonialism with madness, criminality and mental illness. This generalised terrain is a biological sphere of species, a sphere that latterly is rendered in terms of wars for humanity where enemies are represented in discourse not as political enemies but as the "inhuman" or the "evil", whose destruction is not so much a destruction of political will, or political aspiration, but a destruction that serves the survival of humanity at large. War in the age of biopolitics comes to acquire an existential element, rendered as it is in terms of the existential moment of exception, the moment of crisis.

Drawing on Foucault's analytics of war, I have also argued elsewhere that war in the late modern context constitutes a technology of control, a tool drawn upon in the control and regulation of populations and their relations globally. What I am referring to as the matrix of war is hence constituted by a series of interconnected practices, from war, to invasion, to incarceration and deportation, to torture, to state-building, that involve states as agents, the bureaucracies of states, as well as international institutions, both intergovernmental and non-governmental, quasi-official and private, recruited in the service of a global machine that is highly militarised and hence led by the United States, but that nevertheless involves alliances that may shift with time. Those targeted involve states, networks, communities, as well as individuals. In a late modern condition that is interlaced with the matrix of war, distinctions relating to the inside and outside, peace and war, security and war, policing and war, seem to disappear in a complex array of discourses and practices where the political is somehow banished into governmentalising practices the remit of which is global in reach and defiant of limits, boundaries, and distinctions. What is important to highlight here is that boundaries do not disappear. Rather, they are reinscribed through practices of violence, of control, and every instance wherein an "other", the enemy within and without, is targeted in the name of humanity. War is hence implicated, as we will see below and in the following chapters, even in practices associated with the construction of peace. Nevertheless, the critical moment in this analysis, and again as we will see later, is located in the reintroduction of distinctions and limits.

These limits become apparent when we consider how boundaries are reinscribed, how distinctions are redrawn. We find that when we reintroduce the "international" into Foucault's analytics of power, analytics that are temporal rather than spatial in their orientation, confined as Foucault himself acknowledges, to the liberal western polity and its shift from the seventeenth century to the late modern twentieth, we find that "sovereign" power, the power to kill, far from giving way to the government of the life of populations remains core to such government. Its expression is, however, directed at populations elsewhere. As Paul Gilroy points out,

As far as orthodox histories of European statecraft are concerned, problems like the disappearance of public torture are often understood to identify a significant stage in the development of a new type of power: capillary, biopolitical, and primarily directed toward the management of population. Against this assumption, the history of colonial power overflows with evidence that suggests that a distinctive association of governance with military power and martial law should be identified and that this association with distinctive forms of governmental calculation changed the workings of institutional complexes like the army and medical practice, as well as the professional thinking of colonial administrators, planners, and managers. There were different biopowers at work in these colonial histories, and they did not remain sealed off from the mainstream at the distant ends of the imperial system.[57]

Modernity and its late manifestations are hence experienced differently when looked at from the angle of the colonised, past and present. The topographical reinscription of imperialism and the "racial ordering of the world" is not simply applicable in relation to Europe's colonial past, but is currently being articulated in the twenty-first century colonisations and their expressions through a heady mix of military power, carceral power, confinement, administration, acquisition, and the "training" of local populations into societies amenable to self-discipline, self-regulation, and self-government (referred to variously as "state-building" or "nation-building"). Just as Europe's colonial past is intricately linked to the transformations in regimes of power in Europe, so late modern interventions into the societies of others come ultimately to serve the acquisitive logic of structures of domination, whether these are expressed regionally or globally. Race, now expressed in terms of cultural difference, is as much part of this logic as it was in the colonial past.

The global matrix of war is hence constituted by a complex array of practices which have implications for our reconceptions of the international as a distinct social, political, and juridical arena. We see from the above discussion that the matrix of war is built around three distinct types of war: new wars that are local but draw upon a globalised social and economic arena, network wars that are transnational in their workings and view the global as the remit of their operations, and wars of intervention the remit of which is humanity, whether represented in discourse in terms of the protection of human rights of local populations affected by the extremes of violence or in terms that see the human as embodying global humanity as a whole. Thought of in terms of practices of power, we see these practices being manifest in terms of the power to kill, the power to discipline, and the power to govern or to regulate relations at the level of populations. When we consider global relations of power interlaced with the matrix of war we can see that those engaged in the violence of new wars and network wars may possess the instruments of violence and may draw upon a global arena for purposes of material gain or political mobilisation, they nevertheless lack the latter forms of power, namely the power to produce docile bodies or to govern populations, though they may aspire to ultimately possess such power.[58] It is practices of war associated with response mechanisms to new wars and network wars that reflect relations of power that are global in reach. Wars conducted in the name of humanity, whether locally manifest in the form of wars constructed as humanitarian, or wars that are globally manifest in the form of the war against terrorism, suggest not just a sovereign capacity to kill, but the power to discipline and to regulate social life. These modalities of power are not confined to the boundaries of states, but see their purview of operations in global terms, suggesting a reconception of the international beyond the inter-state and towards a global articulation that seeks its defining moment in "humanity".

Conceiving the international in human rather than in inter-state terms has profound implications for the institutions of modernity, primarily the state. For the realm of the human as such to constitute a political and juridical arena is to conceive of the possibility of a cosmopolitan legal framework that transcends the state. Every enactment of war for humanitarian purposes comes therefore to reconstitute the international in cosmopolitan terms, suggesting the gradual genesis of a domesticated global order enshrined in what Habermas refers to as cosmopolitan law. War in this rendition, as we will see in the next chapter, is seen to serve the purpose of peace, a cosmopolitan peace.

If we look into the practices that constitute the matrix of war, however, we see that invocations of humanity are discursive formations that are also constitutively built on the notion of the "monstrous" or the "inhuman", the enemy other against which global society must be defended. War in this sense comes to service the perpetuation of antagonism and conflict, wherein the concept of the human acquires a distinct profile. This latter frame seeks the legitimisation of war in terms of prevention and pre-emption wherein enemies are always potential or even abstract, and being so, always drawn widely, and by consequence communally. Practices that constitute the so-called war against terrorism, for example, are framed in terms that seek to transcend time and space, suggesting the absence of boundaries and limits. Many of the practices associated with this particular war take place in transnational, often indefinable spaces; practices especially apparent in secret confinement, the use of torture, deportations, extraordinary rendition, as well as the bombardment of populations in Iraq and Afghanistan. I state elsewhere that "The paradox of the current context is that while the war against terrorism in all its manifestations assumes a boundless arena, borders and boundaries are at the heart of its operations...these boundaries and the exclusionist practices that sustain them are not co-terminus with those of the state; rather they could be located and per-petually constructed upon the corporeality of those constructed as enemies, as threats to security."[59] Violence in this context comes to con-stitute a mode of control, a technology of governmentality wherein the enactment of war is at the same time a mode of discipline and pacification wherein political conflict is subsumed into practices of control taking place in a global sphere of operations.

Practices constituting the matrix of war are hence intricately related to modalities of power that are global in reach. Invocations of human-ity appear at first hand to transcend the primacy of the sovereign state, suggesting instead the human realm as an arena of intervention. As we see above, such intervention may come in the form of the humanitar-ian war the purview of which is distinctly local in orientation, or in the form of a war without limits (the pre-emptive war) the remit of which is global. Both forms suggest significant implications for articulations of power internationally and the ways in which these come to impact on the sphere of the international as a social, political, and juridical arena. While these implications will form the subject matter for chap-ters that follow, the following concluding section highlights the elements that relate the matrix of war to emerging relations of power.

War, politics and the global

By far the predominant transformation in relation to war is its spatial and temporal manifestation. All of the descriptions of war provided above, from Hardt and Negri's "global state of war", to Waltz's "hege-monic" war, to James Der Derian's "network warfare", to Mary Kaldor's "new wars" suggest some global reach, whether this is achieved through the overwhelming military and intelligence capacities of the United States as hegemon or indeed "imperial" power, or through the workings of globalised transnational networks whose capacities centre on communications networks, informal interconnections, and communal mobilising potential. This global reach is especially pertinent in discussions of the so-called "war against terrorism", wherein those involved in antagonistic confrontation, from the United States' Administration and its allies to the Islamic networks involved in violence project an understanding of their conflict precisely in global terms, viewing the global as their terrain of operations. Such a global rendition of the confrontation has, as we witness above, permeated the discourses of knowledge surrounding contemporary warfare, so that the global, the civilisational, the cultural, are reiterated in the field of knowledge, reinforcing the antagonists' articulations of the bases upon which this ever escalating conflict is built.

As the global becomes the terrain of confrontation, the inside/outside distinction disappears and with it a number of other certainties that we have come to associate with modern subjectivity and modern reason, namely the sovereign state, citizenship, the public/private divide, the secular nation as the primary mode of affiliation, the distinction between war and criminality, war and security. This does not mean that boundaries disappear. Boundaries are inscribed biopolitically and corporeally upon the body of the other targeted both as individual and as carrier of a wider population deemed enemy. The locations of such inscriptions, or such constructions of enemy others, are defined widely and transnationally, visible at times while at others taking place in clandestine locations beyond the witnessing reach of the public sphere. Moreover, such inscriptions are not just confined to the actions of governments or leaders of clandestine organisations; they reach the neighbourhood, the street, the locale, the region, and all those spaces in between. The global aspect of late modern war is no longer simply international, but connects the proximate and the distant, the familiar and the foreign where the global terrain of confrontation reaches the everyday and the routine.

The global terrain of confrontation also has a temporal articulation, so that distant events have immediate impact, such is the "compression of time and space"[60] that defines globalised socio-political relations. No longer can events that take place in distant areas such as the Israeli-Palestinian region be confined to their own boundaries, but emerge in every household through television and computer screens, providing narratives of this protracted conflict that over time have become global narratives, mobilising and recruiting affiliation for the sides involved, reinvigorating communal connections based on religious belief or national and cultural identity, creating in their wake transnational connections that in themselves generate a new form of political subjectivity, beyond the state, beyond the secular nation, beyond the immediate population. Such are the ramifications of the global terrain of this particular confrontation that what local, or even regional, narratives defined the conflict and its various grievances, are now expressed globally. As Mary Kaldor rightly pointed out, writing in the immediate aftermath to the events of September 11th, 2001, "We are, I fear, on the brink of a global new war, something like the wars in the Balkans or the Israel-Palestine war, on a global scale with no out-siders to constrain its course."[61] Similarly the events in Afghanistan, Iraq, and elsewhere, are aspects of this global terrain and cannot be confined to their local spaces, for once again, the narratives surround-ing these wars have global reach and hence are located globally in their consequences.

What does the compression of time and space in relation to war mean for our understating of contemporary war and its transformative impact upon global politics? The modern conception of the nation-state stresses its monopoly over the means of violence and to do so through the successful control of bodies and populations internally. Crucial in Foucault's analytics of war and power is the transformation he records from sovereign power towards the government of social relations, where sovereignty gives way to the government of popula-tions. However, as postcolonial theorists such as Paul Gilroy and Gayatry Spivak highlight,[62] this conception of the temporal shift in articulations of power fails to account for the colonial experience, wherein the sphere of the international, the sphere of the other, is always already implicated in transformations taking place in the liberal state located in the West. When the Foucaultian picture is extended to the global arena it refocuses attention on violence as a mode of control.

However, it also focuses attention on the historical transformations that liberal governmentality has instituted in relation to mechanisms wherein the capacity to be self-governing subjects is enshrined in law, in the development of human rights regimes, in the development of the welfare state, in conventions against torture and genocide, and other forms of global practice aimed at the protection of individuals and populations against the excesses of arbitrary power. This raises the question of how violence is legitimated in contemporary global rela-tions. Humanity is now invoked as the basis for the legitimisation of violence. While such a construction enables a conception of war as the constitutive moment for a cosmopolitan peace, it at the same time

comes to constitute a matrix of war wherein enemies come to be constructed as the monstrous or the inhuman, suggesting a depoliticisation of conflict. War comes to be an ever-present condition, having a
more diffuse, transnational manifestation wherein the other of humanity is primarily defined in cultural terms, raising questions relating the
present to the colonial past.

The shift of temporal emphasis here is to focus on the continuities
that relate the present to the past, suggesting that one framework of
understanding that might contribute to our understanding of late
modern war, its transformations, and transformative impact might be
located in postcolonialism. According to Derek Gregory, "What has
come to be called postcolonialism is part of this optical shift. Its commitment to a future free of colonial power and disposition is sustained
in part by a critique of the continuities between the colonial past
and the colonial present. While they may be displaced, distorted, and
(most often) denied, the capacities that inhere within the colonial past
are routinely reaffirmed and reactivated in the colonial present."[63]
Crucial to an understanding of late modern warfare is the question of
the cultural processes implicated in both the political economic structures of domination and in the violent manifestations of such domination. Political, economic, and military power are represented and
reproduced through structures of meaning that are drawn upon in the
enactment of practices that reinforce power and the discourses of its
legitimisation.

The above postcolonial reading of the present raises, according to
Gregory, two important questions that are central to the interests of
this investigation: "Who claims the power to fabricate those meanings?
Who assumes the power to represent others *as* other, and on what
basis?" And secondly, "What is the power of those meanings? What do
those meanings *do*?"[64] The postcolonial reading of the present is then
based on the idea that understanding the present must at once incorporate the colonial past, a past that enables, discursively, and institutionally, the colonial articulations of the present, including variously,
the degradation of other cultures or their idealisation; both implicated
in the "othering" practices that reinforce supremacy, and, in relationships of power, practices that range from violence and subjugation on
the one hand and domination on the other. Gregory refers to "amne-
siac histories" that deny the continuities linking events such as those
of September 11th 2001 and the subjugations of the colonial past and
the neocolonial economic and political domination that describes the
colonial present. The so-called "war on terror" according to Gregory is

the "violent return of the colonial past, with its split geographies of 'us' and 'them', 'civilisation' and 'barbarism', 'Good' and 'Evil'".[65] The temporal and the spatial are then formative aspects of the "arts of memory", forms of articulation that reengage with the past as they contemplate the present. The "global war on terror", for Gregory, comes to form a "series of spatial stories that take place in other parts of the world", namely Afghanistan, Palestine and Iraq. It is, furthermore, "one of the central modalities through which the colonial present is articulated."[66]

As we will see in the following chapter, the universal can only make sense in terms of the particular, and in terms, furthermore, that assume the subsumption of the particular. As Rob Walker points out, the problem of modern political community is precisely the negotiation between universality and particularity and "how universality and particularity might be rearticulated without capitulating to the modernist presumption that the different must always be resolved into the same."[67] The challenge is to conceive of this relationship in terms that suggest equality of access to the universal, wherein the sphere of the global is constituted in cosmopolitan terms that do not imply the subsumption of the other. Seen in this light, conceptions of the human enable discursive formations wherein the cosmopolitan is not defined in acquisitive terms, but is rather a product of emerging modes of global consent. To legislate for peace is in this sense to articulate the conditions of possibility for a conception of the juridico-political framing of the international in distinctly human terms. Doing so, however, presents its own distinct challenges, its own moments of violence. This is the subject matter for the next chapter.

3
Late Modernity, War and Peace

The concept of history, in which progress would have its place, is emphatic, the Kantian universal or cosmopolitan concept, not one of any particular sphere of life. But the dependence of progress on the totality comes back to bite progress.

Theodor Adorno[1]

One of the most instrumental of treatises on war, Clausewitz's formulaic representation of war as the continuation of politics, obscures ontological commitments that see war as formative of mature subjectivity and nationhood. Here the Hegelian commitment to war as the ultimate expression of complete individuality in relation to the state brings forth the experiential aspect of war and its place, in Hegelian thought, in the formation of the individual as citizen.[2] In direct opposition to this discourse is Kant's antipathy to war and his preference for a civic peace underwritten by the pacifying effect of law. Kant's *Perpetual Peace*[3] seeks to relegate war to the past, so that the modern, fully rational, progressive individual emerges as the author of a lasting peace that is the universal marker of progress against reaction, of civilisation against barbarism, of the civic order of the modern state against the chaos of the state of nature. What is historically significant about Kant's treatise is that it becomes the baseline of liberal thought, and specifically liberal democratic thought, where a direct relationship is construed between a democratically constituted civic peace within and a predisposition for peaceful relations with other like states. If democratic societies eschew war through the pacifying mechanisms of a democratically ratified law, then war must somehow be relocated at the limits of democratic space and, if such space expands through institutionalised, law-governed relations between states, then peace acquires a universal, perpetual character. Significantly, while Kant himself sees the possibility of such relations between "republican" and "non-republican" states, later renditions inspired by Kant are not as anti-pathetic to war and indeed articulate a distinct support for military intervention in situations deemed to constitute humanitarian emergencies. Liberal democratic thought, when rendered internationally, takes from Kant the notion of a civic peace and expands this to the global arena at large, seeking a global juridical order that might make war a thing of the past. In the discipline of International Relations, this position is primarily expressed in liberalism, which takes the position, against realist and neorealist thought, that the internal structure of states, namely the presence or otherwise of democratic institutions, impacts upon state behaviour and has historically contributed to peaceful relations between democratic states. Liberal and cosmopolitan thought in International Relations, specifically that related to peace, will be covered in the following chapter. What is important to highlight in this context is that their articulations in "democratic peace theory" and "cosmopolitan democracy", recognise foundations in Kantian thought.[4]

The aim of this chapter is to explore first and foremost a conception of "peace" as a distinctly modern idea, associated with a concept of progress. The challenge of peace is firmly located in a branch of modern thought wherein the social sphere is primarily determined by the recognition of individual liberties protected in law. This is then a juridical understanding of peace; that law functions as a third force in the social sphere and regulates social interaction. The pacification of the social sphere is, in this framework, taken to the international sphere, wherein the possibility of peace comes to be associated with the emergence of legal frameworks that supersede the sovereignty of states thereby linking humanity in a universal terrain sustained beyond a merely moral set of obligations. The modernity of this conception of peace lies in its emphasis on individual rights and, furthermore, the idea that such rights are juridical in character. This raises a number of fundamental questions that are core to this study. The first set of questions relates to this juridical understanding of peace and how it might relate to war. This relationship is crucial, for it points to an understanding of the processes involved in the *movement* from the condition of war to that of peace. The second set of questions shifts from this temporal relationship to the *spatial* terrain wherein the juridical understanding of peace is situated. This second concern points to the implications of this assumed relationship between the "modern subject" and the "peaceful" subject and their locations in the spatial distribution of power globally. While this latter theme is the subject of investigation in the next chapter, of interest in the present context is how different conceptions of the modern can lead to very different ideas on peace, its possibilities, and locations. While this chapter concentrates on political thought, the next explores the international relations of these ideas, concentrating in particular on the international political sociology of war and peace in the present late modern context.

The modernity of peace

In a previous book, *Discourses on Violence*, I argued that peace "remains as enigmatic a concept as it is in achievement."[5] The assumption I made then was that theories and practices concerned with the question of peace constituted the "emancipatory" component of reflection, in that seeking to understand the conditions of possibility for war and violence in the human condition was primarily the expression of a concern with ideas relating to the transformation of this condition, so that peace may be possible, so that we might imagine capacities and processes that might move societies, across the signifying divides of state and culture, and despite the differential distribution of enablements and constraints, towards the prioritisation of peace, and hence, an end to violence as a mode of human interaction. Clearly then, any such emancipatory agenda makes the assumption from the outset that thinking of peace and its possibilities is distinctly progressive in orientation and hence distinctly modern in outlook; that thought on the question of peace is not just concerned with the conditions of its possibility but at the same time with the discursive and material or institutional conditions which constrain its realisation. In this progressive agenda, peace comes to acquire a meaning that transcends its end to violence conception, seeking as its targets the discursive and institutional continuities that render war itself a persistent and legitimised presence in the human condition. However, even as I elaborated my arguments in relation to the possibility of peace, I attempted against all odds to resist the spectre of Walter Benjamin and his edicts – in his context related to social democracy – against any totalising conception of history:

> Social Democratic theory, and even more its practice, have been formed by a conception of progress which did not adhere to reality but made dogmatic claims. Progress, as pictured in the minds of Social

Democrats was, first of all, the progress of mankind itself...Secondly, it was something boundless, in keeping with the infinite perfectibility of mankind. Thirdly, progress was regarded as irresistible, something that automatically pursued a straight or spiral course. Each of these predicates is controversial and open to criticism...The concept of the historical progress of mankind cannot be sundered from the concept of its progression through a homogeneous, empty time. A critique of the concept of such a progression must be the basis of any criticism of the concept of progress itself.[6]

Raising this spectre now in the present writing, I see ever more clearly the implications of my arguments, so that reflecting on these now at the present juncture of history, the desire is to hold on to some conception of peace while resisting any totalising remit in its actualisation.

In that earlier rendition, I argue that an emancipatory conception of peace challenges the discursive and institutional underpinnings of war as a social continuity. Locating peace in an emancipatory conception of politics, placed emphasis on three elements, namely the public sphere, participation, and the recognition of the individual's capacity to assert difference set within wider social relations. Borrowing from Habermas's conception of discourse ethics, the ethos is distinctly Kantian, while the application acknowledges a Hegelian inter-subjective setting wherein communicative practices realise their constitutive potential in understanding. Recognising that language is a medium of understanding as well as domination, a conception of peace based on communicative practices places emphasis at one and same time on uncovering the distortions associated with differential power and the legitimising practices associated with organised force as well as defining a social matrix that is enabling of free and equal expression. Like Linklater, in his conception of an expansive, dialogical community as the basis of the post-Westphalian condition,[7] these reflections on peace that I articulate in 1996, are premised on the possibility of social transition towards conditions wherein dialogical recognition can form the basis of both mutual understanding across the divide of situated conflicts and define the tools wherein political interaction could be defined in emancipatory, cosmopolitan terms. Both elements in turn were seen as contributing towards uncovering the structures of domination implicated in exclusionary practices.

This rendition on peace is, as is apparent from the above, distinctly modern, distinctly agency led, recognising the distortive potential of tradition, dogma, and relations of power, and seeking the transformation of social relations towards institutionalised guarantees for the individual's capacity to articulate difference. The ontological basis of this conception of peace is hence modern, progressive in outlook, and perhaps expressive of a faith in the human potential for imagining that things may be otherwise. Now in the present, remembering the spectre of Walter Benjamin, and following Foucault in understanding the subject of communicative practices as always already in and of relations of power, the above rendition comes to be clearly expressive of a particular and situated mode of articulation. Moreover, the modernity of peace reveals, as we will see later in this chapter, the constituent other of peace, namely violence. Before this, however, I want to return to the formative moment in a modern conception of peace, namely Immanuel Kant.

The modernity of peace as a concept finds its most powerful, but at the same time, problematic rendition, in Kant. This section explores Kant's contributions to a distinctly modern conception of peace. It then moves to Habermas as the contemporary voice that must remain central in any debate on peace and its conditions of possibility. The analysis elaborates the Habermasian position and its recent articulations, suggesting, in a move that marks a departure (or I should say development) from my last visit to this subject, that this Habermasian discourse is itself replete with both possibilities and difficulties when considered in terms of its implications for global politics. The difficulties, as will be illustrated in the second section to this chapter, are also intensely modern in their genesis.

Two formative texts provide the backdrop for considering the place of war, and hence of peace, in the modern project and its late manifestations as we experience them in the present. These texts are Immanuel Kant's *Perpetual Peace* and his *Idea of History with Cosmopolitan Intent*. Both texts in many ways provide the intellectual context for recent renditions on the so-called "liberal peace project" in its various guises. Paradoxically, both texts at the same time provide the intellectual context for critical and cosmopolitan thought, suggesting some parallel or even mutually dependent trajectory that connects these schools of thought as political projects. Each school of thought, the Kantian and the cosmopolitan, requires its own elaboration and exposition, but none can be initiated without a look back, a reexamination, perhaps a revision, of Kant's original texts and their implications for our present-day global politics. Such reexamination requires some work of detection whereby the relationships between war and peace, war and politics, peace and politics, are somehow located, identified, delved into. To do otherwise is to deny this particular project, and its author, its location in the context of modernity and the critical ethos that modernity in many ways enables. In commenting on Kant's text, "What is Enlightenment", Michel Foucault states: "Thinking back on Kant's text, I wonder whether we may not envisage modernity rather as an attitude than as a period of history. And by 'attitude' I mean a mode of relating to contemporary reality...A bit, no doubt, like what the Greeks called an *ethos*."[8] Such a critical ethos allows a rereading of formative texts, allowing some inroad into the ways in which subsequent renditions draw upon these foundational voices, voices such as Kant's, that have been subject to "application" in the late modern context.

Of primary significance in Kant's conception of "peace" is its reliance on law as the pacifier of the state of nature. Peace is in this sense emergent of prohibitive rules that define its conditions of possibility. Understood in this way, peace is not simply a concept that applies to the cessation of hostilities, or indeed the end of war, but describes a complex set of conditions that are primarily societal. The external peace between states is made possible through certain arrangements within the state; the outside is wholly dependent on the inside, and in particular, its institutional arrangements. Of crucial significance here is that "peace" is at once rendered political, is, in other words, a product of distinctly political arrangements and not simply a product of moral judgement, though this too is a factor. The sovereignty of the state is upheld in that the state alone may be constituted as possessing what we might refer to as the agency for peace. This is significant, for it suggests peace as a *process* and not simply an end-state. The condition of sovereign statehood is, according to Kant, of the "strictest sort"[9] and prohibits the forcible interference "in the constitution and government of another state" as long as the state remains a coherent whole wherein its conflict is as yet undecided. State autonomy is also crucial as guarantee of what might be considered proper behaviour in time of war so that a future peace is rendered possible. In this sense, proper behaviour (that which prohibits, for example, the use of assassins or "poisoners") ensures that war is not transformed into a "war of extermination".

It is in the "definitive" articles that Kant's assumptions on the agents of peace emerge. For here in this section we find that while states may be equal in their sovereign autonomy, they are not equal in their capacity to participate in the processes that lead to the realisation of peace. Such capacity can only be guaranteed through the state's *internal* arrangements. For parties to possess agency for peace, they must exist in what Kant refers to as a "legal civil state", for only such a state can provide the guarantee against the state of nature, which always constitutes a threat. Hence all the definitive articles assume that "all men who can at all influence one another must adhere to some kind of civil constitution."[10] Hence Kant's contribution to the modern legacy, a legacy that recognises not just the autonomy of states in relation to each other, but distinctly links the autonomy of the citizen to the constitution of the state and the wider global order. To be an agent of peace, or more properly of *perpetual* peace, suggests adherence to one of three conditions that include a constitution based on the "civil right of individuals within a nation" (*ius civitatis*), one based on the "international right of states" (*ius gentium*), and one based on "cosmopolitan right" applicable to individuals and states "regarded as citizens of a universal state of mankind" (*ius cosmopoliticum*).[11]

Kant asks whether only the republican constitution can lead to a perpetual peace. The reason Kant gives for an affirmative answer to this question is as follows: "If, as is inevitably the case under this constitution, the consent of the citizens is required to decide whether or not war is to be declared, it is very natural that they will have great hesitation in embarking on so dangerous an enterprise."[12] In terms of government, the "republican constitution" is one where executive power is separate from legislative power and is built upon equal citizenship under the law. The legal underpinnings of the republican constitution are in themselves paralleled by the concept of the "international right" of states establishing a "federation of peoples". Once again Kant juxtaposes the "peace of political order" with the "violence of the state of nature", as highlighted by James Bohman and Matthias Lutz Bachmann.[13] Kant's rendition on the primacy of law as a guarantee of peace is here starkly illustrated in his reference to the "lawless freedom" of the state of nature: "We look with profound contempt upon the way in which savages cling to their lawless freedom. They would rather engage in incessant strife than submit to a legal constraint which they might impose upon themselves, for they prefer the freedom of folly to the freedom of reason. We regard this barbarism, coarseness, and brutish debasement of humanity." However, the rulers of states often seek to defy any external constraint, aided by "sorry comforters", the philosophers and diplomatic historians who provide the justifications for war.[14]

What is significant in Kant's rendition on "peace" is its association with "right", and as indicated above, the concept of right applies to citizens within states, to states in the international order, and to citizens in a cosmopolitan order. This last suggests, for Kant, the existence of what he calls a "universal community" which "has developed to the point where a violation of rights in one part of the world is felt everywhere."[15] Furthermore, "The idea of a cosmopolitan right is therefore not fantastic or overstrained; it is a necessary complement to the unwritten code of political and international right, transforming it into a universal right of humanity. Only under this condition can we flatter ourselves that we are continually advancing towards a perpetual peace."[16] These are then stages of development that gradually take the human being from the state of nature towards a global rule-governed condition wherein war becomes a thing of the past. The formula is progressive in its temporal rendering just as it is universalising in its ambitions. More importantly, it is modern and being so is based on a particularly modern notion of subjectivity and the capacity of human reason everywhere to generate the conditions wherein the social sphere may be rationalised under the pacifying guidance of law. The modernity of Kant's doctrine of perpetual peace is premised on his doctrine of progress, a doctrine that associates progress with a global, and hence human, spatiality. In his *Idea for a Universal History with a Cosmopolitan Purpose*, Kant expresses his understanding of progress as clearly defined in universal and indeed cosmopolitan terms:

> The highest purpose of nature – i.e. the development of all natural capacities – can be fulfilled for mankind only in society, and nature intends that man should accomplish this, and indeed all his appointed ends, by his own efforts. This purpose can be fulfilled only in a society which has not only the greatest freedom, and therefore a continual antagonism among its members, but also the most precise specification and preservation of the limits of this freedom in order that it can co-exist with the freedom of others. The highest task which nature has set for mankind must therefore be that of establishing a society in which *freedom under external laws* would be combined to the greatest possible extent with irresistible force, in other words of establishing a perfectly just *civil constitution*. For only through the solution and fulfilment of this task can nature accomplish its other intensions with our species.[17]

The conditions of possibility for peace are then those associated with human progress which in turn is conceived in universal terms. Crucially, these are terms that, in their critical understanding of limits, are very specific in their understanding of the social formations which enable the realisation of the human potential.

This distinctly modern, and cosmopolitan, conception of peace is taken up by Habermas and "applied" to the conditions of late modernity. As we will see below, Habermas's applications continue to rely on Kant's juridical conception of peace and its constitutive reliance on a conception of right: civic, international, and cosmopolitan. However, it is this last element, the cosmopolitan, that Habermas takes up and develops in the context of what he sees as the challenges presented both by the shifts of our contemporary understanding of the cosmopolitan idea and its achievements and by the distinct challenges presented by globalisation. These challenges emerge both from the unequal nature of the effects of globalisation and the globalised nature of the risks and dangers experienced by present day society.

The cosmopolitan location of peace

In providing an interpretation of the March 2003 war in Iraq, Habermas reveals the meaning and consequences of the juridical approach he prefers in outlining his approach to the problem of war in the twenty-first century. The significance of Immanuel Kant in Habermas's corpus is beyond dispute and provides us with some indications as to the paradoxical relationship that modernity has with questions relating to violence in the human condition. Habermas suggests that the war should not be judged in terms of the consequences of the act, or the "facts" on the ground, for such responses "would succumb to an emotional response to the supposed abstractions of a 'bloodless moralism'"[18] He suggests instead that the war should rather be interpreted in terms of the "neoconservative" agenda in Washington which seeks to offer an alternative, as Habermas sees it, to the "domestication of state power through international law."[19] This alternative "is neither political realism nor the pathos of freedom. Instead the neoconservatives make a revolutionary claim: if the regime of international law fails, then the hegemonic imposition of a global liberal order is justified, even by means that are hostile to international law."[20] Such disregard, according to Habermas, led not only to the United States forfeiting its role as guarantor of "international rights", but reinforced the illegality of the actions taken by the so-called "coalition of the willing." While the motives for the war may be debated, that which Habermas concentrates on is what he refers to as the "truly revolutionary character of a political reorientation."[21] Habermas sees the origins of this reorientation in what Hobsbawm refers to as the "American century", wherein global transformations, from the reordering of Europe and the

Pacific, to the reformulation of Eastern and Central Europe, to the collapse of the Soviet Union, are achieved, or are seen to be achieved by a triumphalist liberalism under the "leadership" of the United States. For the neoconservatives, as Habermas sees it, "what could possibly be better for people than the worldwide spread of liberal states and the globalisation of free markets? Moreover, the road there is clearly marked: Germany, Japan, and Russia were forced to their knees by war and the arms race. In today's era of asymmetric warfare, military might is now more attractive than ever, since the victor is determined *a priori* and can purchase victory with relatively few victims. Wars that make the world better need no *further* justification."[22]

The Kantian underpinning of Habermas's powerful critique of the neoconservative agenda in Washington and its culmination in the invasion of Iraq emerges in his opposition to the "single hegemonic state" imposing through war and a military machine its own vision upon the world, or its own response strategies against those it sees as its enemies:

> There was a time when liberal nationalism saw itself justified in promulgating the universal values of its own liberal order, with military force if necessary, throughout the entire world. This arrogance doesn't become any more tolerable when it is transferred from nation-states to a single hegemonic state. It is precisely the universalistic core of democracy and human rights that forbids their unilateral realization at gunpoint.[23]

Habermas contrasts the "'universalism' of the old empires with what he calls a "modern self-understanding", one that is "shaped by an egalitarian universalism that requires a decentralisation of one's own perspective." Crucially, for our purposes in this context, Habermas argues that such egalitarian universalism "demands that one relativise one's own views to the interpretative perspectives of equally situated and equally entitled others."[24] Habermas finally calls for the further development of international law into a "cosmopolitan order that offers an equal and reciprocal hearing for the voices of all those affected."[25]

Habermas's "international" thought is based on a distinctly Kantian, and liberal democratic, reading. It relies on a "domestication" of the international scene, such that states as well as individuals are subject to the pacifying effects of law, which comes to be the guarantor not just of treaties between states but of human rights, rights that could protect the individual as well as communities against the excesses of state power. The cosmopolitan order that Habermas envisages has a capacity to transcend the sovereign state and as such must be in possession of armed force. Habermas saw the First Gulf War as inaugurating the first step towards a cosmopolitan order that had the force of law behind it. His interpretation of the Kosovo crisis is similarly an instantiation of the cosmopolitan order. War, for Habermas, when fought for rights, inaugurates cosmopolitan law. If rights are to form the universal priority, the sovereign state must be transcended and for it to be so transcended at times must require the use of force. Every instance of such use in the name of law inaugurates that law as cosmopolitan. While Habermas's conception of cosmopolitan law as the basis of an international order is based on Kant, there are significant departures stemming from what Habermas sees as the requisite conditions of the late modern period and its distinct challenges.

Habermas's conception of cosmopolitan law as the basis of perpetual peace shifts discourse away from the sovereignty of states and towards a positive conception of human rights protected under cosmopolitan law. It is precisely the desire to overcome what he sees as the arbitrary impact of power relations on judgement and answerability that Jurgen Habermas advocates a form of cosmopolitan order, and hence cosmopolitan responsibility. It is the combination of the desire for international regulation (the "domestication" of international life) and the increasing significance of the global public sphere that motivates Habermas to call for a post-Kantian cosmopolitan law that may form the basis of judgement and answerability, and that may be drawn upon to legitimise response mechanisms undertaken in the context of extreme violence and violations of human rights. For Habermas:

> Cosmopolitan law must be institutionalised in such a way that it is binding on individual governments. The community of peoples must be able to ensure that its members act at least in conformity with the law through the threat of sanctions. Only in this way will the unstable system of states that assert their sovereignty through mutual threats be transformed into a federation with common institutions which assume state functions, that is, which legally regulate the relations between its members and monitor their compliance with these rules.[26]

The external relations of states are thus transformed into a "domestic relationship between the members of a common organisation." The legal underpinnings of cosmopolitan law come to constitute a global citizenry that is unmediated by the state. For Habermas, "the most important implication of a form of law that bypasses the sovereignty of the state is the personal liability of individuals for crimes committed in the course of government and military service."[27]

Habermas sees the contemporary global context as a "transitional stage between international and cosmopolitan law."[28] The legitimisation of legal norms is dependent on a global public sphere that enables dialogue across the boundaries of cultural affiliation. Habermas is, at the same time, aware of the contemporary difficulties associated with the global public sphere and its capacity to confer legitimacy; the asymmetries emergent from the global political economy, differential access to the media and information technology, and the widespread violation of human rights in the name of necessity. Habermas's distinctly European liberal rendition on the place of cosmopolitan law in global politics is all too clear in this statement: "world views ought not to remain closed off from one another in sectarian isolation. They must discursively engage themselves – not only with each other, but with the intellectual content of European modernity as well."[29] In this way, global politics comes to incorporate categories aimed towards the establishment of a "global domestic policy" for, ultimately, "what other choice do we have, besides at least striving for its realisation?"[30]

Habermas's project is self-declaredly modern in its understanding of the modern subject of politics, has as its underlying premises a Kantian framework wherein peace is associated with the juridical regulation, in what we might understand as liberal democratic conditions, of both domestic and international life. Habermas takes the Kantian project further, in that he seeks not simply the federation of sovereign states, but the transcendence of sovereignty into a global arena of citizens understood to possess rights irrespective of their locations in distinct cultures or states. Habermas is then calling for a cosmopolitanism that seeks a juridical approach to global politics. It seeks to define judgement and answerability in terms of laws that protect human rights, laws that he insists encompass the global terrain as a whole, a terrain that has a capacity to confer legitimacy to any action, such as military intervention or sanctions regimes, undertaken in the name of the protection of human rights. Such global domesticity is built upon a global citizenry that is unmediated by the state and that is, instead, composed of sovereign, unitary beings that have a capacity to unproblematically relate word and deed, reaching agreement through rational, deliberative interaction free of manipulation and coercion.

Three elements emerge from Habermas's distinctly modern approach to the problems of late modern political violence. Firstly, he propounds a juridical approach to conflict, placing primacy on human rights as the legislative force both in the legitimisation of internationally sanctioned use of military intervention and in the acquisition of wide public support for such action. Secondly, the political authority requisite of any such intervention derives from international institutions, specifically the United Nations. Where this is absent, as was the case in Kosovo, other international institutions such as NATO come into the frame. Thirdly, the global legitimisation of conduct is also dependent on global modes of communication that might instantiate a global public arena of judgement and consensus. In relation to this arena, Habermas clearly draws from his discourse ethical approach to communicative practices, but moves further in suggesting that global civil society institutions come to form the vehicles through which virtual participation might take place. We found, in the above analysis, that Habermas's approach is clearly Kantian in its understanding of war and peace and is self-declaredly European liberal democratic, in its advocacy, not just of cosmopolitan law as the regulative ideal for the global order, but of a global sphere constitutive of rational deliberation and mutual understanding.

We can therefore see that Habermas's account of a cosmopolitan approach to the juridification of international life provides a blueprint from which we might begin to think about the political and social processes surrounding responses to violence. However, we might also argue that the moment of law, as portrayed by Habermas, is at the same time a moment of the violence that instantiates this law. This becomes especially apparent when we see that Habermas's understanding of cosmopolitan law is to directly relate its genesis with moments of violence, such as the military intervention in Kosovo. The judgement of law, when enacted globally, comes to be founded on the moment of violence, is brought into being with the decision to use violence. Hence Habermas's support for the war over Kosovo, for here we had an international military response, enacted under NATO's remit though led by the United States and the United Kingdom, aimed at the protection of civilian populations. The immediate purpose of the war against Serbia may have been the protection of the human rights of the Albanian population of Kosovo, nevertheless its other more long term consequence, for Habermas, is the constitution of what he understands as cosmopolitan law. Any war, taking place in the name of the protection of human rights and acquiring global legitimacy, is precisely another moment in the constitution of cosmopolitan law. Based on this exposition, it is not too difficult to see the reasons for Habermas's support for the military intervention in Kosovo and his condemnation of the invasion of Iraq. Where the former, for Habermas, acquired wide international legitimacy as a response to ethnic cleansing, the latter was expressive of a hegemonic move that lacked such legitimacy. Nevertheless, violence, in the form of sophisticated and western military intervention, comes to form the constitutive basis of a cosmopolitan law that binds humanity, so that the wars of the future, the only wars that can be fought legitimately, according to this viewpoint, are those that may clearly and unambiguously claim humanity as their ultimate purpose. As far as Habermas is concerned, where military intervention for Kosovo could make such a claim, the invasion of Iraq could not.

The ontological basis of Kant's conception of peace is the rational self, and it is precisely reason that forms the basis for the institutionalisation of peace as a universal project. The modern subject of reason is at the same time the peaceful subject, author of the transition from the state of nature to a social framework based on rights, a framework that in the Kantian view extends from the civic constitution that guarantees the rights of the individual citizen to the federation that guarantees the rights of all in a community of humankind. Kant is, however, reluctant to shed the sovereignty of states and rejects the idea of a world government as representing cosmopolitan right. In defining the ways in which reason determines the condition of peace, Kant ultimately retains the notion of the sovereignty of states relying instead on the capacity of reason, as manifest in the free and equal constitutional state, to legislate against war, to prioritise the mutual interests requisite of commerce and trade between communities, and to enable the public sphere to act as constraint against the bellicose ambitions of leaders. While Kant inaugurates a juridical conception of peace, he ultimately relies on moral reasoning as the linchpin of peaceful relations between states. It is this element, or this limitation to how far Kant is willing to extend law into cosmopolitan space, that brings Habermas into the frame. For peace to make juridical sense, according to Habermas, it must be backed up by the force of law.

Conceptually, the notion of a "perpetual peace" constitutes only a symptom of a "cosmopolitan order": "Kant must still solve the *conceptual problem* of how this order could be thought of from the viewpoint of law."[31] What is specific to cosmopolitan law and how does it differ from international law? Furthermore, how does the latter relate to the end state, peace? Within the Kantian perspective, the state of nature, a state of war, compels states to form themselves into a federation governed by international law. Such law regulates the behaviour of states, but does not diminish their sovereignty in relation to the initiation of war. In the Habermasian perspective, wars of a certain kind, humanitarian wars, transform the global arena into a cosmopolitan order. Clearly, Habermas is here distinguishing what he sees as "humanitarian" wars, such as the war for Kosovo, which he associates with transformation towards a cosmopolitan order, and wars such as the invasion of Iraq, which he associates with the neoconservative agenda that seeks transformation through the point of a gun. I will return to this differentiation later.

Habermas seeks to establish the difference between international law and cosmopolitan law. The latter "resembles state sanctioned civil law in that both definitively end the state of nature."[32] According to Habermas, Kant uses the idea of the social contract as having ended the state of nature between individuals to suggest that the "state of nature between warring states now comes to an end". According to Habermas, in *Theory and Practice*, published two years prior to *Perpetual Peace*, Kant refers to a "law of peoples" as a condition of "enforceable public laws to which each state must submit."[33] Kant's position two years later is firmly of the view that cosmopolitan order is different from the legal order within states, given that states retain their sovereignty and do not submit to "the public coercive laws of some supreme power."[34] Instead of a world republic, there emerges an "enduring and voluntary association." For Habermas, "Kant never explains just how this union is to be permanent, the feature on which a civilized resolution of international conflict depends, without the binding character of law based on the establishment of something analogous to a constitution."[35] He suggests there must be an element of "obligation" without which peace as an enduring condition cannot be realised, remaining instead a "hostage to an unstable constellation of interests that is likely to degenerate and fall apart, much as the League of Nations did years later."[36] Kant relies on each government's "*moral* self-binding."[37] There is in Kant, therefore, a clear distinction between the external sovereignty of states, which enables states to defend their integrity of borders by military means when needed, and internal sovereignty, which "refers to the capacity, based on the state's monopoly over the means of violence, for maintaining peace and order by means of administrative power and positive law."[38] According to Habermas, "this classical-modern world of nation states remains an unsurpassable conceptual limit" to the conception, let alone the creation, of a "cosmopolitan constitution."[39] Given Kant's "limited horizon" he cannot provide any "moral motivation" wherein states would form such a constitution. Given this difficulty, Kant makes a move that locates the creation, or feasibility, of a cosmopolitan order in a "philosophy of history with a cosmopolitan intent."[40]

Habermas's contribution to our understanding of a distinctly cosmopolitan conception of peace and war in the contemporary period cannot be over-estimated. His critique of the limitations, as he sees them, of Kant's rendition on the perpetual peace is based on a dialectical reading of the historical condition and a set of arguments that seek to show the primacy of rights in any conception of peace. Indeed, so paramount is Habermas's preoccupation with human rights that we can assume peace as such to be a secondary concern. Human rights become the basis of cosmopolitan law and their protection is governed both locally and internationally, with the latter making the case that the

> point of cosmopolitan law is that...it goes over the heads of the collective subjects of international law to give legal status to the individual subjects and justifies their unmediated membership in the association of free and equal world citizens...The most important consequence of a form of law that is able to puncture the sovereignty of states is the arrest of individual persons for crimes committed in the service of a state and its military.[41]

That cosmopolitan law has coercive backing is a point of view reflected in Habermas's call for the "prohibition against intervention in international law" to be revised.[42]

Crucial to Habermas's rearticulation of the Kantian project of peace is his emphasis on the universal claims to validity of human rights. It is this element that pitches Habermas against Carl Schmitt and for the argument he presents in favour of military intervention in the name of human rights. This argument is crucial for it defines the conditions which, in late modernity, have contributed to the transformative potential of war in the inauguration of a cosmopolitan peace, if Habermas is to be taken to the implications of his argument. Habermas's reflections on the Gulf War of 1991 are revealing in this regard. The Gulf War showed the United Nations "carrying out a global domestic policy" in authorising the use of military force, enabling the "allies" to act as "deputies of the world organization".[43] While this particular war was but a "hybrid" in the gradual movement towards a

cosmopolitan order, the war against Serbia, while remaining unauthor-
ised by the UN was nevertheless conducted in the name of human
rights and was again constitutive of the gradual institutionalisation of
cosmopolitan law. Arguing against the "scepticism of a self-destructive
critique of reason, one that senses behind every universal validity
claim the dogmatic will to domination of a cunningly concealed particularism",[44] a point of view expressed by Carl Schmitt, Habermas
seeks to argue at one and same time for the universal validity of rights
and the possibility for consensus across communities of culture on
issues relating to the "norms of coexistence".[45]

The modernity of a conception of peace which sees its most radical
expression in Immanuel Kant find its apotheosis in late modernity in
Habermas's reframing of the Kantian project precisely within the
context of late modern globalised social and political life. The progressive agenda found in Kant is replicated in Habermas and taken yet
further towards the institutionalisation of the protection of human
rights at global level in the form of a gradually emerging cosmopolitan
law that in a sense binds the universal validity of human rights. The
gradual acceptance, through dialogue, of the validity claims relating to
rights will finally enable the emergence of a global consensus on situations that call for a cosmopolitan response, namely the protection of
rights of individuals and communities alike. Every such instance
of intervention in the name of this emerging cosmopolitan law is itself
an instantiation of the validity of this law in the global arena. Hence the
imperative of intervention in situations such as the Gulf and specifically
Iraq's invasion of Kuwait and the Iraqi regime's genocidal attacks on its
own Kurdish population, the situations in other conflict areas, including the Balkans and specifically Kosovo, the conflicts in Somalia and
elsewhere, all representing situations of emergency for communities
targeted in the name of exclusionist identities and nationalist or fun-
damentalist modes of identification. Every response to such situations
is but one further step in the institutionalisation of cosmopolitan law
as the realisation of a juridically pacified global order.

The dialectic of peace

Looked at from the cosmopolitan viewpoint, it is difficult for any
emancipatory position to dispute Habermas's call for the establishment
of regulative frameworks that might enable judgement relating to
answerability in conditions of the extremes of violence and human suffering, as witnessed in places such as Kosovo, Rwanda, and elsewhere in

conditions where civilian populations come to form the primary targets. It is also possible to draw, from Habermas's conception of the public sphere and the extrapolation of such a conception to the global terrain, ideas relating to the global public sphere as potentially forming the site wherein opposition to violence and exclusion might find expression and mobilisation. This, we will investigate further in the sixth chapter of this book. However, it is also possible to delve into what might be referred to as the "dark side" of Habermas's conception of cosmopolitan law, and his juridical understanding of war and peace. For violence, as manifest in high technology warfare, comes to form the basic requirement for the instantiation of Habermas's framework for global domesticity, a domesticity replete with violent and exclusionary practices. We have seen this in our analysis of the global matrix of war in Chapter 2. We do so here specifically in relation to the moments that Habermas sees as instantiations of law.

Habermas's critical thought has been drawn upon in providing a conception of peace, that peace may be defined in terms of dialogical, communicative practices that are constitutively built upon the mutual recognition of subjects engaged freely and equally in deliberative and reflexive practices, practices that might potentially locate conflict in the social arena wherein the grievances that generate strategic action may be subjected to the legislative ideals of consensus-forming deliberation.[46] This conception of peace relied heavily on Habermas's proceduralist ethics, as formulated in his discourse ethics, and on his critical reflections on the public sphere. As we have seen above, these elements of his critical thought remain pertinent to our reflections on the potential of the global public sphere to emerge as the location of contestation against the totalising practices represented in the use of violence and exclusionary practices. We also recognise, however, that Habermas's reworking of Kant's *Perpetual Peace* into a notion of cosmopolitan law sees the instantiation of such law in military interventions that, for Habermas, have the basis of their legitimisation in human rights law and the protections that this body of law confers to populations targeted by the extremes of violence. Thus, humanitarian intervention, for Habermas, comes to form the constitutive moment of cosmopolitan law. The violence of war, when enacted in the name of humanity, begets law, transforming the global condition into a "domesticated" rule-governed arena.

Some might seek to subject this Habermasian understanding to a Schmittian reading, suggesting that war, rather than inaugurating cosmopolitan law, is in actuality a moment of decision inaugurating the power of the sovereign. The power to decide, according to this perspective, is the ultimate form of power. War, according to this framework, is not the product of legitimate practices of international institutions, but is, rather, the product of concrete decisions made by the pre-eminent power of the day, a sovereign entity that has the capacity to transcend established law.[47]

A leading expert in legal theory in the Weimar Republic and the Third Reich, Schmitt provides an anti-liberal position on war and peace and represents, according to Hans Joas, the "militarist" counter-tradition in 1930s' Germany.[48] War for Schmitt remains a real possibility "for as long as the concept of the enemy remains valid". The "political" is revealed only in the "extreme case" of a "conflict to the death, and only in that situation can we recognise what determines the substance of the political entity and what, therefore, is the decisive authority to which all other bonds must defer."[49] Sovereignty is ascribed only to this authority, which ultimately has the authority to decide on the state of exception or state of emergency. His critique of liberalism is that every argument about values is in actuality an attempt to exercise power. Both the concept of the "rule of law" and the just war doctrine are about the exercise of power and hence the determination of the enemy. As Hans Joas points out, "By completely subordinating the normative to the question of its political meaning in specific situations where decisions are required, Schmitt robs the political of every inherent normative dimension."[50] War is hence about an "existential threat to one's own way of life."[51] In a devastating critique of the Schmittian perspective, a critique that must be kept in mind in any call on Schmitt as a critique of the cosmopolitan project, Herbert Marcuse refers to Schmitt's "totalitarian political theory" as expressing a form of "political existentialism" wherein

> the existential appears essentially as a contrast to the "normative", i.e. as something that cannot be placed under any norm lying outside it. From this it follows that one absolutely cannot think, judge, or decide about an existential condition as a "non-partisan third party"...There is no fundamental or general criterion in existentialism for determining which facts and conditions are to be considered existential. That remains left in principle to the decision of the existential theoretician. But once he claims a state of fact as existential, all those who do not "participate and partake" in its reality are to keep silent.[52]

Schmitt's rejection of the normativity of the rule of law and his interpretation of the constraining or enabling role of international institutions as merely expression of dominant power prevent any consideration of the place that the normative has historically played in global institutions such as the League of Nations or the United Nations. The invocation of humanity, for example, in the struggle against apartheid in South Africa, or the support and recognition of self-determination struggles, conferred global capacities to those organisations involved despite the opposition of the powerful. It is therefore both totalising and ahistorical to claim that humanitarian motives are but the instantiations of sovereign power. Schmitt's existential understanding of war, his dissolution of state and society, and his organic conception of communality are elements of a framework of thought that indeed culminates in the reduction of politics to the extreme conditions of confrontation. It is as such unhelpful in seeking an understanding of the relationship between wars conducted in the name of humanity and the instantiation of law as defined by Habermas and other liberal thinkers.

Writing of war in the twenty-first century seems somehow to defy earlier expectations of a modernity devoid of violence, an era marked by human progress towards a rationally ordered world based on universal reason as the baseline upon which human interactions, from the economic to the social, could take place. The very meaning of modernity constitutively implied human liberation from the shackles of religious dogma and arbitrary rule, so that human agency could flourish content in the knowledge that, under certain economic and political conditions, the emancipation of the human condition would be manifest universally, was indeed within the realm of achievement. The modern era, its ethos and institutions, came to represent the potential that could be reached by all, a potential driven by technological advancement and economic and social interactions governed by the rule of law.

Perhaps the text that best places modernity into historical perspective is Horkheimer and Adorno's *Dialectic of Enlightenment*. Any conception of the relationship between the modern and violence, the modern era and its associated myths of progress and peace can initiate the analysis with this all-too-important text. Its significance is not simply confined to its place as one of the foremost texts emerging from the Frankfurt School of critical theory. Rather, its rendition on the Enlightenment provides those of us located in a distinctly late modern condition with the tools that might aid in the understanding of the forms of violence that dominate our era today. Horkheimer and Adorno provide for this present analysis a formative text that points to certain thoughts on the very notion of transformation; that the human condition may indeed be transformed so that progress rather than reaction could be the defining moment of a universally ordained state of being. It is indeed this text that allows us a glimpse into the intricate relationship between modernity's association with a perpetual peace, a discursive association, and the violence that came to be the very product of this association.

Horkheimer and Adorno see the apotheosis of the "programme" of the enlightenment in Francis Bacon and his celebration of technology as the essence of human knowledge, a form of knowledge that is instrumental:

> On the road to modern science, men renounce any claim to meaning. They substitute formula for concept, rule and probability for cause and motive. Cause was only the last philosophic concept which served as a yardstick for scientific criticism: so to speak because it alone among the old ideas still seemed to offer itself to scientific criticism, the latest secularisation of the creative principle. Substance and quality, activity and suffering, being and existence...science managed without such categories.[53]

Calculative certainty becomes the linchpin of the Enlightenment: "For the Enlightenment, whatever does not conform to the rule of computation and utility is suspect." The human subject's epistemic agency is paramount and its subject matter is the "calculability of the world".[54] The "dissimilar" must be comparable and the diverse reduced to the one. Instrumental rationality is the defining feature of what constitutes the modern subject, whose "awakening" comes at the price of acknowledging "power as the principle of all relations".[55] Horkheimer and Adorno see science as being located at the heart of such instrumentality and science itself dissolves distinctions, seeking fungible categories and "universal interchangeability."[56] The Enlightenment "excises the incommensurable" and seeks conformity. The overwhelming picture that emerges is of an Enlightenment as "mythic fear turned radical. The pure imminence of positivism, its ultimate product, is no more than so to speak a universal taboo. Nothing at all may remain outside, because the mere idea of outsidedness is the very source of fear."[57]

What we gain from Horkheimer and Adorno's account of the modern, enlightened self is the image of an age wherein science, instrumentality, the relation of word and deed, are but the reified myths of an age dominated by the requisites of the market place. Enlightenment, however, has its dialectic, in that it is itself premised on a certain mythology, despite its efforts to demythologise. The sacrifice of the individual is at the same time the birth of the sovereign self, the self-awareness of the latter is at the same time an acknowledgement of systemic knowledge that seeks the subsumption of the particular in the whole; the invocation of progress is at the same time the moment of violence perpetrated against the incommensurable, the non-conforming, the feared outside of outsidedness. Here in this text we find some clues that might direct us towards understanding the persistence of violence in late modernity and its impact on subjectivity, identity, politics, and hence collective life.

At the same time, the text makes some questionable assertions that could be subjected to critique on further reflection, a critique that has implications for our current concerns with war and peace. Habermas's defence of modernity is instructive here for it allows for a conception of modern rationality, modern frameworks of thought, that transcend particularity and hence the necessary association of particularity with the fear of the outside. The possibility of critique comes to rely at one and same time on the situatedness of the individual self and hence of meaning or understanding as well as the capacity to transcend such situatedness and hence to overcome the determinations of tradition. In a context of a late modern life that is paradoxically steeped in discourses that seek to rejuvenate the discourses of tradition, an ontological perspective that enables the self precisely to transcend appears to be the only possibility of transformations that enable the agency or the capacity to imagine that things could be otherwise. What Habermas asserts as a modern ontology is one that is a step removed from Kant's as well as Horkheimer and Adorno's, namely a human rationality that is located in the social sphere, in other words, in inter-subjectivity. This has significance in relation to Habermas's defence of the concept of human rights as a distinctly modern concept; in other words, one that is understood in universal juridical terms and not just moral terms. Habermas's ontological stance is well summed up by Thomas McCarthy when he states: "The internal relation of meaning to validity means that communication is not only always 'imminent' – that is, situated, conditioned – but also always 'transcendent' – that is, geared to validity claims that are meant to hold beyond any local context and thus can be indefinitely criticized, defended, revised."[58] Habermas's critique of Horkheimer and Adorno starts from this baseline assumption when he states that the achievements of modernity remain unrecognised in *Dialectic of Enlightenment*. The following statement is again indicative of Habermas's later articulations of his liberal democratic thought and the trajectory that this took in relation to his thoughts on the "international":

> The *Dialectic of Enlightenment* does not do justice to the rational content of cultural modernity that was captured in bourgeois ideals (and also instrumentalized along with them). I am thinking here of the specific theoretical dynamic that continually pushes the sciences, and even the self-reflection of the sciences, *beyond* merely engendering technically useful knowledge; I am referring, further, to the universalistic foundations of law and morality that have *also* been incorporated (in however distorted and incomplete a fashion) into the institutions of constitutional government, into the forms of democratic will formation, and into individualist patterns of identity formation; I have in mind finally the productivity and explosive power of basic aesthetic experiences that a subjectivity liberated from the imperatives of purposive activity and from conventions of quotidian perception gains from its own decentering – experiences that are presented in works of avant-garde art, that are articulated in the discourses of art criticism, and that also achieve a *certain measure* of illuminating effect (or at least contrast effects that are instructive) in the innovatively enriched range of values proper to self-realization.[59]

While reason may have an instrumental content, this instrumentality is simply one aspect of the complex interplay of the inter-subjective manifestation of communicative practices and the diversity of their articulation in modern societies, articulations that find expression in the institutions of modernity as well as in aesthetic experience. For Habermas, Horkheimer and Adorno's text "holds out scarcely any prospect for an escape from the myth of purposive rationality that has turned into objective violence."[60]

Habermas and later, ontologically similar, defences of modernity, its subjectivities and institutions, express, perhaps, a too complacent and too optimistic a vision of cultural modernity and its constitutive articulations in subjectivity and modern institutions. Indeed if we look no further than Zygmunt Bauman's *Modernity and the Holocaust* or Michael Mann's more recent *The Dark Side of Democracy* we find the genesis of the extremes of violence in the very practices that Habermas hails as the emancipatory expressions of the culture of modernity and its institutions. For Bauman,

> the Holocaust was not an antithesis of modern civilisation and everything (or so we like to think) it stands for. We suspect (even if we refuse to admit it) that the Holocaust could merely have uncovered another face of the same modern society whose other, more familiar, face we so admire. And that the two faces are perfectly comfortably attached to the same body. What we perhaps fear most, is that each of the two faces can no more exist without the other than can the two sides of a coin.[61]

Michael Mann similarly presents a picture of modern democracy that conflicts with Habermas's more optimistic vision. Writing in the more recent context of newly democratising states, Mann sees the dangers associated with the constructed contiguities of the demos and the ethnos, contiguities that define the conditions of possibility for instances of "ethnic cleansing" and other modes of the extremes of violence witnessed in late modern Europe and elsewhere. For Mann,

> Modern ethnic cleansing is the dark side of democracy when ethno-nationalist movements claim the state for their own ethnos, which they initially intend to constitute as a democracy, but then they seek to exclude and cleanse others. There was also a dark side to socialist versions of democracy. The people was equated with the proletariat, and after the revolution cleansing of classes and other enemies might begin.[62]

What is clear from the above is that the modern subject envisaged by Habermas as the peaceful, rational subject is undoubtedly a subject located in the European context. While Habermas calls for cross-cultural dialogue and understanding, his starting point is the subject of European Enlightenment. Others may be brought into this realm of modernity and hence peace through dialogue, and specifically dialogue that is defined in distinctly ecumenical terms. It is as if the subjectivity of the other can only be discerned in terms of religion and tradition. If we ask at the closing stages of this chapter, who has the capacity to be agent of peace in the Habermasian worldview, we find a representation that firmly locates the agency for peace within the liberal democratic West. While the difficulties (increasing xenophobia, nationalism, global poverty and the hegemony of neoliberalism) are acknowledged by Habermas, nevertheless the ontological baseline of peace is the rational self located in the west:

> A peaceful world order would be possible only on the premise that internal factors within the powerful industrialized nations render them in less and less of a position to act externally as belligerent states. Kant maintained that only those states that had achieved an internal republican constitution could band together into a federative order of peace. We too can only hope that the populations of the world's social welfare democracies gradually develop into liberal political cultures, that they grow accustomed to institutions of freedom and develop majorities with pacifistic mentalities, so that they can no longer be mobilized for wars in the classical sense.

Habermas argues that a global "overlapping consensus" is possible, involving the world's religions, that the "content of the moral principles embodied in international law is in harmony with the normative substance of the great world historical prophetic doctrines and metaphysical worldviews."[63]

Conclusion

Any discourse on peace assumes the possibility of transformation, of societal progression towards the institutionalisation of modes of interaction that undermine the enabling conditions for violence while generating the possibility for dialogical resolutions to grievance underpinned by law. Such transformations assume, as I indicate at the outset, no less than the transformation of social arrangements into those that guarantee a free and equal public sphere, participation in discourse, and the recognition of individual agency situated in wider social relations. The underlying framework for this conception of peace lay in Habermasian discourse ethics, its Kantian foundations set within the context of inter-subjective social relations. In the rereading of Kant and Habermas I provide in this chapter, the question that becomes most pertinent to our present condition relates to the location of agency in what I want to refer to as the capacity to "legislate for peace". Considering where such agency lies places the spotlight on the relationship between peace and progress, peace and humanity, and peace and violence.

In earlier attempt at reflections on peace,[64] the agency for peace was located in the inter-subjective setting of free and equal communicative practices taking place within a pluralist public sphere. The stress in this early study was on the political agency of individuals recognised as being constituted within wider social continuities while retaining a capacity to make a difference. That this was a Hegelian framing of subjectivity articulated in Kantian spirit, to borrow from Habermas's conception of his discourse ethics, was in no doubt as I applied Habermas's theory of communicative practices to my own concerns, namely understanding the structures of domination generative of violence and defining the conditions wherein such structures may be subject to transformation. Imagining peace as the object of such transformation, even as the spectre of Benjamin had a haunting, if invisible presence, was too compelling an ending to a volume devoted to understanding violence. The ending to that volume is in turn too compelling a start to this, written in the context of continuing violence, now not simply confined to societies in the throes of breakdown, nor to protracted conflicts the ongoing violence of which is almost normalised, but having a wider, global, span of operations involving state as well as non-state actors in global transnational spaces where the very definition of war can no longer be confined to its traditional battlefield sense. The spectre of Benjamin comes to have an all too visible presence in this rereading of Kant's treatise on peace, and its Habermasian articulation in the form of cosmopolitan peace underpinned by cosmopolitan law.

As the chapter indicates, where Kant holds on to the sovereignty of states, which he views as all too important in enabling the genesis of a federation that is at once both the product and the condition for perpetual peace, Habermas sees state sovereignty as the obstacle to the realisation of cosmopolitan law. The latter is in turn the guarantee, ultimately, of the positive realisation of human rights set in the context of a domesticated international sphere where all, individuals and states, are subject to the rule of law. Habermas's cosmopolitan peace is rendered possible through the force of law, and such law is instantiated in every act of war conducted for humanitarian purposes. The agents of war, if defined in distinctly humanitarian terms, in this reading, are at one and the same time, the agents of peace, for peace is by implication defined in terms of the pacifying effect of law defined in cosmopolitan terms. As stated earlier, Habermas clearly sees the United States as the "pacemaker of progress towards a cosmopolitan order vested with legal powers, overriding national sovereignty, to prevent aggression and protect human rights";[65] a role that the United States appears to have forfeited in its illegal invasion of Iraq. Nevertheless, the agent of cosmopolitan peace is, paradoxically, a sovereign state whose actions are preferably sanctioned by the United Nations, as the embodiment of an international legal order. For Habermas, "since the end of the Second World War, the idea of perpetual peace has taken on a more tangible form in the institutions, declarations, and policies of the UN (as well as other international organisations). The challenge posed by the unprecedented catastrophes of the twentieth century has also given new impetus to Kant's idea. Against this sombre background, the World Spirit, as Hegel would have put it, has lurched forward."[66]

The world spirit in Hegel represents the culmination of historical stages of development wherein humankind emerges as the location of reason. However, problematically, and devastatingly, for Habermas, as Hannah Arendt points out,

> The best that can happen to any individual in the Hegelian revelation of world spirit is to have the good fortune to be born among the right people at the right historical moment, so that one's birth will coincide with the revelation of the world spirit in this particular period. For Hegel to be a member of historical mankind meant to be a Greek and not a barbarian in the fifth century B.C., a Roman citizen and not a Greek in the first centuries of our era, to be a Christian and not a Jew in the Middle Ages, etc.[67]

Clearly, in the Hegelian system, humanity experiences different stages of historical development and there remains what we might refer to as the other of progress, those inscribed, therefore, as the other of peace.

Nevertheless, the march of the world spirit, if represented as it clearly is in Habermas's reading, in the increasing institutionalisation of legally pacified international relations, bringing forth a cosmopolitan peace, where cosmopolitan law comes to form the guarantee for the protection of rights, has seen its culmination in the emergence of international practices that no longer view state sovereignty as the barrier to intervention in situations of extreme violence and social breakdown. The reconciliation of philosophy to the actualities on the ground was especially apparent in UN operations that, in the early 1990s, transcended traditional remits of peacekeeping, moving into responsibilities associated variously with elections and governance, as indeed occurred in operations from Namibia, to Cambodia, to East Timor, to name but a few. However, it was military interventions in the name of humanity that are, as will be seen in the next chapter, significant in the transformations we witness in global politics.

4
War, the International, the Human

Why isn't anything going on in the senate?
Why are the senators sitting there without legislating?
   Because the barbarians are coming today.
   What's the point of senators making laws now?
   Once the barbarians are here, they'll do the legislating.

C.P. Cavafy[1]

With the end of the Cold War came the inauguration of a new conception of war, one that sought to invoke humanity in its justifying discourses. The very construction of this form of war as "liberal" attaches to it a certain normative meaning; that war, when undertaken by particular states, is a progressive force globally.[2] Intervention in distant lands would from henceforth be undertaken for the protection of other populations, those under threat from their own kinsmen and governments, requiring protection and rescue in the name of international responsibility and human rights. From the First Gulf War, to subsequent actions against Iraq, to the interventions in the Balkans, to Sierra Leone, Somalia, and then, in the post-September 11th context, Afghanistan and Iraq, the "rescue" of populations has been at the forefront of discourses of legitimisation around war. In wars that made a significant shift away from self-defence as the primary legal basis of war's justification, this moral imperative rendered human rights a constitutive element of war and the political processes surrounding questions of intervention.

It would be all too easy to adopt a perspective on the question of so-called "humanitarian war" that simply provided a realist critique of the moral claims surrounding such interventions. To frame the debate in this way would simply state that the interventions of the 1990s and into the present are either conducted in the name of other populations and their rescue or for the purpose of very real and very tangible interests centred variously around power, order, security, or even geo-strategic resources. In reference to Carl Schmitt's anti-liberal critique, we might suggest that he who has the power to define what is legiti-mate prevails in the justifying stakes surrounding war. Schmitt's inter-pretation of war is influenced by his decisionism, his concentration on who makes the decisions:

> Of course, everyone wants justice, morality, ethics and peace, no one wants to do wrong; but the only interesting question *in concreto* is always who decides in each specific case what is right, what peace consists in, what the threat to peace or a breach of the peace is, how it is to be eliminated and when a situation is normal and "pacified", etc. This *quis iudicabit* shows that within the law and the general commandment to be moral a dualism lies concealed that robs these concepts of the ability to stand up to "power" as simple opposing principles and to swing pendulum-like towards it.[3]

The power to define, as Joas points out, "is power in a pre-eminent sense."[4] Schmitt sees international legal agreements to outlaw war as proposing a "discriminatory" concept of war wherein those involved are not accorded equal recognition but confer to one party the claim to fight an aggressor "in the name of humanity" as a whole. Neutrality in this situation is no longer possible, for the struggle is one between police and criminal where "every form of behaviour must imply taking sides with order or disorder."[5]

As the debates surrounding the military intervention against Serbia and the more recent invasion of Iraq show all too clearly, this dualistic (hegemonic interest versus cosmopolitan humanitarianism) formula of representations appears in some sense to exhaust the language sur-rounding these particular wars. The aim of this chapter is to explore the political consequences of wars fought "for humanity". In part-icular, it concentrates on the juridico-political consequences of such wars, their implications in relation to the constitution and reconstitu-tion of political community, and their location in relation to how we conceive of the "international" as a distinct sphere of politics. The first section concentrates on the implications of so-called liberal wars in the reconstitution of the international. It frames the debate between con-ceptions of the international in terms of the system of sovereign states on the one hand and those that transcend the state, moving towards the "human", on the other. Exploring these questions in the first section enables a move towards an understanding of wars of intervention in terms that suggest a constitutive role for war in the late modern period wherein the very act of military intervention is not so much associated with motivation – which might suggest instrumentality – but with the constitution and reconstruction of identities. In suggesting this constitutive role for war; that war brings forth or establishes identity of the interveners and the intervened upon, so to speak, I explore wars of the recent past in terms of various missions that form the core of the discourses surrounding these wars; to civilise, to modernise, to democratise. Each is in turn associated with a global remit that seeks to rationalise, to render readable and calculable a global terrain that persists, despite the odds, in its refusal to be subject to such technologies. The chapter further argues, in the second section, that beyond war's constitutive role in the formation of identities, the use of military force in the name of humanity is also one further moment in the constitution of the *global* terrain in distinctly juridical terms, so that those identified as the lawful may easily be distinguished from the "lawless", thereby transforming wars into policing operations. This perspective seeks a transformation of conceptions of the "international" in terms of humanity and applauds military intervention in support of the human rights of populations. The consequences of what may be referred to as cosmopolitan wars are profound, for they suggest not just the establishment of a temporary truce between combatants, but a wholesale transformation of social and political relations both domestically and internationally. One tool of such transformation is understood in terms of "state-building", a tool that, as will be explored in this section, in liberal terms, seeks to create the normative conditions for peace, but placed in Foucaultian terms, comes to be constitutive of global relations of power that seek to discipline conflict and dissent emerging from other societies. The third section highlights the dangers and contradictions implicated in interventionist conceptions of the cosmopolitan, dangers that become apparent in the ways in which boundaries are redrawn, exclusions reestablished, so that the terrain of such practices is now rendered in global as opposed to local terms. What emerges from discourses that seek to modernise, civilise, or democratise, is a conception of a world rendered in hierarchical terms, those that can claim the right of judgement and others who cannot, those within the law and those located beyond the law, those worthy of protection and others not so deserving; all suggesting a hierarchy of worth and a hierarchy of worthiness the remit of which is hegemonic domination. A different conception of the cosmopolitan emerges from such an interrogation, one that subjects itself to imminent critique, one that recognises its own limits, its own particularity as a political discourse, a theme that I will to return to in Chapter 6.

Reconstituting the international

The attribution of motivation to state actors in their interactions at global level is a central feature of rationalist discourses in International Relations, whether these are located within the realist/neorealist or the liberal sides of the debate. Where the first attributes to states interests which the state then acts upon, the second argues that such interests have a wider, more collaborative location, and are hence subject to constraint. Nevertheless linking both approaches is the idea that an understanding of state interests reveals the motivations behind their actions. This rationalist understanding starts with the ontological assumption that states are "persons" and being so may be assumed as coherent and consistent beings whose calculations reveal the underlying motivations behind their actions. Instrumental rationality is hence key to both approaches, even as the latter, liberal, approach tends to be more responsive to the claims of international institutions and international norms. If the story of state interests ends here, we can see how it is possible to frame humanitarian wars in terms of a dualism, wherein one approach, the realist, can claim that the purpose of all wars is defined by the individual interests of the state, while the other, the liberal, can claim that wars may be fought beyond the interests of the individual state, serving instead, the commonality of interests shared by humankind.[6] The ontological baseline remains rationalist to the core, for the latter approach again assumes a rational actor, coherent and consistent in its desires to save others.

The design of the United Nations Charter clearly places primacy with the sovereign state, unambiguously prohibiting in Article 2 the use of force or its threat against the independence and territorial integrity of other states. However, the Charter is also enabling of the use of force in strictly limited circumstances, namely those construed, *by the Security Council*, to constitute acts of aggression or threats against peace, wherein such use aims at the restoration of international peace and security (Articles 39 and 42). Where states have a right to transgress is in situations of "self-defence" (Article 51). Running in juxtaposition to this state-centred design of the international is a historic "human" element centred upon the protection of human beings as such. Since the Geneva and Hague Conferences of 1899 and 1907, there have been conventions that seek the restriction of behaviour in time of war, norms and rules that prohibit the infliction of unnecessary human suffering. Codified in international laws of war,[7] including the Geneva Conventions, such prohibitions provide the legal baseline from which judgement may be formed on the violations of the laws of war and, latterly, human rights norms. With ethnic cleansing, systematic rape, genocide, the use of amputation, and other direct modes of intimidation directed against civilian populations, wars such as those in the Congo, Sierra Leone, the Balkans, and elsewhere came to represent clear cases of the infliction of mass suffering upon individuals and communities alike. In more recent situations of war and violence, Geneva has once again become a matter of great controversy in relation to the invasions of Afghanistan and Iraq, and the treatment of prisoners in camps such as Guantanamo, prisons such as Abu Ghraib, and others places used for the confinement of individuals seen as terrorist suspects by the United States armed forces.[8] Thus, humanitarian law and human rights law come to form the basis upon which both the judgement of conduct by combatants may be formed and the grounds upon which those perpetrating crimes of war and crimes against humanity may be indicted in courts of law, such as the *ad hoc* courts established for the former Yugoslavia and Rwanda, or (possibly in the future) the International Criminal Court. There is then a historically tense relationship between a conception of the international that places primacy on the limits of the sovereign state and that which seeks to define conditions that enable the transgression of such limits in the name of the human and hence the universal. Both conceptions are distinctly modern, both seek a positive definition in law and in the workings of governmental institutions, domestic and international; both, in other words, seeks to draw the "limits", to quote Walker,[9] of politics, of community, and of the international. It is this tension that raises fundamental questions relating to the politics of the international and the human.

As far as the realist perspective is concerned, the norms established by the laws of war and human rights law do not so much constrain the behaviour of states as provide the basis from which states, as self-interested actors, may draw the legitimising language for the justification of their actions, both in time of intervention and during hostilities. They do not form the motivation for conduct, in other words, but may be drawn upon by rational actors in their efforts to mobilise support. What is significant here is not the body of law that restricts behaviour or that forms the basis for potential indictment of those deemed to be in contravention of the laws of war. Rather, it is this discourse acting as a legitimising tool for the conduct of states acting within the anarchical condition of the international system. Discourses around human rights and humanitarianism are in this sense an additional tool in the armoury of states that seek to defeat their enemies for purposes other than the alleviation of human suffering. This Schmittian perspective is clear in its articulation of a position that rejects the juridification of war and hence the application of universal norms that may be applied equally within the global arena. This perspective rejects the view that such juridification may limit violence or form the basis for state behaviour, arguing instead that the invocation of such laws lies in the hands of those who hold the reigns of power, and hence those in whose capacity it is to proclaim the identity of those accused of crimes against humanity.

There is clearly a problem with the attribution of humanitarianism as an unproblematic motive for armed intervention into states or conflict zones, given the very real possibility of other interpretations centring on relations of power. Nevertheless, some authors will unproblematically refer to particular interventions as humanitarian, listing situations as diverse, not to mention controversial, as Iraq, Somalia, Rwanda, Sierra Leone, Bosnia, and Kosovo.[10] However, according to Danilo Zolo, "to qualify a war as 'humanitarian intervention' is a typical ploy for self-legitimisation by those who wage that war. As such it is part and parcel of war itself, an instrument of military strategy in the strict sense, used to obtain victory over the enemy."[11] Humanitarian motivations, or the articulation of such motivations are a means of acquiring wider support for action that bears the very highest of costs, and is hence about the manufacture of consensus around war. With the globalisation of politics and communication, according to Zolo, "the universalizing of humanitarian motivations is an effective rhetorical instrument" so that a "world public opinion" may be pitched against a deviant regime, constructing that regime as enemy of humanity at large. Quoting Schmitt's statement, "whoever invokes humanity is trying to cheat", Zolo sees the motivation for the war over Kosovo as a distinct move on the part of the United States to exercise its "hegemonic will" and "wield absolute planetary authority" against the United Nations Charter, international law, or indeed the consensus of other members of the United Nations.[12]

Zolo provides a powerful critique of the "claims" of humanitarian intervention, claims that, in the name of international ethics, undermine the workings of an international legal order defined in terms of the sovereignty of states. Drawing a line from Kant's *"Perpetual Peace"*, to Kelsen's "legal pacifism" to Habermas's "radical-isation of Kantian cosmopolitanism", Zolo argues against the view that "modern war" can be viewed as a form of "legal sanction" deter-mined as such through the criteria of just cause.[13] If the "primary function of law, and of international law in particular, is to submit the wielding of power to general rules, and, hence, to standards of proportion, discrimination and restraint in the use of force, it follows that in the nuclear age war must be considered incompatible with law, *legibus solutum* (outside the law)."[14] High technology warfare, as enacted from the skies, must always remain outside the law, an act of exception, both in terms of a sovereign state definition of international law and in terms of the "international legal subjec-tivity of individuals" as rights holders, for war generalises, treats populations as mass, denies individuals their right to life, their rights of *habeas corpus*, and equality before the law. Herein lies the historically tense relationship between the international defined in terms of state sovereignty and the human defined in terms of the rights of individuals; the aporias that are always already constitutive of the sphere of the modern international.

In exploring the conditions of possibility that render a humanitar-ian discourse a workable tool in practices of legitimisation, we might turn to another author who comes close to Zolo's analysis, but pro-vides a critique of the juridical approach to war. If we look to Michael Dillon's Foucaultian interpretation of the increasing recourse to humanitarian law, we see that the "flight to law" is a means through which conflict is rendered outside of politics; liberal-ism's "depoliticisation" of contestation.[15] International attempts at the criminalisation of social and political violence constitute a "depoliticising manoeuvre" that is expressed in moralising terms, but constitutes the translation of politics into administration and policing. International criminal law is, therefore, not merely about prosecuting war criminals. It is, according to Dillon, about an image of subjectivity that depoliticises conflict and circulates a particular form of order and meaning. It is related to the primacy of global liberal governance and its allied processes of capitalisation, con-sumerisation, militarisation, and globalisation. Global liberal gover-nance is, in this reading, an agent of international capital and humanitarianism is confined to policing the local conditions that global capital is involved in engendering. Following Michel

Foucault's understanding of liberal governmentality, Dillon suggests that politics comes to be equated with the science of government:

> This appeal to a "community" of the *jus gentium* is not, as is claimed, simply the condition of possibility of civilised conduct internationally, however, but a condition of supposability, instead, of correlative orders of governance and violence as well. It effects a subject abstracted from religious, linguistic, racial, ethnic, and other cultural markers of distinctive forms of life. Further, the correlative orders of governance and violence to whose conditions of supposability and imposability criminalisation contributes, also begin to comprise a certain regime of distributive justice in which, some, of course, systematically benefit very much more than others.[16]

The point of connection between Dillon and Zolo is that humanitarianism serves purposes other than the immediate declarations of those involved. Where Zolo places emphasis on the will to power of the major global player, the United States and its post-Cold War hegemonic position in global politics, Dillon stresses global liberal governance and its relationship to global capital, where the United States as a state is but one albeit powerful agent. Where Zolo invokes international law to censure the actions of the Clinton and Blair administrations, Dillon is concerned with precisely such invocation, the call to law and its meaning in the continuities of global, social and political life. However, the call to law is always subject to the "repoliticising" question, "why this violence rather than that?", subjecting international law to a "performative misfire" wherein politics is always already allowed "back in".[17] The spectre of Schmitt is also present in Dillon's rendition of humanitarian intervention. According to Dillon, what is taken to be violent and political differs from time to time and from place to place. Political regimes specify what violence is legitimate and what is not suggesting that relations of power politicise certain forms of violence and depoliticise others. The invocation of security, for example, is not simply about protection from violence; it is a claim for the right to use violence. We might use as examples here the current practices associated with the so-called "war against terrorism" or other protracted conflicts, such as the Israeli-Palestinian, where conflict and grievance is constructed in terms of security, legitimising the violence of one and delegitimising the violence of the other. Thus, how violence is signified and how violence signifies depends on the historically specific relations of power, relations that produce a particular subjectivity, one that is individualised and universalised, abstracted from the specific religious, cultural, linguistic, and racial markers that constitute a distinct form of life and hence a distinct set of contingencies that define political struggle. According to Dillon, the functions of the criminalisation of violence internationally are not confined to the "indictment of evil". They include the bringing forth, the constitution, of a moral and political order suitable to the workings of global governance and the global market place. The criminalisation of violence and hence its depoliticisation is not aimed at limiting violence, but at the constitution of a particular mode of subjectivity defined in terms of policing on the one hand and criminality on the other.

Both authors highlighted above challenge the idea that humanitarianism can unproblematically be associated with the use of force in contemporary global politics. Both suggest that the use of force has functions that transcend the immediacy of the human suffering that characterises recent wars, such as the intervention over Kosovo. While Zolo's account suggests that this particular intervention sought to constitute the United States as the paramount power in global politics, Dillon's account provides a nuanced rendition on the constitutive role of violence and its location in relations of power. The use of force comes to contribute to the ways in which power is inscribed on individual and social bodies alike, producing the subject that has the right of judgement and ultimately the right to kill, and the subject who may be killed, the subject who may engage in history and politics, and the subject criminalised, placed within the remit of policing and beyond politics. The conditions that enable the emergence of such subjectivisation are in themselves taken for granted and therefore placed beyond judgement, namely the global neoliberal order that underpins global governance and the global market place.

Writing in the aftermath of the events of September 11th 2001, the subsequent "war against terrorism", the invasions of Afghanistan and Iraq, we see a diversity of voices engaged in a discursive struggle to acquire prominence in the renditions surrounding these events. Contestations relating to a) political authority and the legitimacy to act, b) the legitimacy or otherwise of actions taken, c) the chain of answerability or culpability, all highlighting fundamental issues surrounding violence in late modernity, whether such violence is associated with clandestine organisations or states. The present context is characterised by a dispersal of violence and its agents, so that there are no clear boundaries that might be pointed to as markers of differentiation between war and criminality, the public and the private. The second chapter of this book also indicated the multiplicity of agents involved in what I referred to as the matrix of war and the interstices within which its practices take place. Mary Kaldor's remit is centred on what she calls "new wars", characterising conflicts in the Balkans and Africa in the main, conflicts located within the wider context of the globalised arena. What I refer to as the global matrix of war is also transnational in its workings, transcending the local and the global, and characterised by the indistinction again, between war and criminality, civility and barbarism, legality and illegality. While Kaldor confines her analysis to regions elsewhere, the global matrix of war as a concept seeks to capture a wider conception of violent practices and their association with structures of domination globally. This section argues that while there is an intensification of the desire to regulate international life in the face of increasing fragmentation and uncertainty, these efforts towards, and calls for, regulation must be seen not merely in juridical terms, but as framed and constituted within the politics of representation and legitimisation. As we will see, violence is implicated in the construction of frameworks that seek to "domesticate" the international. However, at the same time, the juridical also becomes the space of politics and contestation and as such emerges as one of the primary location of political agency and discourses and practices that seek to counter the impunities surrounding late modern warfare.

Reflecting on war at the nexus of the international and the human suggests a number of complex and intersecting encounters involving judgement and the accrual of answerability. Each such encounter has a certain specificity defined by its location and that of its participants, while at the same being constituted within a socio-political matrix that defines the limits of the interactive process and the differential enablements and constraints experienced by those involved. This complexity is magnified in the present context of globalised social relations, where the compression of time and space has led to the extension (and expansion) of the boundaries within which judgements are made. These locations of judgement are peopled by a plethora of agents, those who may judge, those who may act, those deemed answerable, those remaining immune from answerability, those who seek the political authority to judge, and those who seek the legitimacy to act. Each is differently located in relation to knowledge and power and hence has a different and asymmetrical capacity to instantiate judgement in the public, inter-subjective, arena.[18] This inter-subjective arena must, in the present context, be conceived as the global public sphere. This global public sphere cannot be viewed simply in terms of communicative practices that enhance understanding and consensus; rather, such communicative practices are understood to be located within discursive and institutional relations of power that limit the terms of discourse.

Political violence in late modernity is perpetrated by states and individuals alike. From its most primitive to its most technological manifestation, such violence sees its enactment and effect in the transnational spaces that intricately connect the local and the global. The judgement of violence in itself has such transnational locations, crossing boundaries and linking the teenager witnessing the violence of war on their television screens to leaders who see it as their purview to use force in distant lands. The globalised arena that so permeates and determines the parameters of violence provides a socio-political context that, as Anthony Giddens, points out, is increasingly abstracted and distanced from the lived experience of the individual self.[19] And yet, this lived experience is situated within and constituted by the matrixes of power and discourse that define the continuities of the present social order. This paradoxical situation, the distanciation of time and space, so that time defies space, places lived experience, despite the abstractions of social systems, in close proximity to events taking place in distant lands, so that political space is itself trans-formed. The individual self is thus present in the local and the global, in the compressed space that ultimately shifts the location of politics beyond the confines of the state and locality and into an arena that is ever-shifting in its mobilising potential. In the globalised context of violence and confrontation, judgement has a multiplicity of locations, some gaining voice, capable of engagement in conduct, others bearing witness, not yet mobilised into the public arena. Just as violence has a globalised context so too does the judgement of violence.

Reflecting on the present, we come to understand that judgement and answerability are in this context situated within and constituted by complex systems of meaning and structures of domination wherein there may be a disjuncture between the political authority to judge and the legitimacy to act. The subject of judgement cannot be uniformly defined, either as the Kantian cosmopolitan being or the situated self of communitarianism, both of which seem to suggest the existence of formulaic response mechanisms (powered respectively by reason and community) that comes into gear whenever and wherever rules are violated.

If we conceive of judgement and answerability in distinctly political terms, we begin to recognise these practices not in abstract and formu-

laic terms, but in their concrete manifestation in language and relations of power. It is within this context that questions relating to the
reconstitution of the "international" as a distinct juridico-political
space must be located. Invoking the international brings into the frame
practices that instantiate the international in terms of the sovereign
state and relations between sovereign states on the one hand and
those that frame the international in terms of humanity at large;
the national, the international, and the human, respectively. How the
international is framed must hence have profound implications for
the reconstitution of political as well as juridical space, a matter that
was recognised by the post World War II political leaders whose design
of the emerging global order comprised at once both sovereign self-
determination and humanity. That the United Nations Charter encapsulates a framework for "international peace and security" that is statist
to its core while at the same time institutionally enabling codified protections for the human, in the form of the Geneva Conventions, for
example, bears testimony not to the inherent conflict between these
two practices, but to their mutual constitution.[20] However, those who
seek to define the international in terms of the human seek to reconstitute the global terrain so that the sovereign state no longer constitutes
a limit to international action, that in a context of "new wars" and
"network wars", the juridico-political framing of the international
system must enable both intervention in the name of rescue and pre-
emptive intervention in the name of security.[21] As pointed out by
Richard Falk, the two main challenges to the Charter's prohibitions
against the use of force other than in situations of self-defence include
"alleged humanitarian emergencies, and expanding claims of defensive
necessity".[22] What are the arguments that frame these challenges and
what are their consequences globally?

We saw in the last chapter that Habermas advocates the instantiation of cosmopolitan law as a positive mechanism designed for the
protection of the rights of those targeted by the extremes of violence.
The reframing of the international in human terms is particularly
located within the purview of liberal and cosmopolitan thought in
International Relations, but has also emerged within the discourses of
the United Nations, and especially its recent Secretaries General,
Boutros Boutros-Ghali and Kofi Annan.[23] Where both Secretaries
General seek a form of discourse that enables a moment of reconciliation between state sovereignty and intervention in the name of human
rights in times of emergency, the discourses of liberal and cosmopolitan International Relations move much further in their conception of

the international arena as a space differentiated in accordance with domestic, social and political formations and yet unified in a universal remit, that of the *gentium*. It is precisely this dual conception of the international; on the one hand constituted by a hierarchy of social and political formations and on the other a universalising space rendered in the form of humanity at large, that implicates liberal thought in the violent practices of the present and their ramifications globally. The attempt to obliterate limits in the latter frame comes to reconstitute, redraw boundaries elsewhere, inscribed in terms that differentiate the modern and the un-modern, the civilised and the un-civilised, the democratic and the un-democratic, so that the remit of international action is by definition aimed to civilise, to modernise, to democratise. Let us delve into this discourse, the conditions of possibility that have enabled its emergence as a dominant frame of reference, and its implications for social and political life internationally. Such an exploration is necessary, for the attractions of this discourse at first sight derive from its claims relating to the legislation for peace; that it defines the conditions wherein societies and relations between them may be transformed so that war is rendered a thing of the past, so that atrocity, such as that witnessed in Rwanda and elsewhere is never again treated with indifference or tolerated.

Any attempt at the reconception of the international beyond the inter-state system seeks to shift discourse away from sovereignty as a formative moment in modern understandings of politics and political space. That the construct "sovereignty" immediately points to a bounded political community wherein political authority is at once both delimited territorially and self-determining in relations with other like entities is so powerful and deep rooted a framing device that the sovereign state, while being a historical contingency is at the same time a constitutive moment in any discourse on the international and modern attempts at its regulation as a social and political space. As Martin Shaw points out, "This concept of exclusive territorial authority is the principal modern idea of the state."[24] Such assumed exclusivity is, however, tempered historically both by the development of "different layers of authority" and global transformations that "have made national sovereignty increasingly contingent upon observing universal standards of human rights, so that sovereignty is not so exclusive any more."[25] While this historical sociology of the state and of international relations challenges unitary or even naturalised conceptions of sovereignty as the taken-for-granted regulative force in international relations, and indeed we might claim that throughout modernity capital has in many senses transcended the state as the regulative force globally, nevertheless the idea of sovereignty has developed into a powerful "hermeneutic category", according to Neil Walker, that enables a conception of a distinct polity and a distinct political community so that politics and law may be conceptualised in both domestic and international terms.[26] Despite what we might understand as the gradual relocation of political and legal authority, downwards to ever more federated national systems and upwards to international institutional arrangements, the state remains, as Hirst and Thompson emphasise, a powerful enabling as well as constraining element in globalised social, economic, and political life.[27] Historically, practices associated with constitutionalism have also assumed the remit of law as emanating from and constitutive of the delimited political entity which is the state that in turn enables the emergence of a body of law, namely international law, created by sovereign states as a mechanism to regulate relations between them.[28] Crucial questions begin to emerge when the line of demarcation between the domestic and the international comes under challenge both historically through the gradual transformation of social, economic, and political life, and conceptually, through frameworks of knowledge that seek to redefine political community ever outwards beyond the confines of the state, frameworks that are in tune, so to speak, with liberal as well as cosmopolitan agendas in international politics. For such transformations raise fundamental questions relating not just to the meaning and constitution of political community, but to legality and exceptions to the rule; the latter potentially enabling humanitarian intervention and/or pre-emptive action. These two elements – the transformation of political community and the rearticulation of international legality – are, I want to argue, mutually implicating and being so have profound implications globally.

The pace of change that modernity inaugurated from the eighteenth century to the present was never equal, emerging as it did during an era of imperial expansion by European states into the rest of the world. The inter-state system that later emerged in the postcolonial era, while formally constituted as a system of like units, namely sovereign states, was hence never equal in terms of each state possessing sophisticated and rationalised means of social control wherein the government of social and political relations could develop into routinised and bureaucratised systems underwritten in law. While much attention has, in the past, been paid to the economic inequalities of the international system, it is inequalities in domestic systems of government that are now coming under increasing scrutiny. We might therefore imagine the transformation of political community towards ever expansive locations, this imagination is, however, always subject to the historical trajectory of social development, the temporal differentiations of which bring us back to the heart of the dualism between universalising discourses that seek to redefine political community in terms of humanity and particularistic discourses that recognise the tensions emergent from difference. Much of the argument, however, has sought to frame this tension in terms of cultural difference, as if to suggest that culture *per se* is a constraint on dialogue or even the possibility of translation between different forms of life or indeed political and social formations and arrangements. While cultural difference is clearly significant, and I will deal with this question in the following chapter, what is of crucial significance is the differentiation in forms of governance defined in terms of rationalised systems of social control that ultimately sees the shift in social power, as Michel Foucault's analytics of power indicate, from centralised sovereign power towards rationalised systems based on the government of all aspects of social relations developed to such a degree of sophistication that self-government comes to form its formative moment. While this historical trajectory may apply to the European polity, the clear absence in the analysis concerns the international, namely Europe's colonial relationship with the rest of the world. The project of modernity is as much about the emergence of ideas and practices relating to emancipation as it is about colonial domination.[29] The unequal pace of change that modernity inaugurated sees its apotheosis in late modernity, where we witness not just the ramifications of global inequality, but more profoundly, the rejection in some societies – not necessarily defined nationally – of the modernising project. Any conception of the transformation of the juridical and political framing of community globally faces this dual narrative of the project of modernity.

Drawing on E.H. Carr, Andrew Linklater seeks to articulate a project that is intensely modern in its orientation and ambitions. Like Carr, and like other cosmopolitans, including the author of this text, the sovereign national state, defined in terms of its exclusivity, is historically seen as the source, not just of conflict and warfare, but of modes of inequality and exclusion structurated in social and political life. Linklater identifies the progressive agenda in Carr, an agenda that seeks the transformation of the state structure and the expansion of political community beyond the state. As Linklater clearly and rightly points out, such an agenda was not confined to Carr, but indeed was central to Marxist thought on the state and the potential for internationalism emergent from nationally transcendent class affiliations. Nevertheless, Carr provides a baseline from which we can investigate the implications of any attempts at the expansion of political community. As Linklater points out, Carr's *Nationalism and After*[30] highlights three stages "in the evolution of modern state structures". In the first stage, the mercantilism of the eighteenth century, "absolutist states competed with one another for economic and military power."[31] The second stage emerged in the nineteenth century and dissolved national economies from military power thereby inaugurating the free movement of goods and labour sustained by newly formed liberal state structures. This period also witnessed the spread of nationalism and the emergence of new national states which were ultimately incorporated "as equal members of the society of states without any serious disturbance to world peace. Nationalism and internationalism were balanced as a result for the greater part of the nineteenth century."[32] The third phase saw the destruction of this balance, however, and the crisis of the period 1914–1939, emerged as a result of three phenomena, namely "the socialisation of the nation, the nationalisation of economic policy and the geographical extension of nationalism", thereby destroying "the liberal conception of the coming peace." According to Linklater, Carr provides an image of the nation-state that is entirely at odds with Hegel's celebration of the state as the apotheosis of the modern ethical ideal:

> Carr described the collapse of the moral equilibrium which lay at the heart of Hegel's progressivist account of the modern state. Fine balances between the individual and the community, economic self-interest and welfare provision, national sovereignty and international legal responsibilities were destroyed by the state's sudden lurch towards exclusionary practices which were directed against minority groups and aliens...This was the period in which the state's monopoly control of the instruments of violence, its economic powers, and its ability to make national identity the highest political identity were remarkably unchecked, as were its status as the highest court of legal appeal, its exclusive right of representation in international organisations and its assumed sole right to bind the whole community in international law. The fusion of territoriality, sovereignty, citizenship, and nationality reached its zenith in this period.[33]

Writing in the aftermath of the Second World War, Carr argued that state structures could be transformed so that power was neither vested in the exclusive hands of the few internally nor for the benefit of the great powers externally. Driven by an "ethic of welfare international-ism" and "respect for cultural difference", the "post-national state" would be cosmopolitan in orientation and willing participant in inter-national arrangements that were no longer bound by the sovereignty of the national state. Carr's rethinking of political community, enables, according to Linklater, both a conception of citizenship that is cos-mopolitan and a post-Westphalian framework wherein "like-minded societies are keen to establish closer forms of political cooperation to integrate shared ethical norms into the structure of social and political life."[34]

The post-Westphalian framework redefines the international so that sovereign right is no longer the linchpin of relations between political communities, but gives way to cosmopolitan right as a result of histor-ical modes of resistance against state power. The conditions of poss-ibility for the transformation of political community towards the post-Westphalian order centre on certain "moral resources" possessed by certain societies. These resources include "constitutionalism, the ex-tension of democratic possibilities and the evolution of more sophisti-cated understandings of the social and economic preconditions of dialogic communities."[35] While constitutionalism is associated with political liberalism, its formative elements, namely the rule of law, accountability and individual rights, may be enshrined in international legal frameworks where individuals, communities, as well as states can be subject to international law. However, Linklater wishes to move beyond this "solidarist" conception of global organisation sug-gesting that "internationalising the achievements of constitutionalism enforces respect for human rights by punishing serious violations. Extending the rule of law so that all individuals including fellow nationals can be brought before international courts of law when they are suspected of human rights violations marks the transition from a solidarist conception of world politics, in which states retain the form if not the substance of sovereignty, to a post-Westphalian global order in which significant national powers are transferred to international legal authorities."[36] States which block development towards a post-Westphalian order ultimately fail to "contribute to the unfinished project of modernity"[37] and in doing so impede the development and evolution not just of a global public sphere wherein social and political struggles seek precisely such transformations, but of what Held refers to as a "global covenant", wherein political community covers cosmopolitan space.[38]

The drivers behind the transformations that Linklater envisages include progressive social movements, but they are primarily societies that are already in possession of the "moral resources" that drive progress towards a cosmopolitan global order, namely those that already exhibit constitutional modes of governance, democratic accountability, and sophisticated understandings of dialogical communicative practices. These then are the capacities that may be drawn upon in any project that seeks the transformation of political community towards the cosmopolitan arena. However, as we see from the above, this project is not merely dialogical, though this element is clearly an integral aspect of it. Significantly in terms of the reconception of the international, it is also primarily a juridical discourse, for its ultimate aim is not simply cross-societal understanding, but frameworks of law, namely cosmopolitan law, that renders individuals and states equally subject to a global legal order underpinned institutionally through the workings of international courts. Let us then look into the juridical arguments for transformations of the international and their consequences for war and peace.

As Linklater states, the core premise of the post-Westphalian order is that "significant national powers are transferred to international legal authorities."[39] Clearly, such a transfer of authority is fundamental to the redefinition of the sphere of the international from one based on the sovereign equality of states to one that is defined in terms of humanity at large, and in particular the equalities between individual humans enshrined historically in human rights conventions. With increasing recognition that the protection of such rights could not be guaranteed by the state and indeed, as pointed out by Boutros-Ghali, the state itself was often the source of insecurity and violence against its own citizenry, emerged an understanding that the protection of human rights be enshrined internationally through the workings of the United Nations and its institutions. While this organisation, as stated earlier, has historically been concerned with the preservation of "international peace and security" between states, it nevertheless has, since the end of the Second World War, also been concerned with what is now referred to as "human security", enshrined in a number of human rights related conventions, covering the laws of war as in the Geneva Conventions, to the prohibition of torture, to the convention against genocide, to name but a few. The "human" element, therefore, has always sat, if often uncomfortably, with the sovereign state element. This tense relationship reaches its zenith, however, when questions of enforcement emerge, and specifically in relation to the use of force in the name of human rights. Clearly, enforcement measures such as economic sanctions have, in the past, been ratified by the Security Council in relation to Apartheid South Africa, or later, in relation to Iraq, to name but two examples. What is significant about the present period is that the use of military force in the name of the protection of human rights on the one hand, often referred to as humanitarian intervention, and in the name of pre-emption on the other, brings into sharp focus the political and juridical consequences emergent from this rearticulation of the international.

For the question that emerges in this context relates to the driver of such rearticulation, the location of agency or "political authority" in the transformation of the international away from the exclusive terrain of the sovereign state and towards a cosmopolitan order under-written by law. That such authority may be located in a multiplicity of sites, from international institutions, to coalitions of states, to a complex network incorporating these and a panoply of specialised non-governmental organisations has already been shown to be a possibility in situations such as Bosnia or East Timor where an inter-national civil service took charge of governance functions literally shaping, or disciplining, previously conflict-ridden societies into new social formations. While there is much in the literature that stresses the importance of such transformations in establishing the authority of international institutions over and above the sovereign state, what is clearly at stake remains the question of agency, defined in terms of both the material capacity to instantiate intervention coupled with the legitimacy to act. International institutions may be redesigned into more representative frameworks, the crucial element in decisions relating to the use of force centres upon the possession of the material requisite of any military operation, a fact that has clear ramifications in terms of the ultimate location of sovereignty. Given this asymme-try, therefore, the question of legitimacy emerges, raising significant questions relating to the mechanisms through which such legitimacy is established. One way of answering the legitimacy question is to suggest the existence of commonly held interests that are globally col-lective and hence transcending the particular interests of separate states. These may, for example, be defined in terms of a collective interest in security, suggesting security as a "public good";[40] they may be defined in terms of the protection of individual human rights realised within a cosmopolitan jurisdiction;[41] and they may be defined in terms of the protection of the free movement of goods and services in the global market place. Such collective interests can come to constitute transnational ties that potentially form political community across the signifying divide of state and culture suggesting commonly held stakes in the enhancement and reenforcement of such ties. Note the immediate problem in such constructions; the conflation of interests and identities, or that the latter may somehow be a product of the former suggesting that political community may emerge from commonly held interests. However, it is the construction of such collective interests that now comes under scrutiny, for these are not pre-given interests, but are a product of socially manufactured "goods" the construction of which can be construed in terms of relations of power, ideology, or even culture. When questions relating to the location of agency and hence political authority are considered, the legitimacy to act comes into the frame, and such legitimacy may be construed, as indicated above, through the force of international institutions such as the Security Council of the United Nations, or through the construction of global collective interests the stakes generative of which come to constitute global ties and global affiliations that then accrue legitimacy to particular agents. Legitimacy defined in terms of collective interests in particular "public goods" remains a problem, however, in that such interests are held to constitute political *community* which in turn has the capacity to confer legitimacy to the conduct of particular states.

Another different approach to the accrual of legitimacy to conduct when such is not derived from the workings of the United Nations and hence the international sanctioning of conduct focuses on the *identity* of the states involved in the use of force. As we saw in the last chapter, Habermas clearly identifies the agents of peace so to speak as those states which possess liberal democratic constitutions. Indeed Kant's *Perpetual Peace*, which forms the basis of Habermas's thinking, identifies the republican constitution as that which enables pacific relations due to the tempering effect of democratic publics. Habermas attributes the pacific nature of liberal democracies primarily to their constitutionalism and their respect for human rights. Linklater in turn attributes distinct "moral resources" to liberal democratic states, and specifically those that "have replaced the competition for security and power with novel experiments in joint rule by drawing on domestic preferences for the politics of publicity, dialogue and consent."[42] More recently, theorists of the liberal democratic peace have reinforced the core idea here: that liberal democracies possess the moral resources to act in the name of humanity even in situations where formal legality may be missing.

Nowhere is the claim for the moral legitimacy of liberal democracies in the international system more clearly articulated than by Ann Marie Slaughter. Her discourse derives from liberalism in International Relations. Drawing particularly on Andrew Moravcsik,[43] Slaughter's vision for a transformed international law relies on the key element in liberal international thought, namely state-society relations: "Liberal theory explicitly takes domestic regime-type into account in its analysis of State behaviour. If the relevant universe for scholarly analysis is State-society relations, then the scope and density of domestic and transnational society, as well as the structure of government institutions and the mode and scope of popular representation, will be key variables."[44] Furthermore, "By taking account of these variables, in contrast to the uniform assumptions of State identity made by Realists, Liberal theory permits more general distinctions among different categories of States based on domestic regime type."[45] This then is Waltz's "second image", which he rejects on the basis that any theory of the international system must start with the assumption that its constitutive units are like entities. By contrast, Liberal thought in International Relations highlights the domestic governance arrangements of states, enabling this to be a primary variable in the explanation of state behaviour not just towards its own citizens, but externally in relations with other states and international institutions. Slaughter looks to scholarship that investigates the so-called "democratic peace" or the "liberal peace" which argues that liberal states create a "zone of peace" wherein they are "far less likely to go to war with one another than they are to go to war with non-liberal states."[46] What concerns Slaughter is not so much that there might be variations in the mode of explanation for the liberal peace phenomenon, if we can call it such, more that it provides a mode of distinction to be construed between different types of state, distinctions that, either in Realist thought or, what concerns Slaughter, in classical international law, are not made.

The list of attributes that distinguishes liberal from non-liberal states includes "peace, liberal democratic government, a dense network of transnational transactions by social and economic actors; 'multiple channels' of communication and action that are both transnational and transgovernmental rather than formally inter-state; and a blurring of the distinction between domestic and foreign issues."[47] Two elements stand out in Slaughter's version of liberal international thought that are of significance to the present discussion. The first is that, like

Slaughter's cosmopolitan counterparts, the aim is to redefine the international so that state sovereignty, or more accurately sovereign independence is no longer taken as the formative regulative principle of the international system and its juridical and political framing. In this context, Slaughter advocates what she refers to as "disaggregated sovereignty", where the state "is composed of multiple centres of political authority – legislative, administrative, executive, and judicial" that can interact transnationally in servicing the representative and regulative requirements of the individuals and groups constituting transnational relations. The second crucial element is that the revised international law that Slaughter envisages, one that, defined in terms of its component parts, indeed may function as a blueprint for the post-Westphalian political community is that liberal states are its agents and subjects, that such states alone have the capacities necessary for its implementation.

There are many differences in the genesis of the cosmopolitan view of political transformation beyond the sovereign state and Slaughter's application of liberal international thought to a reconception of international law, that will not be covered here.[48] Despite such differences, it is undoubtedly the case that Slaughter provides juridical form to the post-Westphalian political community envisaged in cosmopolitan international thought. While the latter pays due attention to cultural diversity and respect for difference, nevertheless it shares with Slaughter the elevation of liberal democratic states as agents, not just of the "liberal peace", though this is crucial, but of an active transformation of the international into a cosmopolitan sphere of operations whereby an emphasis on human rights and the mechanism for securing such rights becomes of paramount importance. While the emphasis in both approaches tends towards a shift away from the exclusivity of state sovereignty and towards a conception of the international in terms of a transnational polity underwritten by transnational juridical arrangements (the "disaggregation of sovereignty" hypothesis), nevertheless both rely on a certain understanding of the global arena which places the liberal democratic state in a hierarchical relationship to other states. When this distinction is taken as the dynamic force behind the transformation of the international into a transnational, cosmopolitan political community the liberal democratic state is conferred greater legitimacy in the international sphere. Where such states take part in missions involving the use of force, they are assumed to do so in the name of rescue and human security, and must hence be conferred legitimacy. Capacity and legitimacy come to form the twin elements that define agency in a late modern context wherein war comes to be the formative, constitutive moment in redefining the sphere of the international into a liberal global polity, one that is rule-governed and domesticated, enabling the enactment of regulatory practices that cover not just economic and financial transactions, but matters relating to conflict and security. War itself is, in these circumstances and frameworks of knowledge, a regulatory practice, a technology of government that aims at the wholesale transformation of societies as well as the international system as a whole. Liberal thought and practice dominates the discourses and practices of international relations in the present late modern context and enables, through discursive formations, the legitimisation of the use of military force and calls for the redesign of the juridical basis of international life so that intervention takes place not just in the name of rescue after the fact, but for the active prevention of imminent harm.

Governing the international

The international as a distinct political sphere has historically, at least from the emergence of modernity, been defined in terms of relations between sovereign states whereby the regulation of mutual relations was variously based on a balance of power stand-off or a pluralist norm-governed condition in which states defined interest in terms of their regulated interactions.[49] Historically, both realist and liberal internationalist discourses could live with this conception of the international sphere. In more recent times, and for reasons highlighted earlier, what might be called the hermeneutic primacy of the sovereignty principle has shifted significantly in favour of redefining the international sphere in terms of the human element; hence the emergence of human rights and human security as the basis of the emergence of a seeming liberal consensus, or we can even assert, liberal dominance in contemporary discourses and practices in international relations. Post-Westphalian political community underwritten by cosmopolitan law is, through various international developments, from the establishments of war crimes tribunals in Rwanda and for the former Yugoslavia, as well as the creation of the International Criminal Court, coupled with other manifestations of the disaggregation of sovereignty, appears to be an already unfolding possibility. I argued above that one consequence of such a reconception of the international is the emergence of a hierarchy of states, so that some are accrued legitimacy while others are not, some are considered fully developed into cosmopolitan societies while others are not, with the result that this reconception of the international is the production of a "liberal hierarchy", as Christian Reus-Smit has argued, pointing especially to Francis Fukuyama and others in International Relations, as promulgating a picture of the international that is indeed based on the above differentiations.[50] How does the reconception of the international in terms of the human impact on the regulation of conflict, and specifically violence in international politics?

That war is not merely the continuation of politics by other means but is transformative of social and political life is clearly evident when considering the place of so-called humanitarian intervention in global politics. The core principle of such intervention is that the sovereignty of states should not be an obstacle to military intervention, or even occupation, where the state commits mass violations of human rights, such as ethnic cleansing or genocide. As we have seen above, the prerogative of international institutions such as the United Nations is to pronounce such situations as constituting crimes against humanity and providing the international legitimacy for the use of military force in the name of this humanity. Humanitarian intervention is hence associated with so-called "failed" or "weak" states; states that are deemed to lack the proper governance mechanisms and institutional frameworks that enable states not only to govern relations internally, but to act in accordance with the rules and norms of the international system as a whole.[51] The construct of the "failed" state performs, therefore, a number of functions. If a state is deemed a failure, it is as such disqualified from the rights associated with sovereignty, the right to conduct its internal affairs independently of interference by other states or international institutions. If a state is deemed a failure, it is as such removed from the realm of law and its protections, its resources, including its population, subject to possession and control by others. The concept of the failed state is not only used by governments such as that of the United States, which may seek legitimacy for its violations of the rules governing state sovereignty, but has come to form a significant aspect of the International Relations literature, which might refer to "weak", "failed", or even "quasi" states,[52] states that are not only incapable of governance internally, but are, through social breakdown, a source of emergent and deadly conflicts, most of the victims of which have been civilian populations. In Francis Fukuyama's terms, "Weak or failing states commit human rights abuses, provoke humanitarian disasters, drive massive waves of immigration, and attack their neighbours. Since September 11, it also has been clear that they shelter international terrorists who can do significant damage to the United States and other developed countries."[53]

Looking at the legacy of conflicts such as Somalia, Bosnia, Kosovo, Rwanda, Liberia, Sierra Leone, Congo, East Timor, and Afghanistan, it is difficult to disagree with Fukuyama when he states that weak states have been the source of serious international crises that have invited in one way or another international responses, from limited commitments of troops, to full-scale military intervention, to the wholesale takeover of the function of government from local actors. It is also difficult to disagree with critical thinkers such as Andrew Linklater, that any response to such conflicts must be governed by judgements relating to the degree of harm committed against civilians than by traditional concerns with sovereignty. The collapse of government institutions, the takeover of swaths of territory by warlords and armed gangs, the subjection of civilian populations to the sheer terror of mass amputations, systematic rape, and large-scale murder in the form of massacre and genocide, cannot but be understood in terms not just of the failure of states to govern, but of a failure of the modern state in its ultimate purpose, namely the protection of its own population. However, it is also difficult to dissociate or somehow extract the so-called failed state from wider global responsibilities implicated in the production of the conditions generative of the deep-rooted structural, and in some instances, policy-based, harm inflicted upon the mass of populations forming societies deemed failed.

The construct of the "failed state" is, nevertheless, based on two assumptions: the first associates such a state with the loss of sovereignty, and the second normatively rejects sovereignty as the defining force of a late modern, post-Westphalian order, an order that recognises the transcendence of human welfare and well-being beyond the boundaries of the state. The interventions of the 1990s, from Bosnia, to Kosovo, to Sierra Leone, and elsewhere were seen as missions of rescue committed on behalf of the other, interventions made possible precisely through the weakness or breakdown of the states involved. These interventions confirmed what might be termed a disjuncture between sovereignty and legitimacy; the former could no longer function as the source of legitimacy for a state and its authorities. From the actions of individuals (Pinochet, Milosevic, Sharon, Hussein), to the conditions of states (Somalia, Afghanistan, the former Yugoslavia), judgement on legitimacy could no longer be made on the basis of sovereignty or the right to non-interference, but in terms of conduct in relation to human rights.

We may therefore interpret the interventions of the 1990s as turning points in the reconstitution of the global order away from sovereignty and towards a conception of humanity that redefined obligation in terms of solidarity with the other,[54] irrespective of the other's location on the terrain of the global. However, we might also understand such interventions in terms of the primacy of war in the formation and transformation of discourses and practices that come in turn to reconstitute the global order. This latter understanding of humanitarian intervention is concerned with the discursive and institutional transformation of the terrain of the global and not simply, though this is important, with the normative concern with human rights. War has a central place in such transformation and any critical rendition on global politics must provide an understanding of war as centrally implicated in emerging forms and ideas relating to governance at global scale, relating to the construct of humanity, and relating to the construction of the "other" of humanity; for it is the case that (and once again the spectre of Schmitt emerges) when wars are fought in the name of the human, the enemy must by necessity constitute the inhuman. When wars are fought on behalf of the human, the human becomes the terrain of governance, when the human becomes the terrain of governance, the structural transformation is monumental, for the state alone is no longer the administrative unity that holds legitimate monopoly over the means of violence and is as such the basic unit of an international order of sovereign states. Sovereignty has shifted elsewhere, its locations both multiform and not as yet settled.

The shift in sovereignty brought forth by the cases of humanitarian intervention highlighted above raises the question of governance and the agencies involved in such governance. In the case of states deemed failed, the location of government shifts away from the local arena and towards an international constellation involving international institutions and other states, acting directly, or through non-governmental organisations. The aim, in places such as East Timor, Sierra Leone, Bosnia, and Kosovo, was no less than "state" or "nation"-building, or "reconstruction", the latter term seeing its application latterly in Afghanistan and Iraq. Each of these cases was or continues to be another moment in the constitution of global governance, a form of governance that at first relies on the military technology of the powerful, but involves a plethora of other agencies, from the United Nations, to regional states, to non-governmental organisations, involved in such diverse practices as the training of a local police force and army to the provision of "gender-awareness training" to local actors, generating in turn the transformation not just of local practices of government, but of cultures as well.

War, when conceived as serving a reconstructive imperative, an imperative that has the welfare of populations as its underlying justification, constitutes the intervener as protector/saviour and the subject population as the protected/saved; the former as possessing the will and the capacity to protect, and hence to design regimes of protection, and the latter as compliant subject, devoid of agency in their own right, incapable of self-protection, victim populations rendered vulnerable through their very construction as victims. The protector/protected relationship is also a power relationship, potentially denying the latter agency in relation to their own protection. The discourse of protection, upon which much of the legitimisation of intervention has relied, places powerful limits on political agency. Clearly, protection may be constructed as a practice of care; saving others is the central defining moment of humanitarianism, both governmental and non-governmental, and forms a central component of all ethical discourse, both secular and religious. However, protection may also be interpreted in terms of its perpetuation of structures of domination, structures that may be manifest across different spheres of social interaction, from the private realm of the family to the most public realm of the international arena. Protection, as we know from Charles Tilly in historical sociology and Carol Pateman in feminist political theory, comes at a price, namely extraction of one sort or another.[55] Where Tilly writes of material extraction exacted in war-making, Pateman writes of the gendered discourse surrounding the notion of protection, namely the historical subjugation of women. Similarly, we can see that discourses of the protection of populations in the name of humanitarianism or care may at first hand suggest agency on the part of the protected (demands for rescue, and efforts at the escalation of local conflicts in order to internationalise these are examples), nevertheless, the discourse of protection suggests both an element of subordination as well as exchange. Once agents enter a relationship defined in terms of protection, the capacity to determine the modalities such protection takes is limited. A hierarchical relationship emerges and has implications not just in the use of violence against the protected, but in practices associated with reconstruction and state-building.[56]

Humanitarian intervention set the stage for a post-Westphalian international political order that is no longer necessarily based on the sovereignty of states as the baseline of legitimacy, but on the judgement of conduct in relation to the realm of the human and its expression in human rights. Intervention could take place in the name of humanitarian emergency and the sphere of the international and the agencies that possessed the capacity to function in this sphere could take over governance functions from states deemed failed or weak, states perceived to be both a danger to their own and to others. The logical steps towards the establishment of what Fukuyama on the Right refers to as an "international imperial power"[57] and what Hardt and Negri on the Left, refer to as Empire,[58] are all too stark – the violent breakdown of states and/or their abdication of internal control; in effect, the loss of a capacity to govern, transformed situations of conflict into emergencies requiring policing operations, and such could only be provided by external agencies, state and non-state, thereby transferring sovereignty from the local to the external – and indicative of the structural transformations that took place in the 1990s and continue to the present. Such structural transformations were, however, reliant on a discourse of legitimisation that drew upon humanitarianism and its requisite constructs, human rights, rescue, emergency, and other modes of signification that transformed the violence of war into a language of protection.

The military intervention over Kosovo and subsequent interventions, including Afghanistan and Iraq, for example, could be fully understood in this context if we look back to the First Gulf War of 1990/91 and the expulsion of Iraq from Kuwait. It was this event, coupled with subsequent bombardments of Iraq, which set the stage for a new type of intervention steeped in a mode of representation that places a premium on language. The Gulf War brought the theatre of war to the mass of the global public, placed representation at the centre of strategic conduct, rendered particular and highly complex weapons systems household names, and legitimised the possibility of war at distance as an achievable option at relatively little human cost to those involved in its prosecution. Related to these features of warfare in late modernity is the additional factor of what David Campbell refers to as the "moral certitude"[59] which unproblematically links the term "just" to deadly warfare. War and humanitarian intervention come to form a mutually constitutive relationship wherein violence and moral agency are as one in a global context that seeks solutions achieved at great speed, and with an anxious eye at a fascinated, viewing public.

The discursive backdrop was then framed around two mutually reinforcing spaces, that of ethics and that of warfare. The conventions drawn upon in the discourses of war are deep rooted and hegemonic in their domination of the signifying practices that surround war.[60] The language of war, framed as it is in constructs of strategy and morality, relies on just war theorising that has its roots in theological as well as secular treatises from Augustine to the present. The epistemological and ontological certainties that surround just war theorising are in themselves indicative of their complicity in violence and the legitimising practices that surround its use in the name of the human. The discourse seeks to identify just cause and just conduct; he who possesses the power to declare war must be certain as to its righteous purpose, and must conceive of war only as last resort. Those involved in the conduct of war must remain certain of its proportionality and its target, distinguishing clearly and unambiguously between combatant and civilian. Those who proclaim the faith must in turn rely on the generals who must remain ultimately responsible for the conduct of war, providing assurance as to the successful outcome of war.

Such is the discursive backdrop that surrounded and legitimised the First Gulf War and was drawn upon in subsequent interventions in the name of humanity. The global public was here subjected to a linguistic phenomenon that brought highly complex technological warfare into everyday discourse. The language of war; "precision bombing", "surgical strikes", and the unfortunate accidents that were "collateral damage", all framed and rendered meaningful in the context of just war as a legitimising and hegemonic signifying practice. The high technology of late modern warfare, "stealth bombers", "patriot missiles", delivered at distance and yet made proximate through video imagery, rendered war an object of fascination. It also made war a subject for scrutiny and moral judgement, effects that saw their apotheosis in the judgement of the Second Gulf War, namely the 2003 invasion of Iraq.

The high technology of late modern warfare is, by necessity, underpinned by a form of ontological certainty centred on instrumentality and strategic intent. Those involved in the decision for war are purposive agents, capable not only of calculative precision, but of certainty as to the ethicality of the act. There is no room here for ambiguity or even reflexivity in a subject who must remain committed to the predicates of rationality. What is crucial in this construction of uniform subjectivity is an apparently unproblematic relationship between word and deed, between intent and outcome. The sovereign subject of the Gulf War and subsequent acts of war could pronounce upon intention and relate this to specified targets.[61] The intention was framed in a highly moral discourse while strategic conduct was portrayed through usage of maps, satellite photography, and video imagery. All presented a uniform subjectivity, precise in its calculations and certain of its righteous place in history. The weaponry of war that enabled this mode of being was itself "smart" in its deadly precision. There is no room here for the "other" of this particular war, the mass on the ground, largely unseen, but demonised nevertheless into its own abject uniformity.

The epistemological and ontological certainties which enabled the Gulf War and made possible the military intervention in the Balkans point to a certain subjectivity that emerges in the discourses and practices surrounding late modern warfare, specifically wars conducted in the name of humanity. The subject here is certain of the justness of the cause and is highly concerned to portray such certainty in representation. Acting on behalf of humanity, its remit is immediately universal, possessing legitimacy that is limitless in space and time, transcendent of geographic difference and historical time. In this universal remit, the subject of humanitarian intervention acts with precision, decisiveness and rapidity; a form of "short, sharp, shock"[62] treatment that must reverse and punish undesirable conduct at little, if any, cost to the side. Such a subject must in consequence rely on highly complex technology that renders war in the absence of actual combat possible. Above all else, the subject in late modern war is an enlightened being, cosmopolitan in orientation, and global in reach. The interventions in the Balkans came to confirm not only the politics of representation surrounding late modern wars fought in the name of humanity, but set in place the structural relocation of sovereignty, so that this could no longer function as the limit to international conduct. The war over Kosovo that started on the 24th of March 1999 and lasted all of 79 days was dubbed a humanitarian war conducted, according to Tony Blair, by a "new generation of leaders in the United States and Europe, who were born after World War II, who hail from the progressive side of politics, but who are prepared to be as firm as any of our predecessors right or left in seeing this thing through." For Blair, this was a just war, fought in the name of humanity and decency, where ethnic cleansing could no longer be tolerated in the heart of Europe:

> We need to enter a new millennium where dictators know that they cannot get away with ethnic cleansing or repress their peoples with impunity. In this conflict we are fighting not for territory but for values. For a new internationalism where the brutal repression of

whole ethnic groups will no longer be tolerated. For a world where those responsible for such crimes have nowhere to hide.[63]

The message was clear and it was to be legitimised through its repeated invocation in the media. In scenes reminiscent of the Iraqi regime's atrocities against the Kurdish population, those that emerged from Kosovo formed the basis of legitimisation for intervention in the name of rescue. Where the former had produced a policy of "no-fly zones" to protect the Kurdish population in Iraq's northern regions and the Shi'ite population of its southern regions, in effect transforming the map of Iraq into three distinct zones, the latter produced an air campaign against Serbia and its forces in Kosovo. In both cases, sovereignty could no longer function as the limit of conduct; such limits had shifted elsewhere into a zone of politics that viewed its remit in terms of the human population in its universality, its zone of operations the global terrain as a whole.

The war over the Balkan skies, its predecessors in the First Gulf War and subsequent actions against Iraq, and interventions in Somalia, Sierra Leone and elsewhere, were performances of a global form of sovereignty that could not only reverse and punish acts against humanity, but rebuild nations and states in accordance with a political rationality based on liberal government. Populations on the receiving end would witness three distinct phases in such nation- or state-building. The first centred around war in the name of protection, the second on the establishment of institutions of government that would govern territories that had in effect lost this capacity, and thirdly, the training of a local population to self-govern afresh. The effects on the production of subjectivity and political agency are paradoxical as well as being indeterminate in a late modern context that defies easy, managerial solutions or totalising frameworks that view the global, and hence the universal, in uniform terms. The discourse, from Bosnia to Kosovo to Iraq is one that aims to reconstruct societies and their government in accordance with a distinctly western liberal model the formative elements of which centre on open markets, human rights and the rule of law, and democratic elections as the basis of legitimacy. The aim is no less than to reconstitute polities through the transformation of political cultures into modern, self-disciplining, and ultimately self-governing entities that, through such transformation, could transcend ethnic or religious fragmentation and violence. The trajectory is punishment, pacification, discipline, and ultimately "liberal democratic self-mastery".[64] Each step in turn services wider, global remits so that the pacified, the disciplined, the self-governing of the liberal order can no longer pose a threat either to their own or to others.

Read from a liberal perspective, what Oliver Richmond refers to as "peace as governance" comes to form the linchpin of "liberal peace";[65] a distinctly Kantian idea that sees its manifestation in late modern international projections of power utilised in the name of humanity. Read from a critical perspective, one that I have already identified as being informed by Michel Foucault as well as other critical discourses in poststructural and postcolonial thought, the rearticulation of the international in terms of humanity throws up what we might refer to as the darker side of humanitarianism and state-building. Revealing this darker side is not intended to reject the liberal peace project altogether; rather, it is to indicate how violence is centrally implicated, not just in its prosecution in the early stages of wars of intervention, but in the actuality of its construction.

I have argued that a central transformation of the late modern era has been a shift in our understanding of the sphere of the international. Realist and liberal internationalist thought have historically relied on defining the international in terms of inter-state relations; a modern Westphalian conception that places a premium on state sovereignty. From this modern conception emerged other derivative ideas relating to the regulation of relations between states, from balance of power systems formative of realist discourse to liberal collective security ideas focusing on the role of international institutions and norms of conduct to which states would adhere. Both discourses were, in turn, formative of discourses of peace and security emergent in the aftermath of the Second World War and institutionalised in the United Nations Charter and limits to war that this Charter placed upon its signatories. Nevertheless, a parallel discourse has also existed, namely one based on the concept of humanity, defined in terms of universal human rights and seeing its realisation in conventions relating to conduct in time of war as well as in peace-time. The human element has hence always been a constitutive element of the international, its realisation emerging to the fore in United Nations sanctions against Apartheid South Africa and later Iraq, as primary examples. Nevertheless, the juridico-political framing of the international remained, one that was primarily constructed in terms of the sovereign equality of states. More recent renditions on the international have, however, sought to move beyond a statist understanding of the international and towards a conception that highlights the human, variously conceived in terms of human rights and human security.

The wars of intervention of the 1990s have clearly shifted the terrain away from state sovereignty and towards a transnational polity whereby intervention could be legitimised, if not legalised, in terms of the remit to protect or rescue. The juridico-political form for such cosmopolitanism emerges primarily in the idea of cosmopolitan law, to which both governments and individuals may be subject and in the name of which military intervention could take place precisely for the realisation of human security. Where states are deemed failed, such intervention has involved a set of practices that, as mentioned earlier, indicate a gradual shift in emphasis from punishment to disciplinarity to the government of populations. These transformations suggest the emergence of a late modern international imperial order built and rendered possible by a hierarchy of states defined in terms of both capacity and legitimacy. It would, however, be a mistake to think of this order in terms of states as agents alone, for it is the case, as many authors writing on the subject of peacebuilding and statebuilding have shown, that these practices also involve international institutions as well as non-governmental organisations in a complex array of interactions and relationships that variously involve local actors.

How do we understand war when the human becomes a terrain of government? Clearly one way of answering this question is to frame it in terms of the liberal peace. Doing so enables a conception of intervening troops as peacekeepers and peacebuilders engaged in saving others. In an age of biopolitics, however, when war takes place it does so, as I highlighted in Chapter 2 of this investigation, and following Michel Foucault, in the name of humanity. War becomes a technology aimed at the government of populations. Michel Foucault's understanding of the transformations of power, from sovereignty, to disciplinarity to governmentality provides pointers to how such transformations are rendered in global terms. For Foucault, we have a tendency to overvalue the state when "what is really important for our modernity – that is, for our present – is not so much the statisation [etatisation] of society, as the 'governmentalisation' of the state."[66] What we witness in practices of intervention associated with state-building is the culmination of the governmentalisation of the state rendered transnationally. However, the missing element in Foucault's rendition is precisely the "international" as a distinct sphere the juridico-political transformations of which are not only of interest in formal structural terms, but have profound implications phenomenologically, that is, in terms of the lived experience of populations targeted. While much attention is paid to the former, specifically concerns relating to the juridico-political transformations of late modern globality, the latter element must also be configured in these emerging cosmopolitan landscapes. The final section of this chapter looks to both elements and how they might be related. This is provided in anticipation of what follows in the final chapters of this book.

Re-designing the international

Oliver Richmond correctly points to a global consensus centring on the "liberal peace" project. He also points to the spectrum of this consensus, from the "hyper-conservative" to the "conservative" to the "orthodox" to the "emancipatory", highlighting the significance of exploring "the graduations of the liberal peace that are being constructed through different types of intellectual and policy analysis, and by different actors, in order to evaluate the effectiveness and sustainability of peacebuilding approaches."[67] While investigations into the policy implications of this spectrum are important, my concern in the present context relates to the political implications of the shift in discourse towards a liberal hegemonic discourse that associates its project with a moral imperative that is global in reach. It would be a mistake to associate this project with Kant, though Kantian universalism has some traces here. Nor would it be appropriate to suggest a Hegelian "end of history" rendition wherein reason's apotheosis comes into universal form. Traces again, for the project is in formation, not yet complete, constrained by the complexity that confronts it as it traverses the global arena.

The project is not yet complete, and may never be. The problem in any discussion of transformation is whether these are merely contingent or structurally transformative. And we have already seen from the above and from previous chapters, that a number of authors precisely suggest structural transformations taking place, in progress. What is evident in the liberal hegemony that dominates discourse in the present is that it clearly and unambiguously centralises some notion of virtue; that a distinct moral imperative is its driving force. Jean Elshtain, for example, suggests that states in possession of a certain level of capability to project power bear primary responsibility for enforcing what she labels the "equal regard" norm.[68] We have already seen this position reflected in the language of humanitarian intervention: rescue, protection, care, humanity, human security, human rights, democracy, progress. This is not simply an intellectual project, but is deeply programmatic in its construction and instrumental in its orientation to the future.

One central element of the project is the transformation of the international juridico-political order so that intervention in the name of humanity is no longer deemed illegal. The focus of attention is the "disaggregation of sovereignty" so that international law is no longer bound with the primacy of sovereign equality between states. A crucial element here is the distinction between legality and legitimacy. As Richard Falk has pointed out, the two challenges to UN Charter strictures against the use of force in circumstances other than self-defence have emerged in relation to the use of force in humanitarian emergencies and in so-called "anticipatory self-defence", Kosovo and Iraq respectively. Falk, pointing to authors such as Jean Elshtain advocating the use of force, summarises the implications of a shift from legality to legitimacy thus:

> In some senses, recourse to legitimacy as a supplement to legality is a discourse that parallels the revival of the Just War doctrine, especially in thinking about the propriety of "war" as a response to the 9/11 attacks. Indeed, supplying content and criteria for legitimating war resembles the process of validating war by reference to the Just War doctrine. In this regard, invoking legitimacy as the basis for validating international uses of force both acknowledges the authority of law as serving normal needs of global society, and its dysfunctionality when extended to govern *selected* exceptional situations. But which circumstances, and by whom identified? And by whom appraised? Is not, in the end, the danger of relying on legitimacy to overcome the inadequacies of legality a means to assert the primacy of politics and the subordination of law?[69]

Reluctant to move into a Schmittian direction wherein actions deemed legitimate are simply a consequence of the primacy of politics over law, the sovereign's right to declare a state of exception, Falk argues for a form of "interpretative flexibility" in law so that the legitimacy of law is sustained while the legitimacy of particular interventions, the recourse to war, for moral and political purposes is sanctioned. Rejecting the view that legitimacy could potentially be defined in terms of "reputation", Falk defends legality in terms of its openness to flexibility in "conditions of humanitarian necessity (Kosovo; Darfur, Sudan) and circumstances of defensive necessity (1967 War in the

Middle East, Afghanistan War of 2002)", and its assertion of illegality where these conditions remain unmet as in Iraq, 2003.[70] While Falk appears to imply that the cases chosen are incontestable, the effort is to suggest that the exception be explained "as reasonable rather than arbitrary."[71] However, the reasonableness of the case relies ultimately on a decision that proclaims the exception to the rule, the moral and political case for such a proclamation. Arbitrariness remains a challenge to any moralising imperative for the use of force in a global order that is asymmetrical in the distribution of power. While interpretative flexibility has been shown to be of value in the workings of an independent judiciary that can, within the liberal democratic polity, hold the executive to account or even to challenge the executive's declaration of emergency or a state of exception, no such facility exists as yet in the global arena, other than the Security Council. However, the controversies relating to Kosovo and Iraq emerged precisely in circumstances where no such legal sanction was forthcoming. Kosovo, in these circumstances, is as arbitrary as Iraq. Both constitute discretionary acts, both acts of exceptionalism.

The significance of cases such as Kosovo and Iraq lies both in the particularity of the political and moral issues surrounding these events, and the constitutive role that recourse to war plays in reinscribing the international as a juridical and political arena centred on humanity and the subject positions produced in this reinscription.[72] Nevertheless, the particularity of the case, indeed its immediacy, can never be dissociated from its consequences across space and time. Hence, while Falk correctly asserts that "legality clarifies the core obligations relating to force, while legitimacy tries to identify *and delimit* a zone of exception that takes account of supposedly special circumstances,"[73] the point is that any such delimitation of a zone of exception is one further violent moment in the reconstitution of the international arena so that what is generated is what Agamben refers to a "zone of indistinction"[74] between legality and illegality, war and criminality, and, as we have already seen, war and peace. There is a prominent tendency in the literature of International Relations to advocate the exceptional "rescue" operation,[75] however, as Martti Koskenniemi has shown, every such operation is but another moment in the reconstitution of the international away from legality and towards exceptionalism legitimised in the name of cosmopolitan right.[76]

What of the subject positions emergent from such exceptionalism? The term, "state of exception" may be understood as the condition of being "under siege". It may, however, also be considered to suggest the suspension of the law. According to Giorgio Agamben, "The state of exception is not a special kind of law (like the law of war); rather, in so far as it is a suspension of the juridical order itself, it defines law's threshold or limit concept."[77] The state of exception suggests the "very limit of the juridical order" and is as such "neither external nor internal to the juridical order."[78] This limit zone, threshold, or zone of indistinction has a performative function in terms of the production of subjectivities precisely located at the limits of law. As I indicated above, the discourses of justification surrounding the illegal recourse to war in conditions of humanitarian emergency or pre-emption, rely on legitimacy; that, for example, these situations call for what is referred to as an overwhelming "responsibility to protect", a moral imperative that calls for a necessary response. Necessity is hence a constitutive element of the state of exception, the former producing the legitimacy for the latter. Discourses advocating the legitimacy of action beyond law are hence reliant on establishing necessity; those with the capacity to act are called upon to do so. However, the action lies at the threshold or the limit of law; neither inside nor outside, a zone of indistinction that, in blurring the boundary between inside and outside, places the subjects involved, the agent enacting war and those on the receiving end somehow beyond the law, generating impunity for the former and subjection beyond the protection of law for the latter. Immediate examples of the workings of the state of exception clearly relate to Guantanamo, Abu Ghraib, Bagram airbase and other locations as yet undetermined, locations of incarceration of so-called "enemy combatants" beyond the scrutiny of law. However, the state of exception also applies to the immediacy of the violence perpetrated in wars declared humanitarian, for it is the case that while those involved in the discretionary use of force are by and large beyond the law while the target populations – for they are populations – are variously rendered the unfortunate casualties of war or remain invisible in any count of such casualties.

Humanitarian exceptionalism, the state of exception called forth and legitimised for humanitarian purposes is implicated in the production of populations targeted as what Agamben refers to as "bare life". There is, however, an intriguing paradox here, for while Agamben uses the term to refer to those incarcerated beyond law, shorn of rights, the condition of humanitarian war, a concept that has no existence legally and is hence always located in a zone of indistinction, inscribes populations targeted as the recipients of care and indeed protection while those very populations are at the same time the recipients of bombardment at distance through high technology warfare that quickly shifts from so-called "smart" bombing to total warfare deploying "dumb" bombs and "shock and awe" tactics. Killing in the name of humanity, for this is what "liberal war" is, constitutes the state of exception that enables what Michael Dillon refers to as "caring to death".[79] The "carers" are always hierarchically positioned, not just in technological capacity terms, but in moral terms, constructed as those engaged in saving distant others, just warriors acting on behalf of humanity at large.

The constructions implicated in liberal wars are only possible through a move involving their dislocation from history, a form of anamnesis that easily forgets the carers' complicity in generating the conditions that are rendered in terms of humanitarian necessity. The carers' moral positioning removes them as the agents "behind the injuries", to borrow Sara Ahmed's words. Ahmed is referring to the linguistic construction of a Christian Aid pamphlet aiming to raise support for its campaign against landmines. However, her analysis is equally as pertinent to situations of liberal war, where the agents of such wars are not only removed from the "chain of events" that historically reveals their complicity in the injuries inflicted against those very populations they aim to save. Only such a dislocation from history, such a politics of forgetting, can generate the moralising discourse that enables liberal wars to claim legitimacy and indeed to enact the state of exception. To borrow from Sara Ahmed again:

> Being moved by the other's pain elevates the Western subject into a position of power over others: the subject who gives to the other is the one who is "behind" the possibility of overcoming pain...The over-representation of the pain of others is significant in that it fixes the other as the one who "has" pain, and who can overcome that pain only when the Western subject feels moved enough to give.[80]

When Michel Foucault asks how it is possible to enact war in the age of biopolitics, when power shifts from the sovereign power to kill to one that aims at the life of populations, his ultimate answer, as we saw in Chapter 2, relies on the division of population along racial grounds; those targeted when wars are fought in the name of humanity are, by definition, deemed the inhuman, the danger against which "society must be defended". The subject of so-called liberal wars is the subject always placed in the position of power and so powerful is this positioning that the subject who cares, saves, rescues, and so on is always the moral subject, somehow removed from its complicity in the history of war and its violence; the agent of injury. The life of the other is saved through injury, through its production as bare life. The other targeted appears to be located somehow beyond subjectivity, shorn of history, and hence dislocated from any space that might be understood in terms of inter-subjectivity and the communicative sphere that confers the subject meaning. Agamben's rendition of "bare life" must hence have highly significant implications for contemporary (global) politics, for it is a concept that appears to be inscribed, by Agamben and others, onto the figure variously of the prisoner, the refugee, the deportee, a population under occupation, and I would add here the population targeted in humanitarian wars. Bare life is hence the embodiment of the state of exception. Understood in these terms, populations "saved" in liberal wars are also constituted as bare life, though the paradox, as I stated-above, is all too evident.

For Foucault, "biopower was without question an indispensable element in the development of capitalism; the latter would not have been possible without the controlled insertion of bodies into the machinery of production and the adjustment of the phenomena of population to economic processes."[81] Foucault's understanding of biopower is hence centrally associated with his appreciation of the two institutional continuities constitutive of modernity, namely the state and capitalism. Where the former is understood not in terms of sovereignty, but in terms of a set of historically situated practices of government, the latter, with its rise from the seventeenth century onwards, is crucially and constitutively built upon the capacities of the former as administrative unity built in turn upon technologies of control productive of such unity. For Foucault, the site of control came to be the population as a whole; the administrative rationale of the modern state aimed at the government of all aspects of the life of the population. As Hardt and Negri point out, it was the necessities emergent from a "global machine" that produced or necessitated the control of populations and their administration within coherent forms of social organisation.[82] The government of conduct from henceforth comes to be channelled through practices that inscribe the population as category; its life, its welfare, its distribution, its fragmentation, the inclusions and exclusions emergent from the diversity of governmantalising practices enacted by a diversity of agencies, both private and public.

In his text, *Remnants of Auschwitz*, Agamben refers to Michel Foucault in suggesting that the latter offers an explanation of the degradation of death, "an explanation that ties it to the transformation of power in the modern age."[83] As I indicate earlier, sovereign power is, from the seventeenth century onwards, transformed into what Foucault refers to as "biopower". The ancient right to kill and let live is transformed into the formula to make live and let die. Agamben refers to Foucault: "While in the right of sovereignty death was the point in which the sovereign's absolute power shone most clearly, now death instead becomes the moment in which the individual eludes all power, falling back on himself and somehow bending back on what is most private in him."[84] There are two models of power here; the ancient sovereign power of life and death, and modern biopolitical power which centres on "making men live". Sovereign power and biopower are here differentiated, a differentiation that, as Agamben points out, gives rise to a series of oppositions: individual body/population, discipline/mechanisms of regulation, man-body/man-species, that "at the dawn of the modern age, define the passage from one system to the other."[85] For Agamben, writing of Nazi Germany, the sovereign power to make live coincides absolutely with the sovereign power to kill, "such that biopolitics coincides immediately with thanatopolitics."[86] The distinction Foucault makes between sovereign power and biopower becomes, for Agamben, a "zone of indistinction", a zone that incorporates within it a series of other indistinctions that define the exception.

Agamben's claim is that he sees in Foucault the implications that Foucault himself failed to elaborate: the co-presence of life and death. In reading *Society Must Be Defended*,[87] Agamben's emphasis is on Foucault's rendition on race and racism. Racism allows biopower to mark a break in the biological continuum of the human species, reintroducing a principle of war in the system of "making live", in other words, the possibility of war in an age of biopower. Agamben once again quotes Foucault: "In the biological continuum of the human species, the opposition and hierarchy of races, the qualification of certain races as good and others, by contrast, as inferior, are all ways to fragment the biological domain whose care power had undertaken, they are ways to distinguish different groups inside a population. In short to stabilise a caesura of a biological type inside a domain that defines itself precisely as biological."[88] The emergence of biopower inaugurates a people into a population which then multiplies in the division of the population into separate and distinguishable races. According to Agamben, the caesura mark out zones which coincide with increasing degradation. In Nazi Germany, the Aryan is distinguished from the non-Aryan, the non-Aryan is transformed into the Jew, the Jew into the deportee, the deportee into the prisoner, until the caesuras reach their limits in the camp, culminating in a condition where it is no longer possible to distinguish caesuras.[89] The moment wherein it is no longer possible to distinguish caesuras becomes the moment of "bare life". Agamben refers to Hitler's concept of "a space empty of people", designating a "biopolitical intensity" through which people pass into a population and a population, ultimately, into the "Musselmanner". The camp becomes the manifestation of biopolitical power, the manifestation, in other words, of modern power. For Agamben, this is not just a manifestation of modern power, but a reflection of the present late modern condition. Bare life is the culmination of biopower.

For Agamben, sovereign power is the progenitor of biopower, or biopolitics: "The production of the biopolitical body is the original activity of sovereign power."[90] What is clear in Foucault's rendition, however, is the intimate relationship, and indeed mutual dependence, of the state, and agencies associated with the spread of capitalist production and exchange globally. The state and capitalism's global entrepreneurs are mutual clients, and seen from a historical and sociological perspective, which of these precedes in terms of decision or articulation of power becomes historically determined and situated rather than being subject to a teleological relationship. Biopower, or the "government" of populations emerges through practices that may be centrally determined (through the sovereign juridical power of the state) and/or dispersed in an array of locations and enacted through a diversity of agencies. The subject of biopower in Foucault is fully the subject capable of self-government, ever shifting as well as subject to constraint within the trajectories of power. The subject of Agamben's bare life, however, is devoid of subjectivity and its existential complexities and differentiations.

Operations of power for Foucault are interlaced with practices that seek the removal of the subject deemed "other". Such removal is historically manifest through a diverse array of practices from incarceration to deportation to full-scale violence. Foucault's rendition on this removal of the subject must be located in his understanding of the nexus between war and power, where the former takes life and the latter confers it, or more precisely, gives it form. According to his *History of Sexuality*, "Wars are no longer waged in the name of a sovereign who must be defended; they are waged on behalf of the existence of everyone..."[91] Where war takes place, it takes place in the name of the population, and as I argue elsewhere, in the name of humanity at large inscribed in very particular terms, namely the neoliberal global order.

The subject of this order is not simply bare life; rather, this is a subject, in Foucault, that has the capacity for self-government (hence Foucault's understanding of govern/mentality) emergent from relations of power that must assume a subject who can act. The liberal government of populations appeals, as Mitchell Dean points out, "to a notion of the subject active in its own government and presupposes certain types of free subject in the operation of particular programmes of conduct."[92] But, following Foucault, Dean refers to the "illiberality" of the "free subject" towards the "other", differentiated beyond the rationalities of liberal government, the subject inscribed through liberal society's "dividing practices" as the unfree, incapable of self-government. Those subjected as the "unfree" may be construed as the culmination of the state of exception, and hence as bare life in Agamben. They remain inscriptions in Foucault, and hence never fully subjected.

The exceptionalism that defines liberal wars has, as we see in this chapter, a number of implications that are global in reach. The redesign of the international may well be articulated in terms of the emergence of a new form of cosmopolitanism that is based on a universalising project for the transformation of political community beyond the exclusions of the sovereign state. However, we have also seen that borders shift elsewhere just as sovereign power shifts towards a global domain of operations that some would render imperial. The effect on the ground is the production of subjects differentially placed not just in the moral stakes that enable the legitimisation of late modern wars for humanity, but in relation to the state of exception that lies at the heart of such wars. There is then a particularity to the state of exception, wherein the enemy targeted is always reduced to bare life, either killed in order to be saved or killed in order simply to be removed from circulation. Such is the nature of discretionary war whose agents confer to themselves the right of judgement. For Michel Foucault wars rendered in human terms are also wars driven by a racial differentiation of the population. In the late modern context of war, the racial is, in the contemporary period, cultural, and it is cultural differentiation, the cultural profile of the contemporary state of exception and its global war that forms the subject matter for the next chapter.

5
War and the Politics of Cultural Difference

Hegemony ...is a whole body of practices and expectations; our assignments of energy, our ordinary understanding of the nature of man and his world. It is a set of meanings and values which as they are experienced as practices appear as reciprocally confirming.

Raymond Williams[1]

What I have referred to as the global matrix of war is constituted, as I indicate in Chapter 2, of two dominant sets of practices that are in many ways related, though the relationship often remains unacknowledged. These two sets of practices include wars fought in the name of humanity, wars legitimised variously in terms of discourses centred on rescue, care, and human rights; they have also come to include wars and confrontations that are targeted against an enemy deemed to constitute an existential threat. While Kosovo is seen to represent the former set, Afghanistan and Iraq are considered to represent the latter. Nevertheless, as I argued in the last chapter, these two aspects of the global matrix of war are historically related, for they both constitute a mode of exceptional politics that seek to render actions that stand beyond the law legitimate and, more significantly, necessary. Beyond the obvious fact that they have both involved the use of a high technology military machine and that they therefore both represent a mode of asymmetrical warfare that predominantly injures populations targeted, they are both liberal wars, enacted by liberal regimes and, more significantly, in the name of what are represented as distinctly liberal, and cosmopolitan, values. The exceptionalism of these wars is a liberal exceptionalism, self-legislating, self-legitimising, and above all else, universalising in its remit. The discursive landscape and its grammars is one that is framed in terms of progress and civilisation, a battle for modernity itself. The enemy in both forms of war, the humanitarian and the pre-emptive, is seen as bearing responsibility for mass atrocity, and is as such deemed the enemy of humanity at large, its progress and its civilisation.

Of profound interest in the discursive grammars that enable liberal wars is their facility of forgetfulness, a facility that enables the dislocation of the present, so that the attribution of responsibility is always located elsewhere, so that the human costs of a hegemonic neoliberal order and the global military order that sustains it and the ongoing wars that draw from it are not considered as injurious or as complicit. Wars fought in the name of humanity are by definition fought by those whose self-perception is constructed in terms of humanity as a whole, even as gestures are made towards this humanity's constitutive diversity. The civilisational remit, therefore, is what connects Kosovo and Iraq, even as these two cases are clearly also very divergent in many respects. While the last chapter focused on interventionist wars deemed humanitarian and their implications for the rearticulation of the international sphere, this chapter places its attention on the other set of practices I suggest constitute the late modern matrix of war, namely those associated with pre-emption, currently labelled the "war against terrorism". These practices, as we will see below, involve a panoply of operations, including those that have a parallel in humanitarian wars, namely those associated with post-war governance regimes. However, the primary and most significant element in the so-called war against terrorism is that it is transnational in orientation, traversing the domestic/international divide, manifest in practices that include high technology bombardment as much as domestic legislation aimed at individuals deemed a danger to society. It is this transnational character of the practices associated with pre-emption that renders them especially significant in the social as much as the juridico-political framing of the international arena.

The aim of this chapter is to explore the distinctly cultural manifestation of practices associated with the so-called war against terrorism. It seeks to locate the conditions of possibility that have rendered the cultural not just a marker of difference but of enmity and existential threat. While the first section of the chapter explores global conditions that have elevated cultural difference as a significant marker of difference, the second deals particularly with the cultural signification of the matrix of war, arguing that such signification is constituted by two elements, a racialising of the enemy on the one hand and the depoliticisation of conflict through culturalist discourse on the other. The

third section of the chapter looks to the consequences of practices constituting the global matrix of war, consequences that are manifest globally. The analysis throughout engages with critical, poststructural,
and the postcolonial literature to reveal the locations of culture in
systems of knowledge, relations of power, and modes of subjectivity
that might inform our understanding of how culture stands in relation
to questions of war in late modern global politics.

Late modernity and articulations of culture

The global politics of late modernity have come to be overwhelmingly
focused on a confrontation that is imbued with cultural signification.
We saw this to be the case in Chapter 2, where I argued that the global
matrix of war defining the so-called "war against terrorism" is predominantly defined in terms of practices that view the particular other, the
other variously associated with Islam, the Middle East and South Asia
as the source of threat. Practices associated with cultural exclusion, or
indeed cultural targeting, are not simply contained in the war against
terrorism, but have come to be defining features of newly emerging
immigration controls, especially within the European and American
context, and anti-terrorist legislative measures that particularly target
Islamic communities.[2] In a context of a globally defined war, cultural
difference comes to be defined in terms of antagonism and mutual
threat; a situation wherein what at first hand were local grievances
associated with distinct conflict situations such as Kashmir or the
Israeli-Palestinian conflict, have come to constitute a global civilisational antagonism of cultures that pits western liberalism against Islam.
Huntington's "clash of civilisations"[3] thesis comes to see its realisation
in a twenty-first century global confrontation that is daily reinforced in
discursive as well as institutional practices.

In any critical exploration of the present, the paramount question
has to centre on the triptych that appears and reappears in this
volume, namely power, knowledge and subjectivity. That power is
always implicated raises questions relating to the frameworks of
knowledge that turn real and actual grievances into global cultural
confrontations. As each enactment of violence takes place so too
each succeeds in its own way in the diminution of grievances associated with local and protracted conflict situations that have for long
required resolution. However it is not simply these modes of
globalised violence that diminish these very real political conflicts of
territory, identity, and self-determination. Systems of knowledge pro-

duced and reproduced in a self-perpetuating political economy of knowledge are equally implicated, for the emergence of such a field of research within the western academy as "international terrorism" and "new security studies", or constructs such as the "Arab mind"[4] reinforce a framework of knowledge that essentialises culture and suggests the world faces a problem of terrorism that is distinct from the political conflicts and grievances that underpin violent conflict behaviour anywhere. That such violence is enacted in the name of Islam and that it is represented in systems of knowledge as "Islamic" terrorism itself comes to reinforce a distinctly culturalist reading of events and hence what is in effect a depoliticised reading. In this context, culture comes to matter not because it matters in essence, but because it has come to be interpolated in discourse *in place* of political conflicts of recognition.

We must therefore ask how culture, or cultural difference, has come to matter in global politics and specifically in relation to questions of war and peace at global scale. Culture may well be a discursive ruse utilised in a convenient play of power that seeks to diminish political conflict and transform such conflict into a global problem that associates violence with the cultural other. Cultural affiliation, when articulated in terms of religiosity, may also be used to perpetuate antagonism and to undermine secular modes of political organisation and expression. However, cultural difference is also a basis of mobilisation against domination and hence comes to represent not just a discursive ruse for the activation of enmity, but a form of political subjectivity that seeks recognition. Any ideas on the transformation of global relations from war to a condition of peace must then take culture seriously, especially as at the heart of any political discourse that has a cosmopolitan worldview is the idea of pluralist recognition.

When the aspiration is to legislate for peace globally, the global as a terrain of interaction comes to mean the universal, and the universal as an all-encompassing category, must somehow contain the particularities that in actuality constitute the cultural diversity that is the defining feature of human existence. The achievement of peace, its cosmopolitan realisation, appears at first hand to come at the expense of difference, specifically the form of difference that is culturally defined. We saw in the last chapter that humanitarian intervention is often premised on claims to universal legitimacy, being first and foremost defined in terms of the protection of human rights against the extremes of violence witnessed in situations of ethnic cleansing and genocide. Where such interventions have taken place, the aftermath is often centred around what is variously understood as peacebuilding or state-building; the near wholesale transformation of a society and its institutions in accordance with the western liberal democratic model. With cases such as Namibia, Cambodia, East Timor, to name but a few, it might be argued that concerted efforts aimed at the reconstruction of societies can be considered rungs in the gradual effort at the achievement of a triumph for modernisation, liberal democracy, and ultimately a cosmopolitan order that underpins global relations. On the other hand, the assertion of local identities against the imposition of external frameworks, either of governance or of a homogenised, globalised identity, suggest some resistance to these programmes. The question of cultural difference has a powerful presence in global politics, a presence that is not so much the *cause* of conflict, of exclusion, of affiliation, as well as resistance, but a product of signifying practices and relations of power that confer causality to cultural difference.

There is perhaps no stronger a visual manifestation of global cultural confrontation than the United States marine confronting the Iraqi citizen. Barriers of language may be the immediate obstacle to understanding, but other factors, related to the asymmetry of power that stems from occupation, but manifest in radically different forms of cultural expression, contribute to the failure of communications in Iraq to such a degree that the Pentagon now seeks to build "cultural awareness" training into its programmes.[5] That a twenty-first century colonisation can be reduced to a matter of cross-cultural communication is itself testimony to the depolitication of war, invasion, and resistance to occupation. However, within a global arena that witnesses events taking place in Iraq and elsewhere, cultural affiliation, expressed variously through Islam as a binding force in a transnational community of belief or through national affiliation, comes to form a thread that connects the teenager in a northern English town or the Arab city with distant populations in the bombed out villages, towns, and cities that he or she is unlikely to know or experience at first hand.[6] Cultural affinity has become a powerful force in global politics as have exclusions based on cultural difference. What are the conditions of possibility that have so elevated cultural difference as the signifier of a globally defined confrontation?

There is a sense in which cultural difference has in many ways replaced race as the basis of exclusion in contemporary social formations. Race thinking has, according to Paul Gilroy, adapted its discourses so that the divisions between groups are not simply measured in terms of colour lines. As Gilroy states:

> We are, unlike DuBois, now obliged to note that white supremacy is only one among a variety of depressing options in the unwholesome cornucopia of absolutist thinking about "race" and ethnicity. The resolute enthusiasm of postmodern ethnic cleansers and absolutists apparently knows no color lines. Hendrick Verwoerd, Samuel Huntington, Ariel Sharon, Slobodan Milosevic, Osama Bin Laden, Condoleezza Rice, and a host of others have all contributed something to the belief that absolute culture rather than color is more likely to supply the organizing principle that underpins contemporary schemes of racial classification and division.[7]

While racism as a distinct form of political and social exclusion may persist in all contemporary societies, it is the relationship between cultural identification and expression on the one hand and political conflict on the other that is of interest to the present investigation. However, before we can properly explore this relationship, it is imperative that we try to somehow grapple with the meaning of cultural identity and difference to then be able to delve into how culture has come to be interpolated in questions relating to global confrontation.

We can explore the question of conflict and identity in a number of ways. For the purposes of this study, culture forms an aspect of social identity, and brings with it particular practices and modes of understanding that at one and the same time confer identity and suggest frames of identification of distinct groups in society.[8] We may debate the place of cultural identity in relation to ethnicity, religion, or nation. However, what is important in the present context is to highlight the understanding that a distinctly cultural mode of articulation may transcend all of these forms of affiliation so that practices associated with culture may form points of contact between different ethnic and national groupings. Culture in this sense permeates the everyday and the routine just as it is invoked in the most turbulent times. The symbolic orders and frameworks of meaning that confer identity to an individual or community are continually reproduced in social interaction, at one and same time both drawing on established practices recalled through traces of memory and deep-rooted interactions as well as reenacting the situatedness of the individual self. Culture, though ever subject to transformation in its modes of expression, nevertheless forms the taken-for-granted background that enables us to confer meaning to the world around us. However, like other modes of identity, culture remains subject to different modes of articulation and what form such articulation takes is of crucial importance in understanding how cultural difference comes to be related to conflict and antagonism.

Conceptual categories such as culture, class, gender, or even ethnicity, are never completely at one with the actuality of social relations, so that the latter always have the capacity to defy or even escape definitional limits.[9] It is hence difficult to draw upon singular categories of identification to situate an individual self in relation to the social continuities that surround the self. As Homi Bhabha, has argued, understanding the political significance of cultural difference does not emerge from the attribution of characteristics deriving from static points of origin, but is rather dependent upon the practices wherein cultural difference comes into force, where such difference is articulated in inter-subjective settings. These articulations come to form "strategies of selfhood", both individual and communal, that renegotiate identity, and the form, collaborative or contested, that inter-subjective relations take.[10] We might typecast individuals and communities into pre-given categories, but such typecasting is always a product of relations of power and not a product of the modalities through which individuals and communities find cultural expression. Such expression may derive from a complex array of myth, memory and the self-imagery that derives from the symbolic order, but is always in process, always contingent upon the matrices of social and political life. The articulation of a sense of self, therefore, is always a way of providing a marker as a reaffirmation of the individual's location in relation to the social matrix and its structures of signification and domination. Cultural difference must therefore always be seen in relation to the continuities that form the discourses and institutional practices within a given society. While articulations of self provide a marker in relation to structures of signification and domination, they also form a moment of interpretation by the individual self of precisely these structures. Articulations of self are, however, also subject to the typifications that locate individuals and communities in relation to dominant social norms and symbolic orders. Constructions of "self" and "other" emerge from the dynamic that defines self-articulation and modes of representation. Both in turn are constituted within the discursive and institutional backdrop that defines social formations. There is, in this sense, no pre-given subject as such, but a subject who is, in Julia Kristeva's perspective, always "in-process".[11]

However, I want to argue that it is not just the subject of cultural expression who is in process, but the forms of discursive representations that confer a typified social identity to the self. This dynamic of self and other is itself not just constituted within the discursive and institutional practices of social and political life, but is implicated in the reproduction and renegotiation of these practices.

Cultural difference incorporates both self-articulation and representation. Both in turn are situated in relation to a wider constitutive context of symbolic orders, social norms, and institutional continuities, so that difference is not simply a matter of identity, but is located in relations of power. The politics of cultural difference suggests a form of political agency that bases its articulation in terms of cultural differentiation and identification. The spatio-temporal articulation of this mode of politics is, in late modernity, not confined to the domestic sphere, but expands transnationally through the global arena. Stuart Hall refers to this dynamic as the "politics of location".[12] However, this is a mode of politics that is not simply confined to what is traditionally thought of as the location of politics, namely the state, but expands to a multiplicity of locations or spheres wherein contestation and mobilisation might take place. As we will see below, this has monumental implications for questions of governance, in that any effort at the creation of a single governmental space comes face to face with articulations of self that locate the self elsewhere, transnationally, and hence beyond the purview of the state. Political agency, when articulated culturally, transcends the boundaries of the state and the state's efforts at the creation of a coherent political space.[13] Such a disjuncture between a political subjectivity expressed globally and governmental practices that seek to "contain" governmental space within the modern state reinforces Stuart Hall's claim that "Identities are never unified and, in late modern times, increasingly fragmented and fractured; never singular but multiply constructed across different, often intersecting and antagonistic, discourses, practices, positions."[14]

The politics of location is hence no longer bound to the sedimented state, but shifts across the global terrain, so that it is this terrain that forms the backdrop to the mobilisations and contestations associated with late modern conflict and warfare. That the compression of space and time emergent from the globalisation of all aspects of social, economic, and political relations enables the emergence of a political subjectivity that is no longer place bound is one of the most monumental transformations of the recent era and brings with it the fragmentations and uncertainties associated with late modern existence. Conflict and grievance can no longer be confined to locality, but come to form the source of grievance and conflict elsewhere, in locations distant from their points of origin. Cultural affiliation comes to form the mediating force between the local and the global, so that the articulations of self and the modes of representations that typify the individual and community, are manifest in a multiplicity of locations from the local neighbourhood to the city to the state and the global arena. The global becomes a social sphere that sees its articulation in more local actions, mobilisations, and contestations. As Zygmunt Bauman points out, "With time of communication imploding and shrinking to the no-size of the instant, space and spatial markers cease to matter, at least to those whose actions can move with the speed of the electronic message."[15] The "inside" versus "outside" distinction that provided the certainties and domestications of the modern era of the nation-state can no longer hold when the spatial is now defined in terms of the co-presence of the local and the global. The diminution of the distinction between inside and outside as spatial terms has allowed, again as Bauman highlights, "the stretching of conflicts, solidarities, combats, debates or the administration of justice well beyond the reach of the human eye and arm."[16]

The global terrain as a social sphere is, however, too complex to suggest singular modes of cultural expression, even in the most antagonistic of times. While the Islamic communities of northern England may express affinity with their Palestinian or Iraqi counterparts, there are no pre-given ethnic or cultural identities that may be drawn upon to somehow "profile" communities. Rather, the negotiations of self incorporate both local and distant settings, local affinities as well as transnational solidarities. If there is one powerful element that emerges from the postcolonial literature it is that of questioning the idea of pre-given ethnic and cultural identities, suggesting instead the theme of "crossing-over", "hybrid subjectivity",[17] and the ever present refiguration of narratives of self and modes of articulation. While the politics of representation, as David Campbell has shown,[18] may seek to typify individuals and communities into singular modes of identity, drawing on constructions that variously negate or even vilify the other so represented, the lived experience, especially of migrant or exile communities is far more complex and fragmented in its affinities and loyalties.

Such complexity and fragmentation must, however, be located in relation to structures of domination in global politics, structures that are not only implicated in practices of exclusion, but in the generation of adversity borne of the imposition of practices associated variously with missions to modernise, to civilise, to liberalise, to democratise, and so on. As Michel Foucault reveals, history itself becomes a technology, a tool in relations of power, deployed in the production of truth and the exclusions generated through such production. When history becomes a technology, the practices of exclusion that such a technology instantiates come to revolve around those who possess legitimacy in renditions of past and present and those denied such representational access. Historical technologies are hence not merely centred upon glorifications of the past, as is evident, for example, in forms of nationalist discourse, but arhe social and political turning points of past and present and what, ultimately, matters for the future. Relations of power are hence formative of the historical process, the construction of its turning points, and the discursive practices invested in these turning points. Any consideration of transformation, or of historical breaks, is then related to power so that particular events acquire the status of a historical break. For Michel Foucault, analyses of power must move beyond the dichotomy between structure and event, for events differ in their "capacity to produce effects".[19]

The mobilisation of cultural modes of affiliation must then be considered in relation to structures of domination in global politics. For this is the context within which culture matters in relation to questions of war and peace. It is undoubtedly the case, as a number of authors in International Relations have shown, that culture has always been a significant if ignored factor in this Anglo-American discipline.[20] What is significant for the present context is the unravelling of how culture as a distinct mode of political expression comes to be mobilised in a global terrain of confrontation. The rendition accrued to particular events is hence always situated within the complexity of cultural practices linked with the capacity to mobilise material and human resources in the stakes for legitimisation. The narrations associated with particular events, the dominant discourses surrounding them, are hence not simply a matter of language, but of relations of power and the distribution of forces in the struggles for discursive hegemony in history and its transformations. For Foucault, "The problem is at once to distinguish among events, to differentiate the networks and levels to which they belong, and to reconstitute the lines along which they are connected and engender one another."[21] The issue is not one of symbolic field but of power, for "The history which bears and determines us has the form of a war rather than that of a language: relations of power, not relations of meaning."[22] Cultural difference is not *per se* a relationship of struggle or confrontation; it only becomes so within the context of power and domination.

In the context of late modern political and social life, cultural difference may simply be an instantiation of the great diversity of human existence and the multiple forms of expression and experience witnessed in the great global cities, such as London or New York. Travel, migration, and instant communication render diversity a distinct form of lived experience so that late modern subjectivity comes to be somehow "in tune" with difference and potentially open to pluralist, hybrid modes of being. This, perhaps, was the optimistic vision for a late modern twenty-first century where humanity could be seen as one in its drive for consumer capitalism driven by the achievements of information technology and the dominance of the global market place with material goods and brand names that connected populations across the global terrain. Cultural difference, in this frame, could be seen as the benevolent face of a cosmopolitan global order emergent from the possibilities of communicative interaction. Much of the shock of the events of September 11th 2001 and July 7th 2005, in New York and London respectively, stemmed from the fact that these indeed are global cities, containing within their borders cultures, ethnicities and nationalities literally from across the world. When the cosmopolis becomes a target, it is as if the whole of humanity in all its lived diversity is the target, becomes the other to those perpetrating the act.

Any reduction of current, global, conflicts, including the invasions of Afghanistan and Iraq, and the wider "war against terrorism" into a cultural confrontation is itself complicit in a "clash of civilisations" discourse that is akin to the ancient hatreds framework that sustained the Balkan conflicts. While there are a number of issues related to distinctly local conflicts, that form the basis of the current global confrontation and its capacity to mobilise, there is nevertheless a significant element associated with cultural difference that imbues these global antagonistic relations. The background conditions emerge from the features of late modern social and political life. According to social theorists such as Anthony Giddens and Manuel Castells, one of the central elements of late modernity relates to culture and personal identity. The shift in the organisation of global patterns has, as one of its most significant factors, that of cultural transformation, a transformation so profound that the defining dialectic of late modern life is that between the global and the local. The institutional and phenomenological aspects of late modernity are interlaced with cultural articulations of difference in the face of universalising discourses and practices that are perceived as posing an existential threat to local life. However, as Zygmunt Bauman, amongst others, has highlighted, the late modern condition, and specifically, those elements related to globalised social and political relations, is differently experienced by different sectors of the global population.

Modernity and its late modern manifestations has historically been experienced differently across the globe, suggesting that modernity's institutions, namely the nation-state and capitalist production and exchange, have been interlaced with local and very specific conditions. Many aspects of such conditions may be hostile to capitalist production and to the naturalisation of the nation-state over and above other modes of identification. Indeed a glance at the Middle East shows a postcolonial period of modernisation driven by a centralised and secular state and experienced across the span of civil society institutions from educational establishments to literary circles. The formative debate during this era of modernisation centred upon the dialectic between modernisation and tradition, between the rationalising imperatives of state-controlled production and social relations and a religiously defined realm of tradition with its pre-scribed rules of interaction, from the economic to the personal.[23] What is important to stress is that the manifestations of modernity and its concomitant identities differ with social context and the dynamics in force locally. Nowhere is this differentiation in the experience of modernity and its institutions more apparent than in relation to the modern state and what we might refer to as the "experience" of sovereignty. While the occidental conception of modern political community has been constructed around the limits of the sovereign state, the postcolonial state experience has been predominantly defined in terms of the constitutive vulnerability of such limits. In relation to the postcolonial state, conceptions of political community, of justice, of legitimacy, as the basic tenets of politics, could never be defined simply in relation to the state, but were historically always somehow located elsewhere, in local communities as well as transnational spaces. In terms of representation, postcolonial societies always emerge as anomalies or failures with respect to modernity and its organising principles. As Inayatullah and Blaney point out, in specific reference to the liberal peace project in International Relations, "In this updating of modernization theory, the relationship between liberal democracies and their ex-colonies is staged as a kind of 'morality play' of purity and pollution. That is, the cultural conceptions of Western liberals are constructed as normal or natural in relation to today's 'barbarians', the marginalised and anarchical peoples and regions, perpetually on the road to mature liberal selfhood."[24]

Marking difference: race and the elevation of culture in the matrix of war

I have indicated elsewhere and in the second chapter to this book that Foucault's understanding of war enables a conceptualisation that moves the terms of reference beyond this term's traditional battlefield sense. The term "war" has an excess that blurs the boundary between spaces of war and peace, the battlefield and the social realm. Nowhere is this conception of war more apparent than in the contemporary global matrix of war and specifically with practices defining the so-called war against terrorism, for here we witness an array of practices ranging from invasion, to extra-judicial assassination, to incarceration, to the use of torture against detainees, to deportation, to increasing association of migration with the terrorist threat, to the increasingly interventionist modes of surveillance, all constituting the actualisation of a state of war, a state of exception, globally rendered. All such practices are represented in discourse as necessary security measures brought forth for the protection of society and "our way of life". Nevertheless, these are practices that possess a distinct cultural profile wherein the other deemed a threat or danger to society is the subject variously associated with Islam, the Middle East and South Asia suggesting a particularity to the state of exception and its impact upon lived experience.

Edward Said is a foremost theorist and writer on the politics of cultural difference and its location in relation to conflict and antagonism. Writing at the outset of the First Gulf War, he states: "For decades in America there has been a cultural war against the Arabs and Islam; the most appalling racist caricatures of Arabs and Muslims have conveyed that they are all either terrorists or sheikhs, and that the region is a large arid slum, fit only for profit or war."[25] There is, in this dominant discourse – and Said is writing before the events of September 11th 2001 – a form of abjection that denies the other's alterity or complexity: "The very notion that there might be a history, a culture, a society – indeed many societies – to be thought of as interlocutor or as partner has never held the stage for more than a moment or two."[26] Julia Kristeva writes of the "abject" as that which "disturbs identity, system, order. What does not respect borders, positions, rules. The in-between, the ambiguous, the composite."[27] The indefinable and the complex denied indefinability or complexity is precisely that "being opposed to I"[28] whose being constitutes an existential threat. What is crucial in what we might refer to as the politics of abjection is that the abject is not merely excluded or discriminated against, but denied a presence in discursive articulation.

Cultural theorists, including Spivak and Said, write of a form of violence that is inherent in the very practice of representation. Spivak writes of the "epistemic violence of imperialism"[29] where the colonised disappear from view or are only brought forth through the actions of the coloniser. Like Spivak, Said is interested in the epistemic violence that is inherent in a politics of representation that confines the colonised subject to a space of negation, a space of non-presence. Drawing on Frantz Fanon's *Wretched of the Earth*, Said writes of the spatial separation of the violence of the colonised space and the "cleanliness, the well-lighted streets of the colonialist town, A European town, violently implanted in a native society."[30] When violence is used, it is legitimised in the name of "rationality – civilisation". The practice of violence is hence always implicated with a politics of representation; discursive practices that are always already violent. For Said, the "discursive formation" that captures the "structure of cultural domination" of the Arab and Islamic world is "orientalism", a system of representation that has its origins in European imperial rule and that sees its violent and somewhat cruder rendition in American texts, from the popular to the scholarly, renditions that represent the Arab in a "gesture of abject defeat", variously stereotyped as "camel-riding nomad", oil sheikh or terrorist. For Said, such epistemic violence is enabled by a positivist social science discourse that denies complexity a space in its epistemological rule-book:

> One of the striking aspects of the new American social science attention to the Orient is its singular avoidance of literature. You can read through reems of expert writing on the modern Near East and never encounter a single reference to literature. What seems to matter far more to the regional expert are "facts", of which a literary text is perhaps a disturber. The net effect of this remarkable omission in modern American awareness of the Arab or Islamic Orient is to keep the region and its people conceptually emasculated, reduced to "attitudes", "trends", statistics: in short dehumanised.[31]

A discursive formation that abjects the other is hence also a dehuman-ising discourse that underpins practices of violence. To suggest that there is a direct causal link between the epistemic violence that Said writes of and the present direct violence currently enacted in the Middle East would constitute a grotesque over-simplification of the issues at stake in the present juncture of history. What can be stated is that the politics of representation, the epistemic violence that Said and Spivak refer to, produces particular enabling or permissive mechanisms, feeding into modes of discourse as well as practices that continue to target the other through direct violence and other forms of abjection witnessed more recently in Iraq as a twenty-first century mode of colonisation and in camps such as Abu Ghraib and Guantanamo.[32] While discursive practices, to use Judith Butler, are speech acts that injure, these feed into and enable the targeting of direct violence against the other.[33]

There is, in recent times, a resurgence of interest in the British Empire and other imperialist projections of power. The debate focuses on particular revisionist readings of Britain's rule over its colonies and whether such rule may be interpreted as "progressive" in parts.[34] Such calls for a rewriting of the historical record must be set against equally as recent revelations about the violence of British imperial rule in India and Kenya, amongst other colonies.[35] Discourses in the United States centre, as I indicate in Chapter 2, around US Empire in the present, a project more recently defined, or indeed legitimised, by certain neo-conservative commentators as "democratic realism", centred on the exceptionalism of the United States and its global remit.[36] What is significant about these discourses is that they span the Left-Right divide in the political spectrum and, coupled with the legitimising discourses around wars of intervention, rejuvenate what we might understand as a twenty-first century form of colonial politics the primary legitimising tool of which centres on liberal cosmopolitanism. This mode of politics has distinct features that must be highlighted if we are to fully understand its global consequences.

The first feature I want to highlight relates to the projection of power that is core to the colonial project. Just as histories of Britain's colonial rule suggest that a clear element of this rule was the public and open display of power, in the form of public executions, hangings, and the humiliation of "natives", so the high technology mode of warfare expressed in the "shock and awe" tactics of the US invasion of Iraq were aimed not simply at the military defeat of a spent enemy, but for the display of sheer untrammelled power, aimed at a wider regional and global audience. There is an emphasis here on the visibility of such power, indeed the performance of sovereign power, from the "shock and awe" bombardment of a capital city, to the public hooding of prisoners, to the public torture and humiliation of the incarcerated. As I stated in an earlier study, "This spectacle of power has to be analysed in terms, not just of those who are its direct victims, but of the onlooking public at large. The direct violence perpetrated against the former becomes the mode of control of the latter; terror is implicated in both in that while the former suggests direct violence aimed at injury, the latter is generative of fear and through such aims to silence dissent and obliterate politics."[37] The public performance of untrammelled power reconstitutes sovereign power, as Michel Foucault has shown in relation to public displays of torture in seventeenth century Europe, what he refers to as the "economy of punitive power".[38] The sovereign power performed in the contemporary context is expressed in high technology warfare and the technologies of power utilised in spaces of territorial occupation and beyond. Crucial to present day modes of colonisation and their displays of sovereign power is that such display combines with legitimising discourses that constitute the recipient, or target, populations as subjects of humanitarian concern. There is here a double move of life and death, both rendered through a military machine that possesses global reach.

The second related feature of our twenty-first century practices of colonisation that has within it elements reminiscent of past modes of colonial rule centres on the question of race and specifically racism as the basis of the production of bare life in these states of exception. As I indicated earlier in this investigation, Foucault addresses a question to himself in relation to the possibility of war in the context of biopower, the power that seeks the regulation of life; wars fought in the name of humanity. Wars fought are fought in the name of distinct populations, racialised as the dominant race. That the practices constituting the global matrix of war are racially and culturally marked is clearly of significance in the lived experience of individuals and communities of those targeted; however, the significance also lies in revealing the workings of power upon the very corporeality of those targeted, the other conceived in racial and cultural terms. The targeting of the racial other has a long history in the emergence of the modern state and indeed modernity as a whole.[39] In contemporary society, race has its manifestations in deeply-rooted discursive and institutional practices structurated in the routines of daily life, from statements related to migrants and asylum seekers, to racist attacks on the streets, to media representations of the racial and cultural other, to policing operations of "stop and search" that rely on racial profiling, to military practices in distant lands that treat populations under occupation in distinctly racist terms. "Visible difference", to quote Linda Alcoff,[40] is central to epistemic frameworks and systems of knowledge that classify and categorise, that above all form the basis of the self-understanding variously of the liberal subject, the western subject, the agent of rescue, the modern subject, and ultimately the militarised subject of colonising power.

The historical trajectory of the liberal democratic state is clearly imbued with the phenomenon of racism, from its violent colonial manifestation to contemporary modes of exclusion at all levels of social interaction. However, what I want to emphasise here is that culture and race are now interchangeable. Furthermore, the invocation of "race" in contemporary colonial practice does not suggest that race as such is the cause, or indeed the driving force, behind practices of domination; it is however, a constitutive product of such practices, so that populations under occupation, those subjected in the state of exception, come to be classified and categorised in racialised terms, terms that accrue supremacy and inferiority to the occupier and occupied respectively. As Gilroy highlights,

> by "race" I do not mean physical variation or differences common-
> sensically coded in, on, or around the body. For me, "race" refers
> primarily to an impersonal, discursive arrangement, the brutal result
> of the raciological ordering of the world, not its cause. Tracking the
> term directs attention toward the manifold structures of a racial
> nomos – a legal, governmental, and spatial order – that, as we have
> seen, is now reviving the geopolitical habits of the old imperial
> system in discomforting ways.[41]

The state of exception that defines the late modern matrix of war is indeed such a nomos, seeing its apotheosis realised in the projection of military power across the global terrain, generating in its wake forms of domination manifest in a multiplicity of locations, from the imme-diacy of occupied terrain, to attempts at the rearticulation of the global political and juridical order, to governmental practices implicated in the profiling of individuals and communities. However, this racio-logical ordering of the world is also very personal, indeed corporeal, targeted at the body of the other,[42] so that boundaries are no longer conceived as co-terminus with those of defined territories, but as carried corporeally by populations deemed a threat to society.[43] The politics of colonial domination is corporeal (directed at individual bodies) as much as it is biopolitical (directed at the mass of populations). Perhaps we can argue that such domination does not by necessity have to be generative of a racialised domination, that the populations of the other may be deemed rescued from oppressive rule, brought forth into modernity before their time. There will be voices within academe and in the media who can refer, for example, to elections in Iraq bearing testimony to the liberation made possible through invasion and occupation; that Abu Ghraib and other locations of abuse and mass killing were but aberrations in an otherwise liberal occupation.[44] Such discourses must, however, be placed in the context of the history of colonial rule, a history replete with racialised rule and its legitimising discourses.

When cultural difference emerges as the primary signifier of a politics of conflict and confrontation, its conditions of possibility relate at one and the same time to the interaction between discursive formations and the structural transformations associated with late modernity. Where the former suggest a politics of representation that underpins the construction of enmity, the latter point to the dialectical consequences emerging from the dynamics of globalisation and its impact on the ontological securities that provide meaning in lived experience. Both are in turn imbricated with structures of domination that ultimately determine the legitimate, the acceptable, the righteous and the barbarian. The effect is the production of subjects, categorised and spatialised, shaped in accordance with the rationalisations of discursive and ultimately institutionalised modes of identification. In a context defined in terms of a global "war against terrorism", such rationalisations are often interlaced with friend/enemy identifications that then drive the implementation of violent practices in the name of security. As I indicated in the second chapter of this study, the global matrix of war and the exceptional practices that constitute it is experienced differently by different sectors of the global population, where some such sectors are and continue to be subject to profiling based on culture.

Cultural difference and the modernising project

When Michel Foucault is asked by the editors of the journal, *Herodote*, why his investigations "privilege the factor of time"[45] and are not as concerned with spatial differentiation, his response is revealing of the occidental situatedness of his analytics of power, a situatedness that has consequences not just in terms of his periodisation of the workings of power and its transformations from the classical period to the twentieth century, but in terms of the occlusions that the postcolonial literature has highlighted, occlusions that have manifest implications for interpretations of the modernising project and its late modern articulations. Spivak, for example, is concerned that the absence of a spatial differentiation in Foucault's analytics fail to place the spotlight on the relationship between the violence of imperial domination of other societies and the evolution of practices of government in the occident:

> Sometimes it seems as if the very brilliance of Foucault's analysis of the centuries of European imperialism produces a miniature version of that heterogeneous phenomenon: management of space – but by doctors; development of administration – but in asylums; considerations of the periphery – but in terms of insane, prisoners and children. The clinic, the asylum, the prison, the university – all seem to be screen allegories that foreclose a reading of the broader narratives of imperialism.[46]

Foucault himself readily admits to the situated nature of his analytics, but nevertheless reveals a particular geographic sensibility that is of interest to the context of the present discussion.[47] This relates to the distinctly spatial articulation of power:

> The longer I continue, the more it seems to me that the formation of discourses, and the genealogy of knowledge need to be analysed, not in terms of types of consciousness, modes of perception and forms of ideology, but in terms of tactics and strategies of power. Tactics and strategies deployed through implantations, distributions, demarcations, control of territories and organisations of domains which could well make up a sort of geopolitics…[48]

Discursive formations and systems of knowledge form constitutive elements of the tactics and strategies of power and these in turn have a spatial articulation and such spatiality may be located in terms of territory as a distinct juridico-political space, the colony, as the spatial domain of imperial rule, the "archipelago" as the distribution of carceral sites, and so on.

If discursive formations have a spatial element, then those relating to modernity, namely rationality, certainty, progress, civilisation, may be understood in terms of tactics and strategies that assume their projection into a universal arena. If each of these elements is understood as an "empty signifier", to quote Ernesto Laclau,[49] then their substantial content comes to form the basis of historic struggle and contestation, each term is in this sense always of politics and the investments made in seeking the paramount, or indeed hegemonic position in the wider realm of meaning. Nevertheless a gesture of hegemony is at the same time one that suggests the universality, or the unquestionable global pervasiveness of these concepts; that each speaks for itself, can have one uniform meaning. Martha Nussbaum, for example, recognises that humanity as a whole contains a diversity of cultures, but is one nevertheless that is connected through a common rationality that is dissociated from the particularity of cultural context, whether this applies to local practices or to global institutions and social forces.[50] As Sara Ahmed points out, "The presumption of the neutrality of reason as the foundation of the global community works to conceal how reason is already defined as the property of some bodies and not others...Or, it conceals how reason works precisely to universalise from a particular body, with its own histories of production, exchange and consumption."[51]

No such concealment is apparent in modernist discourses that recognise the essential contestability of modernity's discursive formations. An example here is a speech delivered in March 2006 by the United Kingdom Prime Minister, Tony Blair, a speech that went largely unnoticed by the media.[52] The significance of the speech for the present context is its recognition that the substantial content and articulation of modernity are subject precisely to struggle and contestation; ultimately, subject to political mobilisation. There may be a multiplicity of rationalities or understandings of progress; nevertheless the project of modernity suggests that distinct notions of these discursive formations must ultimately emerge as the predominant organising principle of a modern social order. The significance of this speech in terms of the contemporary rearticulations of the international far exceeds his earlier (1999) Chicago speech that I highlighted in the last chapter, a speech that proclaimed a new form of internationalism driving his advocacy of the war over Kosovo. In this later speech, Blair proposes to "link, in values, military action in Kosovo, Sierra Leone, Afghanistan and Iraq with diplomatic action on climate change, world trade, Africa and Palestine." While the economics of globalisation are considered "matured", the "politics of globalisation are not". Arguing mainly against narrow "national interest" motivations for the formulation of foreign policy, Blair's distinct appeal is to interventionism as the basis of recognising the connectivity of humanity and its shared problems. The "fault lines" in terms of perspectives on these matters is one that Blair defines in terms of "conservatives" and "progressives", wherein the former express opposition to intervention while the latter advocate it. However, it is in relation to Islam and its particular rendition by the "extremists" that Blair seeks to confront, for this is not simply a battle relating to terrorism *per se*, but is rather a battle of ideas:

> This terrorism will not be defeated until its ideas, the poison that warps the minds of its adherents, are confronted, head-on, in their essence, at their core. By this I don't mean telling them that terrorism is wrong. I mean telling them their attitude to America is absurd; their concept of governance pre-feudal; their position on women and other faiths, reactionary and regressive; and then since only by Muslims can this be done; standing up for and supporting those within Islam who will tell them all of this but more, namely that the extremist view of Islam is not just theologically backward but completely contrary to the spirit and teaching of the Koran.[53]

The various constructions included in the speech bear testimony to Blair's recognition that there is a substantial and ideologically distinctive content to constructs such as progress and civilisation. The speech is replete with dualisms that are somehow tactically and strategically located in the struggle over modernity's empty signifiers: conservatives and progressives, violence and democracy, the reactionary and the modern. This is a powerful construction, for in initiating the speech from the outset in terms of the dualism between "conservatives" (those opposed to the war in Iraq and critical of government policy) and "progressives", and continuing to formulate the speech in terms of the latter two dualisms, Blair by implication suggests that those opposed to war and the draconian anti-civil libertarian measures brought in through anti-terrorism legislation, are at the same time inadvertently complicit in violence and reactionary politics. Blair's recognition that modernity's organising principles are always subject to contest, and hence politics, emerges clearly when he states "This is not a clash between civilisations, It is a clash about civilisation. It is the age-old battle between progress and reaction, between those who embrace and see opportunity in the modern world and those who reject its existence...this is, ultimately, a battle about modernity."[54]

There are many similarities between Blair and Nussbaum that I will not elaborate here. What differentiates them is far more pertinent to the present discussion, for while Nussbaum seeks to conceal the substantive content of modernity's discourses and their situatedness in time and place, thereby denying their essential location as matters of politics and political mobilisation, Blair, equally concerned with the project of modernity, recognises its location in relation to history and politics. The discursive formations contained in Blair's speech, though in themselves contestable, are recognised by their author as being precisely situated in such contests. Any actions undertaken in the name of progress and modernity, including war, state-building, the alleviation of poverty in Africa, the resolution of protracted conflicts, will inevitably be actions that are subject to the political struggles contained in modernity itself.

That the modern liberal democratic state arose primarily from the debris of war and came to be built upon a gradual pacification of disparate populations as the basis upon which liberal democratic institutions evolved is perhaps a historical model that at first hand appears to lend itself to the contemporary scene. As a number of philosophers and social theorists, from Michel Foucault, to Charles Tilly, to Anthony Giddens, have shown, the modern European nation-state is historically built on war-making, the gradual pacification of internal conflict, and ultimately the shift in relations of power from the sovereign ruler towards a rational form of rule premised on certainty and calculability; that modern government could, in effect, govern individual and collective life to such an extent that ultimately the individuals and communities forming society could ultimately come to self-govern, self-regulate. It might easily be argued that while Kant's project represents an idealist vision inappropriate to the realities of history, accounts of modern European history provide a historical testimony to the successful embodiment, through the panoply of practices of exclusion, surveillance, incarceration, welfare, and so on, of liberal democratic institutions that allow for the self-governing subject of liberal thought. Europe's historical record can arguably provide a model for late modern approaches to state-building that seek the end of conflict.

It is perhaps not all together surprising that the extremes of violence witnessed in places such as the Balkans conflicts, Rwanda, Sierra Leone, the Congo, Darfur and elsewhere raise fundamental questions related to the breakdown of states and social order and their spill-over effects into regional as well as global spheres. Indeed the concept of the "failed" state, though problematic, encapsulates the distinct failure of states, not only in relation to the pacification of internal conflict and strife, but vitally in its capacities to provide for the welfare of its population. From ethnic cleansing to political repression to widespread corruption within government institutions, state failure appears in the above situations at least to create a void within which factions, warlords, and criminal gangs may thrive at the expense of local populations. The "failed" state can hence no longer be considered a "power container" to use Anthony Giddens's definition of the modern state, and as such can no longer be assumed to possess the capacities associated with modern governance. The highly modern, and distinctly rational solution presents itself and centres upon the rebuilding of the state as a modern, rational, form of rule. Furthermore, if the locals lack the capacity to achieve this for themselves, others, external agents, both state and non-state, can provide them with the means of doing so. This then is the late modern programme of state-building. It is distinctly modern, thoroughly rational, and international, or even cosmopolitan, involving as it does an international civil service provided by states, international institutions, and non-governmental organisations. It also comes, eventually, to involve local agents, but only as the reconstituted agents of liberal democracy, fully trained in, for example, gender awareness, equal opportunities, human rights, civil society, and democracy. State-building is as pedagogic as it is about institution-building. It constitutes no less an ambition than the transformation of societies into full and able participants in democracy for the local population, legitimate and law-bound government, peaceful relations with neighbours, and exchange in the neoliberal global market place. The project of state-building is, in Blair's terms, civilisational and it is modern. Being modern, it inherits modernity's legacy, not just emancipation, but also control and the exclusions that emerge when modernity's legacy is contained in one singular, hegemonic narrative.

That a search for certainty and order comes to govern responses to protracted periods of social breakdown and unpredictability is not altogether unexpected. The breakdown, not just of the political order, but of the social sphere in, for example, the Balkans or sub-Saharan locations such as Sierra Leone or Liberia, was so extensive that everyday certainties were shattered. That entire communities and neighbourhoods could be subjected to the extremes of violence at the hands of marauding gangs, more often than not, directed by warlords and factional leaders, and in Rwanda culminating in an organised genocide, called forth global response mechanisms premised on the idea that rational order may be built into the institutions of a regenerated state. In situations of actual as opposed to discursively constructed threats to everyday security – for example, in the case of Sierra Leone, the actuality of mutilation as a weapon of fear – the rational aim of any response is, or should be, the restoration of what in effect constituted ontological security; the right to an everyday life lived in the knowledge that the individual will not be subject variously to mutilation, kidnapping, rape, and murder committed by others, often recruited from within shared spaces and locales. In situations of social breakdown, the aim, as recognised by Boutros Boutros-Ghali, the former United Nations Secretary General, could no longer be confined to a separation of forces in a peacekeeping operation, but had to incorporate measures aimed at the restoration of the social order. The immediate question that such an aim raises relates to the model upon which such a social, and ultimately political, order could be built.

It is in relation to the above question that cultural difference comes face to face with the politics of peace, for the latter comes ultimately to be defined in terms of the government of social relations based on the model of the liberal democratic state; a triumphant western liberal model set against a postcolonial critique that places emphasis on cultural domination. Where the former perspective takes the modernisation of society as the requisite step towards state-building as a response to state failure, the latter interprets the so-called failed state in terms of the domination of the neoliberal global order, a domination that is complicit in the conditions generative of both structural and direct violence. Where the former expresses confidence in a rational modernisation process that establishes a successful modern state, seeing the failed state as symptom of local failure, the latter sees the problem of failure in the imposition of a particular, namely western, project onto other societies. The former takes its queue from a long trajectory of liberal political and social thought, while the latter draws upon critical and poststructural thought in concentrating on the dialectic of the project of modernity and the implications of its universalising discourses.

Liberal social and political thought lies at the heart of assumptions that constitute the state-building programmes seen as the prerequisite of peace in post-conflict societies. The assumption here is that modernity, having transformed European societies from arenas of violence into ordered and successful social, economic, and political formations, could, if implemented in conditions of violence and state failure elsewhere, succeed in rebuilding the modern state in war-torn societies. While there is a tendency within philosophical discourse to assume that the principle of rationality as the basis of human conduct emerged from abstract theorising, it is important to remember, as Stephen Toulmin points out, that the autonomous individual of rationalist philosophy emerged from historical conditions of war and social fragmentation. The modern project, including the emergence of the Westphalian state, was hence the culmination of social, economic, and political processes that were both protracted and differentially experienced within the European context. The rationalist philosophies of what came to constitute the Enlightenment were a product of a long period of turmoil and religious fragmentation, so that certainty came to be preferable to the scepticism and pluralism that had characterised the renaissance period. Thus, according to Toulmin:

> The 17th-century philosophers' "Quest for Certainty" was no mere proposal to construct abstract and timeless intellectual schemas, dreamed up as objects of pure, detached intellectual study. Instead, it was a timely response to a specific historical challenge – the political, social, and theological chaos embodied in the Thirty Years' War. Read in this way, the projects of Descartes and his successors are no longer arbitrary creations of lonely individuals in separate ivory towers...The standard picture of Descartes' philosophical development as the unfolding of a pure esprit untouched by the historical events of his time...gives way to what is surely a more lifelike and flattening alternative: that of a young intellectual whose reflections opened up for people in his generation a real hope of *reasoning* their way out of political and theological chaos, at a time when no one else saw anything to do but continue fighting in interminable war.[55]

In conditions of unending war, "philosophical scepticism became *less*, and certainty *more*, attractive."[56] The legacy is, as we know, the emergence of a rationalist and universalising programme that values instrumentality and certainty; that the human mind has a capacity to fully comprehend the world and to control it. The consequences, as stated by Toulmin have a resonance in the late modern era of our contemporary times: "the devaluation of the oral, the particular, the local, the timely, and the concrete...appeared a small price to pay for a formally 'rational' theory grounded on abstract, universal, timeless concepts..."[57]

The late modern context shows a revaluation of the local and the particular in the face of the universalising imperatives of globalised relations. Such revaluation is manifest in social and political practices while being reflected in an intellectual discursive backdrop that in itself seeks to reinvigorate the particularity of modernity as a distinctly European project. Local assertions of identity come face to face with a modernising project that is itself increasingly recognised as a distinct historical project, indeed a "civilising mission", framed around very particular conceptions of what it means to be a rational self, fully constituted in modernity's defining institutions, namely the modern state and the neoliberal global order. Herein lies the paradox of the late modern revaluation of the local, for while the distinctiveness of the modern project is recognised, that of local practices elsewhere is at once both emphasised in culturalist terms and understood in hierarchical terms that then enable the subjugation of the other. As David Slater argues, "the post-colonial seeks to question Western discourses of, for example, progress, civilisation, modernisation, development and democracy, by making connections with the continuing relevance of *invasive* colonial and imperial power that these discourses tend to evade."[58] Over and above systems of representation, however, is the view that relations of power are both discursive and material, linking directly to a colonial past that sees its culmination today in practices of invasion and twenty-first century forms of colonisation.

Conclusion

This chapter has argued that the global matrix of war is imbued with racial and cultural signification. It argued firstly, that practices associated with interventionist wars, specifically those associated with so-called pre-emptive wars legitimised within the framework of what has come to be known as the "war against terrorism" have rendered the cultural not just a marker of difference, but also of enmity and existential threat. I argue that the elevation of cultural difference in this matrix of war is built at one and the same time around two elements, namely the racialisation of the other in a late modern rendition of colonial politics, coupled with the depoliticisation of conflict through the elevation of a culturalist discourse. The third section of the chapter places late modern war and the place of cultural difference in the context of the project of modernity, suggesting that it is precisely this context that provides the conditions of possibility for both types of war in the global matrix of war, the humanitarian and the pre-emptive, for these come to see their teleology in a programme that seeks the wholesale transformation of societies towards the rational, the modern, the civilised. The "battle about modernity" that Blair proclaims as the link between actions in as diverse locations as Sierra

Leone and Iraq is at the heart of the continuing project of modernity, a project the legacy of which is replete with contest and contradiction; liberating on the one hand and violent in its exclusions on the other. So powerful is this paradox that any universalising project of modernity, including primarily cosmopolitanism, comes face to face with its darker side, a side that, while proclaiming dialogue with the other, nevertheless renders the other absent.

The final, hesitantly concluding chapter of this book seeks to define an alternative reading of cosmopolitanism, one that I label "political cosmopolitanism" that seeks to move the terms of discourse away from the primacy of war and exclusion as defining practices in the transformation of the international. This form of cosmopolitanism places the question of solidarity at the heart of its discourse, seeking a socialisation of the international without the dangers of undermining the self-determination of societies and their distinct modes of expression and affiliation. Nevertheless, this is a cosmopolitanism that is political in its discourse, arguing that while identities are significant, so too is equality as significant as a project both locally and internationally. Nevertheless, each of these categories are recognised as being distinctly located in the project of modernity, a project that has historically and not just metaphysically, elevated the individual self as a self capable of self-constitution beyond the determining remits of locale and culture. Political cosmopolitanism locates its discourse firmly in an imminent critique, therefore, of modernity. It is imminent in that it is constitutively modern, formed in the discourses and institutions of modernity, namely the state understood not just in terms of administrative governance, but as the location of self-determination and equality before the law, globalised modes of production and exchange, globalised modes of communication as exchange, the protections of law at global level, and hence the potential of global solidarities. Considered in these terms, those up against the notion of "failure" are not confined to the societies of the other of the west, but equally include the west.

6
Beyond War and By Way of a Conclusion: Solidarity, the Politics of Peace and Political Cosmopolitanism

> *Cosmopolitanism as it is classically conceived presupposes some form of state sovereignty, something like a world state...For a deconstruction to be as effective as possible, it should not, in my view, oppose the state head on and in a unilateral fashion.*
>
> Jacques Derrida[1]

Conflicts in late modern times are no longer distant isolated events, contained within their own spatiality and temporality, but are immediately present in the global arena, suggesting this arena at one and the same time as a wide and dispersed space for the mobilisation of material and human resources for ongoing antagonisms. From the local wars associated with state breakdown, to the network wars conducted by clandestine organisations, to the wars of invasion conducted by a global hegemon, the complex interconnections that span the global and transcend state boundaries come to constitute the enabling conditions for the conduct of war. This arena cannot simply be conceived in terms of the increasing dispersion of social and political life, but as being differentiated in terms of differential access to regulatory practices and institutions (including those associated with trading and financial links), to material resources, and communications media. What differentiates network and interventionist wars is that the agents involved in their conduct view the global as the remit of their operations. The global matrix of war suggests a global sphere of operations that transcend the inside/outside, domestic/international divide, suggesting the primacy of transnational modes of conduct that draw upon resources that are both domestic and international. However, the global as a spatial terrain is not simply external to the wars of the present, but is a constitutive element of these wars, just as the form that these wars take is constitutive of the global as a distinct juridico-political space.

The research agenda in Conflict and Peace Studies as well as International Relations has shifted in recent times in response to the changing circumstances of global politics. What was long recognised by the early advocates of the former,[2] that diplomatic responses to violent conflicts were inadequate in meeting the demands of just and lasting solutions, came to constitute the inspiration for a more recent and burgeoning research programme in post-conflict peacebuilding and the transformation of social relationships from conditions of enmity to those of mutual recognition.[3] While the early authors placed emphasis on the relational aspect of such transformations, the new research agenda focuses on the relational as well as on the enabling institutionalised mechanisms through which social transformations might be realised. The building of peace came to be synonymous with the building, or indeed rebuilding, of states and their governmental institutions as much as the rebuilding of societal interactions.

Questions of war and peace came once again to constitute core concerns in the discourses of International Relations. While the discipline's very inception was premised on a primary imperative to understand war and the conditions of peace, and indeed much of the discipline's effort has historically been devoted to this research agenda, the driving force behind these intellectual endeavours has in actuality been not so much the question of war, but that of order in an assumed anarchical international system of states.[4] Questions of war and peace were hence of significance when they touched upon order in the international system, when they "spilled over" into relations international. Of crucial significance here were questions relating not just to the constitutive elements of the international system as a system of states, but to the regulative principles that held the system together, so to speak, the institutionalised rules and norms that enabled regularised social relations to take place at global scale.[5]

The primacy of order in the discourses of International Relations had relegated questions of justice to the margins, and in consequence the research programme in Conflict and Peace Studies. Where the latter's focus was aimed at the messiness of lived experience in conditions generative of violence, injustice and exclusion, the former sought to expunge such messiness from its discourses. As Christine Sylvester's powerful critique of International Relations makes all too clear,[6] here was a discipline devoid of "people" and lived experience, so remote from the conditions that touched the lives of millions that it could but seek refuge in taken-for-granted abstractions such as a dehistoricised state and systems of interaction between states. Even normative discourses in International Relations offered formulaic representations of what it means to be in the world, reducing such being to a dualistic cosmopolitan/communitarian divide that once again reflected a discourse remote from the complexity of social and political life and its modes of articulation. Even as feminist, critical, and poststructural discourses in the discipline sought to bring people back into the frame, inaugurating in doing so a wholesale rethinking of its basic tenets, these were, like their Conflict and Peace Studies counterparts, once again considered as somehow concerned with matters outside the core remits of International Relations. This despite the core concerns of critical discourses, namely the workings of power throughout the matrices of social and political life, their implications for the agency of individuals, peoples and their interactions, the subjectivities emergent from conditions within the law and beyond the law, and the historical trajectories that, as Rob Walker has shown,[7] constituted the core dualisms constitutive of International Relations itself, the inside/outside, order/disorder, the universal/the particular, the self/other, the civilised/the barbarian. What is all too revealing is that the orthodoxy in the discipline could abrogate its remit from the messiness of social and political life precisely as a consequence of the alignment of the elements constituting each side of these dualisms: the inside, order, the universal, the self, the civilised as against the outside, disorder, the particular, the other, the barbarian.

The messiness of the world, its uncertainties and fragmentations has, nevertheless, forced itself into the sanitised portals of International Relations so that what have been the concerns of Conflict and Peace Studies as well as critical discourses in the discipline are now core: the historical sociology of the modern state, the political implications of a globalised capitalist order, the human and social consequences of war, the significance of culture and gender in the construction of meaning, materiality and experience, all understood as having profound implications for our capacity to understand the political framing of the international and its locations. While the prevalent tendency is to hold on to the dualisms mentioned above, such efforts are informed by an often implicit acknowledgement, and fear, that the line (/) enabling the dualism is ever shifting, so that the outside is always already in, the other is the self-same, the universal has always been the particular, the civilised has always been the barbarian, except that the first element in each dualism is differentiated in terms of power and the capacity to dominate. The constitutive line (/) enabling these dualism is itself enabled, indeed constituted, by an act of violence, if not physical, then epistemic.

Much of the recent research agenda in International Relations, like its Conflict and Peace Studies counterpart, is informed by the distinct circumstances of deadly conflicts emergent in the post-Cold War era. That the extremes of violence, systematic in their perpetration of acts reminiscent of the Nazi era, could once again take place in the centre of Europe, that civilian populations elsewhere could be targeted by their own governments, that societal breakdown could come at the instigation of the state, that all such could be witnessed the instant they occurred by a wider global public sphere, reinforced the view that our conceptions of the state, political community, the regulation of social and political life internationally, could no longer be remote from lived experience. This research agenda was not just responsive to global conditions, but was in itself reinforced by a post-Cold War environment wherein conflicts could no longer be "contained", either analytically or politically, within the interpretative frame that was the East-West divide. It is precisely in this context that the research agendas of International Relations and Conflict and Peace Studies come to coincide, for much of the agenda that is concerned with questions of war and peace is framed around questions of intervention, international responsibility, the agencies involved, both state and non-state, and the implications of such intervention for our understanding of the locations of political space and political community.

This book has concerned itself with the implications of war and conceptions of peace in the formation and reformation of the sphere of the international. This sphere is, as I have argued, interlaced with a global matrix of war, involving a diversity of agents engaged in distinct, but interconnected enactments of war and antagonism, including wars deemed to be fought for the rescue of others as well as those conducted in response to what is perceived as constituting an existential threat variously to society, humanity, the West, and so on, a threat no longer confined spatially and temporally, but one that is conceived in global and perpetual terms, so that conflicts that we might in the past have considered in local terms, remote and somehow confined to distant places, are now rendered in global, transnational, and all-pervasive terms. The modern legacy faces its own apotheosis in late modernity, so that modernity's efforts at the containment of the uncertain and the messy can now be revisited afresh, and the choice appears to be either a struggle for the project of modernity itself or a rethinking of modernity's legacy, its always dialectical articulation, and its potentials for a reconception of what constitutes a global sphere based on solidarity and mutual recognition. We might, as is the remit of Conflict and Peace Studies, investigate the particular policy frameworks and actions undertaken by agents at local and international levels, and contribute critically to a research agenda that can be drawn upon by policymakers. We might, equally, engage with a rethinking of the sphere of the international in distinctly political terms, suggesting that while war may be implicated in the reframing of the international, there is an alternative grammar, one that somehow has a sense for the articulation of solidarity that is not built on violence. The rest of this chapter explores this possibility. It does so not in the hope of presenting totalising solutions, but in a self-conscious attempt to reinvigorate the political in our thinking about the conditions of war and the possibilities of peace.

The paradoxes of modernity

As I have stated elsewhere in this book, the modern legacy presents, as all critical theorists recognise, the tools wherein we might think at one and the same time about human emancipation from dogma and tradition as well as its consequences in the extraction of the particular and the distinct. We could think at once about technological advancement and its potential for the liberation of humanity from the constraints of nature as well as the consequences of the reification of the technological. Thinking modernity's dialectic is itself a distinctly modern move, enabling an ethos of critique, so that we might acknowledge our distinct situatedness in modernity's discourses and institutions while recognising that these very discourses and institutions are themselves implicated and complicit in exclusion and violent practices. This critical ethos enables the self-consciously modern subject to acknowledge and move beyond that which the struggles of modernity as a distinct historical period enable; namely an appreciation of the human potential to imagine that things may be otherwise, that there is another day to come, and that the very capacity to think this is itself steeped in relations of power and the differential distribution of enablement and constraint that has always defined the inequalities that are of modernity's own making.

Any critical voice is hence self-declaredly modern and engaged, in one way or another, with the struggle for modernity and its legacy. All emancipatory concepts and movements; feminism and the women's movement, socialism and the emancipation of the working class, democracy and universal suffrage, national self-determination and the anti-colonial struggles, the fight against racism and xenophobia, sexual liberation and the struggle against homophobia, all a legacy of modernity, all expressive of a modern subjectivity that sees its expression in different locations across the world, and all contested by reactionary ideologies and institutions that seek not just the revival of tradition, but also the perpetuation of existing structures of domination. The distinctly modern aspect of all of the above struggles is that they all seek their articulation in a positive conception of rights, enshrined in law, and hence all achieved as a result of social and political struggle and contestation, some still ongoing.

The modern legacy is, at the same time, replete with a history of violence and discriminatory practices against those deemed other. Rationalised systems of control, the bureaucratisation of government, killing at technological scale in the Holocaust and in the Gulags of Stalinist Russia, mass killing at distance in Hiroshima and Nagasaki, and latterly in Vietnam and Iraq, a global economic order that constitutively enables the few and impoverishes, and often kills, the many, colonial violence and its latter day articulation, ongoing institutionalised modes of discrimination based on race, ethnicity, gender, sexuality, and class, all constituting the history of modernity and its continuing present, so that there can be no claims to self-righteous comfort, the assumed hierarchy of worthiness or peacefulness that the West accrues to itself at the expense of the other. The struggle for the project of modernity is not just between here and over there, us and them: it is always already here in a global terrain wherein political struggle, political contestation, and political solidarity can no longer be confined and determined by the spatial boundaries of the modern state.

Modernity provides the discourses and institutions enabling of its own imminent critique; the modern state as the principal form of human organisation that populations across the globe have historically aspired to and continue to do so; the modern self as one capable of independent judgement and as holder of rights, and the modern global economic order defined in terms of capitalist production and exchange. What I have referred to as the "human" element is as much an aspect of modernity as are the two institutional continuities of modernity, the state and the global capitalist order. This is a legacy that is replete with tension as modernity's institutions come face to face with the human element, an element that, by definition, transcends even as its recognition is always historical, situated in time and place, despite its Cartesian and Kantian renditions. This human element shifts and moves, having a capacity to defy boundaries, defiant somehow of modern institutional attempts, often violent, at the containment of the human into rationalised, calculable, and predictable forms.[8] The modern state, as the apotheosis of the modern legacy to contain, to pacify, and to rationalise, comes to function, in late modernity, as the primary mediating force between populations and global capital, finding itself in contest with both rampant humanity and rampant globality. The claims of the human, specifically in discourses of human rights have, in the modern period and into our own late modern context, run in juxtaposition with the claims of the state and those of global capitalism. The relationship between these claims has historically been defined in terms of tension and struggle.

States differ in their capacities to function in their historic role as the mediating force between the claims of citizens in human terms and the claims of global capital. The experience of modernity, as I indicated earlier in the book, has differed substantially across the global terrain, so that it is not possible, or indeed ethically or politically acceptable, to comprehend late modern manifestations of modernity without at the same time acknowledging the significance of the colonial legacy as a constitutive aspect of modernity itself and its implications for how we understand the continuities of modern life. For here, or out there, the human was rendered variously as the inhuman or indeed the sub-human, the international conferred no meaning in terms of sovereign equality, and the global was, and in many postcolonial instances, continues to be the source of persistent vulnerability. Just as the "governmentalisation" of the state, to use Foucault, differs substantially in the postcolonial context, so too the capacities of the postcolonial state to defer the claims of rampant globality, so that the various monopolies held by the state, over violence, security, identity, economic activity, political activity, are no longer a certain, taken-for-granted matter and, in a late modern context of globalised relations, such transformations have had implications for states across the globe.

Much therefore hinges on the capacities of the state both as a location of government and as the location of politics, for it is both elements that feed into the claims of the state as mediating force between its citizenry and global forces. It is when government and politics are somehow located elsewhere, beyond the state, shifting both internally and externally, often into a transnational terrain, that modernity's historic attempts at the containment of uncertainty come to unravel, presenting once again dangers as well as opportunities, dangers in the form of the fragmentation of societies, and opportunities in terms of a relocation of politics beyond the state, expressive of potentially new forms of solidarity between the local and the global. However, this relocation of politics is itself replete with difficulties for the modern state and for any secular articulation of politics, as transnational identities and political affiliations shift elsewhere, often into the terrain of the cultural and the religious.

It is the case then that the globalisation of all aspects of social, economic, and political relations render Westphalian associations of relations international with the state highly problematic. Understandings that limit politics to the state remain in denial of the implications involved when we can no longer unproblematically associate the political with the state. Just as the emergence of the modern enabled the abstraction of the subject of politics both from deity and a pre-modern, and hence problematic, locality, so too the late modern shifts the terrain once again, so that what the modern subject perceives as the pre-modern emerges once again in expressions (and elevations) of religious affiliation and the traditions associated with locality. The state as the location of politics, of certainty, of form, legality, and order, is now but one location amongst a number of contenders, some more formal than others, some more ordered than others, some subject to a form of legality and others not as constrained. This does not, of course, mean that the rationalisations associated with the modern state are in any way diminished, as so many authors in the globalisation literature might suggest.[9] These practices are, if anything, enhanced, albeit through transnational and supranational processes that interlink states technocratically in an increasingly bureaucratised global sphere of operations that does not so much challenge the state as entity, but our understanding of the location of politics, the meaning of the political, and by implication, our very ability to engage politically.

The dynamics of late modernity must hence be seen as incorporating both the intensification of the institutions of modernity as well as the emergence of modes of political expression that seek to transcend these institutions. If the state is no longer the sole location of politics, then some element other to the state forces itself into the arena and this element comes into being, is manifest at some location that has its spatial articulation beyond the state, its temporal articulation beyond the modern, a beyond that may be pre and post, the meeting of which submerges the certainties of the modern. Culture, as an arena of collective life, comes into force in these circumstances where the modern state can no longer contain the political.[10] Other arenas of collective life emerge as sites of politics, the expressions of which find voice in the so-called new social movements, in issue-based politics, in lifestyle politics, in increasingly dispersed activities that seek to give voice and in doing so to construct a relocated political space. The "global" as a sphere of interaction emerges or is forced into being, through creativity, through technology, and through the legacy of modern rationality. Some see this arena as an emerging global civil society, containing different articulations of interests, conflicts, spaces of cooperation and so on. Others see this as an inherently conflictual space, seething with primordial affiliations, with structural inequalities, and with the movement of peoples across boundaries, both territorial and cultural.[11]

The modern legacy has, as many authors, from the Frankfurt School to Michel Foucault, have shown, a paradoxical effect.[12] This is indeed the legacy of critique, of a subject universalised in its being, a subject capable of judgement of self and others. The modern subject is, furthermore, the ultimate arbiter of experience, of modern institutions, including the state. The modern subject is, however, at the same time the author of an imposed universality, of violence, of an instrumentality that submerges and at times extinguishes life in the name of all that is constitutive of modern institutions, of modern order, of predictability and certainty. Difference, for the modern, at a particular juncture of history, becomes problematic, has to be contained, rendered readable, compliant. The universal subject of Enlightenment reason becomes precisely the subject of violence, of a colonial order that defines itself as a "civilising mission", so that when its violence is revealed, it finds easy access to the panoply of legitimising tools, primary amongst which is reason itself.[13] The modern, the universal, the civilising, the democratic, the progressive, the scientific, all come to constitute a self-image that has no limits even as it is itself the author of limits, of the boundaries that are constitutively the spaces of exclusion of everything deemed other to the civilised, the progressive, the scientific, the ordered, the predictable, and ultimately the rational.[14]

The late modern may be conceived as the "intensification"[15] of the modern rather than its diminution. The rationalising imperatives of the modern are now, through technological capacity, ever more capable of intrusion into the lived experience of the individual self. While the eighteenth century saw the increasing bureaucratisation of mechanisms of state and its policing operations, these mechanisms in late modernity seek a global remit, so that the global population as a whole may come under the rubric of rationalising technologies that can "read" everyone's profile, recognise all as they move, interact, shop, write, seek information, and disperse knowledge.[16] Technological capacity comes to form the linchpin of a mode of power that has global reach, both servicing of, and enabled by a neoliberal order the imperative of which is itself global. The cultural in these circumstances is manifest in a number of ways, both global and local, so that while the former may suggest the emergence of a "new" cosmopolitan order, cognisant of cultural difference, and emancipatory in its calls for global governance, global solidarity, it is itself borne of the modern legacy, a legacy that sees itself capable of containing the global. The local is in these circumstances the exotic, the private, the traditional, the parochial, and the non-democratic, the non-political. Culture as such comes once again to constitute that which is associated with the other of the modern, the progressive, the universal.[17] This is especially so when culture becomes the site, the location, through which resistance to the globalising imperative takes place. In late modern life, such cultural expression is no longer contained, or indeed containable, in distant lands, but is located in the spaces of the modern, now rearticulated globally and locally, in transnational spaces in neighbourhoods and cities across the globe.

This is the late modern context that presents distinct challenges to any intellectual effort at rethinking the international and the possibility of political solidarity, and hence political cosmopolitanism that is not reliant on enactments of violence or assumptions based on hierarchies of worthiness. In my attempts at the expression and articulation of a distinctly political conception of cosmopolitanism, I start with the premise that the politics of peace, the capacity at once both to resist violence and struggle for a just social order, is not just within the purview of the liberal state or indeed an international civil service, but is primarily located with individuals, communities and social movements involved in critical engagement with the multiform governance structures, as well as non-state agents, they encounter in their substantial claims for human rights and social justice. The politics of peace must then rely on a conception of human solidarity that has a capacity to transcend the signifying divide of state and culture, while at the same time recognising the claims of both. As we will see below, liberal discourses suffer a particular paradox when scrutinised in relation to solidarity, for renditions in liberal thought and practice seek to evade the notion of solidarity while relying heavily on some understanding of social consensus. Both must be considered in the context of the cultural pluralism that defines the human condition.

Solidarity and the international

It is all too easy to situate the politics of peace in relation to the immediacy of warfare and violent confrontation. Even a cursory glance at the history of the conflicts of the 1990s, conflicts that were, as we have seen, constructed as "new wars" or situations of humanitarian emergency, or indeed the Gulf war, hailed as the inauguration of a new global order, suggests that all emerged from ongoing conflict situations which were variously either treated with indifference or in terms of active, if often implicit support of parties implicated in oppressive and violent practices.[18] The politics of peace is then not a politics of emergency, but one based on critical engagement and solidarity with those whose rights are violated both as routine and in the most extraordinary of circumstances. For Hannah Arendt, the "political realm" as she phrased it, "rises directly out of acting together".[19] Solidarity assumes collective action and hence political community. The location of political community becomes of primary significance in rethinking the politics of peace for, in the context of the international, with the conflicting claims that I highlight above, such political community is no longer conceived simply in relation to the state.[20]

Let us then delve into the concept of solidarity and how we might use it in rethinking the politics of peace.[21] The concept of solidarity can have both adversarial and a consensual meaning, neither of which should be excluded from the politics of peace that I want to envisage. The adversarial is perhaps best represented in contemporary thought by Chantal Mouffe who conceptualises the political sphere as a sphere of struggle and contestation. Solidarity in this sense is always a manifestation of particularistic identities and affiliations constructed in the political arena.[22] Identity and collective consciousness appear to be the defining moments of political action. This is hence a conception of politics that is grounded in historical struggle, in the situatedness of the subject of politics. Solidarity comes to encompass a spatial and temporal domain, constructed politically through an active process of mobilisation that takes diverse forms, all of which assume in turn a public arena of communicative interaction. Solidarity historically assumes collective identity, collective action, and articulations of such connections in the public sphere. Such articulations are not only aimed at the recursive rearticulation of solidarity, the reconstitution of an "us", but at one and the same time at the construction of an adversary, constituted as "them", the enemy, the source of grievance, of the barrier against emancipation and self-realisation. Solidarity is hence a manifestly public expression of political identity, indeed it is an expression or even the acquisition of a right to politics, a right to participation, a right to a voice articulated in an inter-subjective setting. Solidarity is, in addition, a politics of presence, of a corporeal as well as a discursive presence that claims a stake in a connection with others deemed to be of a shared identity, strangers in common connected in a sense of identity, purpose, and community. Such a conception of political agency trumps impartiality and consensus in the name of an already acquired position held in opposition to others.

Liberal conceptions of solidarity tend to be consensual rather than adversarial, premised as they are on the institutionalisation of procedural resolutions of social conflicts. When conceived as a distinctly liberal construct, solidarity comes to assume a social remit that is total in its scope as opposed to being applicable in relation to social antagonism. The collectivity is the social realm as a whole, the state and civil society held together in an overarching sense of "a people" connected in democratic relations that ensure the regulation of conflict through agreed upon procedures.[23] This collectivity is a collectivity of autonomous individuals held together through consensus on social institutions and norms the existence of which is not geared towards the fortification of the state but the enablement of the individual as a distinct autonomous entity capable of the conduct of life, of the exercise of freedom, within the constraints of a contracted order. Social solidarity emergent from a liberal set of premises is hence reliant on some notion of social consensus over the institutions of state and their relationship to civil society and the public sphere. This liberal conception of solidarity, when applied in the context of the politics of peace, places emphasis on the creation of institutionalised mechanisms that would render possible the procedural resolution of social conflicts as these emerge in a post-conflict setting. The assumption is that social consensus will emerge with the successful implementation of state-building measures geared towards not just establishing the governmental capacities of the state, but formative of an active civil society sector that can then partake in democratic practices. Whether solidarity emerges as a result of a compromise between different interests or is a by-product of an existing cultural consensus on the value attached to the liberal constitution is important in the context of post-conflict situations wherein the wholesale reconstitution of social formations, their success or failure, comes to rely on the existence or otherwise of an emerging consensus relating to renewed modes of interaction. We might hence argue that different liberal conceptions of social solidarity might point us in different directions relating to the outcomes of such intervention, whether these are based on the encouragement of deliberative procedures, on the institutionalisation of compromise between different interests, or on what Quentin Skinner refers to as the republican model, which assumes some cultural value that the collectivity attaches to its institutions.[24] What is evident from the liberal rendition on social solidarity is that, rather than being a formative moment in the constitution of collective identity, it is a product of institutionalised mechanisms geared towards proceduralist resolutions of social conflict. This conception of solidarity is hence predominantly confined to the limits of the state, wherein social consensus may exist in the domestic setting, but cannot take place beyond this setting in the absence of governmental institutions that are supranational in their workings.[25] The "liberal peace" project may be interpreted in terms of the liberal conception of solidarity, though initial interventions, in solidarity with those targeted in violent and oppressive practices, are clearly adversarial, though they do not have to be violent. Nevertheless, a distinctly liberal understanding of solidarity is one that is based on a certain consensus over fundamental elements that constitute the liberal tradition, namely individual autonomy and hence toleration of different forms of life, individual choices of lifestyle, expression, and association.[26] To accept human interaction as the product of largely voluntary associations is to accept individual liberty as the primary driver of such associations and hence the enabling condition for the toleration of difference and the distrust of arbitrary rule.[27]

Liberalism assumes the existence of an "overriding consensus"[28] that, if not entirely subsuming difference, is nevertheless capable of tolerating it. This assumption of an overriding consensus is evidenced in recent renditions on what constitutes a distinctly European identity, a conception of certain fundamental values that enshrine the points of connection between the diverse societies that constitute the European Union.[29] Indeed as Habermas and Derrida sought to emphasise in the aftermath of the events of September 11th and then as a consequence of US unilateralism, what distinguishes the European project is a certain consensus based on the Enlightenment tradition, a tradition defined by its respect for individual freedom and toleration.[30] The institutional rendition on this celebration of an assumed European consensus came in the form of the European Constitution, where, once again, the assumption of a consensus on core values was reiterated.[31]

What the above indicates is that liberal thought and practice assume the baseline of social solidarity to be located in certain core elements now so deeply rooted that they have come to constitute the very meaning of the liberal democratic state and what constitutes the successful state as such. As Gray notes, while some liberal philosophers might view this in metaphysical terms, those more historically oriented, such as Quentin Skinner, recognise the historical backdrop to present-day political manifestations of ideas relating to liberty and pluralism. What becomes apparent is that the idea of solidarity, rather than being conceived in rationalist terms, is predominantly a product of a historically generated consensus around particular preferences that see their assertion in the face of discourses and practices that violate such preferences. To recognise liberalism as a historically situated set of ideas and practices is to recognise at once both the consensual definition of social solidarity and its historically adversarial genesis. John Rawls, for example, talks of a "sectarian liberalism" as expressing a core set of values underpinning consensus.[32] As authors such as Skinner and Gray make all too clear, the core articulations of liberal democratic practices are indeed a product of historical contest and hence of recognised boundaries. These culturalist understandings bring with them the tensions that emerge in living with other forms of life, where social consensus as a basis of solidarity, albeit one that was historically hard won, comes face to face with the very practices that a liberal self-understanding opposes. In relation to the politics of peace, this liberal rendition on solidarity is in many ways at the heart of hierarchical conceptions of the international system, as I indicated in previous chapters. Such conceptions, even as they seek the expansion of political community beyond the sovereign state, and even as they articulate a recognition of difference, are nevertheless premised on the historical supremacy of liberal modes of being and social organisation. While this may be the case for individuals and populations constituted within a culture of liberalism, it does not bode well in relation to solidarity with others whose historical experience of liberalism writ large is not as celebratory, or indeed as savoury.

Rob Walker's approach to solidarity and the rethinking of political community presents some pointers as to how we might begin to think about global solidarity, or solidarities, as the basis of the politics of peace. The first element that may be drawn from Walker is that articulations of solidarity do not constitute totalising discourses or grand gestures towards establishing a universal remit. Rather, solidarity is a more localised form of expression, localised in terms of the issues at stake rather than in spatial terms. As Walker states,

> It is clear that this is not an ambition to imitate the solidarity of the nation, nor that of a universal class, nor that arising from some abstract claim about the human species as such. Nor is it a matter of conventional relations between states. It is, rather, a recognition that behind the insistence on acting locally is a challenge to rework the meaning of human community in an age in which our vulnerabilities are indeed global in scale while our capacity to act is circumscribed by who and where we are.[33]

Walker identifies three elements that recognise the constraints, as well as enablements, emergent from the structural continuities of social and political life globally: firstly, that global "connections" impact upon lived experience globally; secondly and crucially for the present context, "global structures and connections do not imply an easy universalism, especially a universalism that generates a reading of History as a move from fragmentation to integration from state system to global community"; and thirdly, that despite the impact of global structures, people's lives are indeed lived locally, in relation to local issues, local struggles, even as these are subject to the structures of domination that are of both global and local inception. Significantly, Walker suggests that the claims of global structures to universal worth, and I would add here any discourses that view their worth in universal terms, are but expressions of "forces of dominance" based upon "explicit principles of exclusion".[34]

I want to argue that what I am referring to as the *politics* of peace places emphasis on the political as expressed in solidarity with others. Such solidarity makes no claim to universality, nor is it teleological in outlook. Rather, it recognises that "political community" does not simply arise as a product of structures of domination brought in from elsewhere. Rather, the politics of peace expresses local and often rather invisible acts, expressions of solidarity that are neither hierarchically defined nor suggestive of any claim to universality. Enactments of solidarity, or the agents involved, may be local and they may have come in from elsewhere, both regional and global. This understanding does not assume that involvement results from situations of exception or emergency, though emergency conditions emergent from violence targeted against populations and communities, may call for immediate articulations of solidarity and contestation. There is no claim here for the overthrow of the state or the instantiation of a global community writ large. There is, however, a crucial recognition that the global as such matters as a location of politics.

Cultural difference and political cosmopolitanism

The idea of social solidarity premised on a consensus of fundamental beliefs emerges in conceptions of solidarity that have global aspirations. Of particular interest here are voices that espouse a form of cosmopolitanism that sees the social not in terms of a distinct national community but humanity at large. The cosmopolitan, from the Stoic of ancient Greece to the city dweller traversing the globe, is the individual who could know the world and move, if allowed, within its multiform diversities. Cosmopolitanism does not, however, simply espouse a lifestyle of free movement and association, but articulates a desire for a particular form of polity that extends beyond national boundaries, indeed extends to the global arena as a whole. To suggest a cosmopolitan polity must hence imply the institutional articulation of a global social consensus, an articulation that sees its ultimate expression, as I have indicated in earlier chapters, in a form of cosmopolitan law that has global reach and that is applicable to states and individuals alike.[35] The statute of the International Criminal Court, now ratified in a number of domestic jurisdictions, the Universal Declaration on Human Rights, and the European Convention on Human Rights are but a few examples of a cosmopolitan law emerging that binds humanity across and beyond particularity and locality.

Where consensus is manifest globally, it is hence assumed to be based on agreement on moral norms that enable forms of institutionalisation based on cosmopolitan principles. As Fred Dallmayr points out, such modes of institutionalisation are in themselves enabled by the presence or development of a "general consensus on moral norms"[36] that assume a certain commonality of goals. However another approach to understanding this process is a distinctly historical one, where an emergent consensus is conceived in political and not just moral terms.[37] This conception of cosmopolitanism assumes a more historical orientation towards the production of social solidarity emergent through struggle and political contestation. Where what might be called moral cosmopolitanism assumes cultural difference to be secondary to a universally based consensus, political cosmopolitanism recognises that any form of consensus emerges from historical processes of struggle and contestation. While both approaches seek to recognise difference and assume pluralism, what I am referring to as political cosmopolitanism understands itself as a process that involves what Bonnie Honig refers to as the "inescapability of conflict" and the "ineradicability of resistance" where what is involved are "political and moral projects of ordering subjects, institutions and values."[38] The "universal" in this political conception of cosmopolitanism acquires a meaning that, as we will see later, must be conceived in terms that recognise, as I stated above, the global as a location of politics. The challenge, however, is to conceive of the global as an arena of politics without at the same time reinforcing modes of exclusion and domination based on difference. Writing in relation to the European polity, but having resonances that are relevant for our concerns in the present context, Ash Amin states, "Europe is now home to millions of people from non-European backgrounds, many religious and cultural dispositions, and many networks of attachment based on Diaspora connections and cultural influences from around the world. Europe is as much a site of longings rooted in tradition – regional, national, and European – as it is a site of transnational and trans-European attachments."[39]

For Ash Amin, reflecting on recent invocations of the "Idea of Europe", such calls for inclusions of the other remain inadequate, as they persist in dichotomies that associate universalism, humanism, and reason with a "myth of origin" that is European and cultural particularity, tribalism and religious expression with the non-European other. There is then a "hierarchy of worth"[40] that associates the public or political space with universal categories such as citizenship and rights, and the private sphere with cultural affiliation and practice. In Amin's words, "After 11 September 2001 and all that it has led to in terms of the many rushed and thoughtless associations forged between Islam, rogue states and terrorism, many Western liberals have consciously returned to these core values to propose them with urgency as a new world standard of cohesion and civilisation, against the excesses of Americanism and, above all, the 'terrors' of religious fundamentalism."[41] These reflections have added salience once again in the context of the bombings in London and the subsequent high profile calls on the Islamic community to, so to speak, deal with its extremists. Amin advocates "hospitality" to the stranger and "mutuality" in the construction of a "common public sphere and ethos of solidarity" in the face of a resurgent racism in Europe. But beyond expressions of a rather abstract notion of hospitality in the culturally plural space that is Europe, how do we begin to give substance to the ethos of solidarity that Amin invokes? The following section draws on the work of Balibar to explore a conception of solidarity that is at once human and political, at once positive and negative, capturable and real on the one hand while defying easy capture on the other.

Rethinking solidarity

The location of politics has shifted beyond the state and extends ever outwards to incorporate the global arena as a whole. The movement of peoples and services, the emergence of global networks of interaction, and the increasingly intrusive character of such networks into lived experience, have all rendered the global as a distinct arena wherein relationships of commerce go hand in hand with those that seek the certainties of traditional modes of identity and affiliation. The concreteness of cultural ties come to form the antithesis to the intensification of modernity and what is now its globally manifest institutions and discursive practices. One response, in the context of social solidarity, is to assert a moral cosmopolitanism which, as seen earlier, is premised on a form of transcendent reason that binds humanity irrespective of difference. Another is to suggest a distinctly *political* understanding of cosmopolitanism, which understands the universal as an arena of struggle and contestation. It is in the context of the latter frame that I draw on the work of Balibar, for here we see a conception of the universal that rejects its utopian invocations as well as the state-centric emphasis of liberal thought, suggesting a critical articulation of human solidarity that is also political, one that recognises the ever persistent presence of conflict. Balibar's conception of the universal suggests a form of triptych: universality as reality, universality as fiction, and universality as symbol.

For Balibar, the world and all its interdependencies have come to constitute an arena of interaction whose "limits" have been reached. Such "worldwide-isation" emerges from the expansion of dominant and unified technologies and institutions that have incorporated "all parts of the world":

> There have been stages in the extension and intensification of real universality, until "in the end" a decisive threshold was crossed, which made it irreversible (we might also say: which makes it impossible to achieve any proper "delinking"...; and a moment has also come when *utopian* figures of universality have become obsolete by their very nature. By utopian figures I mean any intellectual plans

of establishing universality by connecting humanity with itself, creating a "cosmopolis" – which was always imagined at the same time as an implementation of certain moral values, precisely "universalistic" values. This impossibility did not arise because it proved impossible to connect the world as a single space, but exactly for the opposite reason: because this connection of humankind with itself was already achieved, because it was behind us.[42]

It is hence no longer a question of creating a world as such; rather, it is a question of transforming it. What is significant here is that real universality is not restricted to economic structures, but "has become political (with the "progressive emergence of transnational strategies, of political 'subjects' irreducible to local agencies, based on a single territory) and cultural and communicative."[43] Real universality defies the utopian vision through the reemergence of ethnic strife and the reassertion of primary identities with cultural origin. However, the politics of identity are "ultimately means of resisting inequality, or universality as inequality."[44] But the dilemma is ever-present, for to universalise such resistance is to reinforce exclusive modes of identification. Real universality in many ways shows up the tensions that confront any political cosmopolitanism, tensions relating to the recognition of difference on the one hand and the struggle against exclusionary modes of expression on the other. To universalise resistance, in other words, is precisely to reinforce an exclusive form of identity, to instrumentalise its modes of expression.

In his second conception of the universal, the "fictive", Balibar adopts a Hegelian perspective to focus on the institutional and representational manifestations of universality; the overcoming of primary and immediate ties by the higher authority of, firstly the Church in the European context, and then the secular state. Fictive universality involves at once both individuation (and hence liberation) and normalisation (hence exclusion). The modern "Hegelian" subject is one enabled to participate in a number of roles, whose identity can shift and develop, and whose life as private individual is largely autonomous. Individuation, or the creation of the individual as autonomous subject, establishes the self as individual in the public sphere of interaction and relationship to higher institutions, including the state. The modern state, its institutions and legal authority, liberates the individual from the shackles of primitive affiliations and turns the individual into a subject capable of an abstract affiliation to the modern, universal, institutions of the state.

The idea of individuation as the product of practices that establish universal institutions such as the modern state is a powerful one as it suggests that social solidarity within the modern state is a solidarity of strangers. However, the second process involved in the historical emergence of universal institutions and representations is "normalisation", the modern subject is not just autonomous, but she is also "normal", conforming, and as shown by Foucault, a product of disciplinary practices that historically have shifted from the pastoral to the repressive, to the sophistication of surveillance practices that ultimately produce the subject capable of self-government.[45] For Balibar, the hegemony of the modern state and its fictive universality is one that is centrally bound by this dual aspect of the modern subject, namely the autonomous and the "normal". The effect historically is at once both inclusive and exclusionary, inclusive in that all are equally subject to the universally applicable law, and hence capable of invoking such universality in the acquisition of rights, and exclusionary in that forms of subjectivity deemed beyond the normal citizen; the foreigner, the homosexual, the ethnic other, the un-integrated, come to be subject to discriminatory practices.

Balibar's conception of fictive universality brings into sharp focus the role of the modern state and the constitution of modern subjectivity. The universalising imperative of modernity and its institutions distances the subject from traditional associations embodied in ethnic, religious, or cultural identities and through such distancing liberates. The process has, historically, been conflictual for, just as the state and the wider community are liberating for the individual, primary identities come to assert difference precisely in the name of community. Within the late modern era, the intensification of the institutions of modernity through their globalisation has led to the reassertion of local, and hence primary identities.[46] Nevertheless, modernity is premised precisely on the separation of the private from the public, the subsumption of the former by the latter. As acknowledged by Balibar, there is a "permanent tension" between primary membership and citizenship, as is clearly the case in the present context of the so-called multicultural state. The implications for solidarity of the "fictive universality" associated with the state is both integrative and conflictual. It is integrative in that, as Balibar highlights, it is "effective as a means of integration – it demonstrates its own universality, so to speak – because it leads dominated groups to struggle against discrimination or inequality in the very name of the superior values of the community: the legal and ethical values of the state itself."[47] As especially shown by a number of feminist authors, this liberating aspect of the modern state is crucial as a tool for the protection of women from traditional practices that specifically target women's lives and bodies.[48] The conflictual consequences are highlighted when traditional modes of identity are either suppressed by the state or come to constitute the location wherein political agency is asserted over and above the state. The imperative for integration, in its individuating and normalising aspects, can historically come to generate the very basis for disintegration. Within the late modern context, such disintegration comes to be manifest transnationally, where primary affiliations or identities transcend state boundaries, finding their expressions in a complex array of connections and networks that span the globe.

The third form of universality that Balibar identifies is "symbolic" or "idealistic" universality. The idea here is that "universality also exists *as an ideal*" wherein claims are "symbolically raised against the limits of any institution."[49] The language of "universal values", having, as Balibar stresses, what Derrida calls a spectral character,[50] can be drawn upon in any solidarity movement. Nevertheless, in terms of the dominated, this spectral quality underpins or constitutes the driving force behind resistance or, what Balibar refers to as "insurrection". The attraction of this conception of universality for Balibar (or indeed any theorists interested in emancipatory politics) is that "it introduces the notion of *the unconditional* into the realm of politics."[51] For Balibar, this idealistic universality has both extensive and intensive aspects. The extensive argues against the relativisation of rights, for example, while the intensive suggests that equality and liberty are not just interlinked but mutually constitutive concepts. To suggest the existence or the desire for liberty constitutively suggests the desire for equality, for there can be no differential distribution of liberty. The insurrectional moment of ideal universality is the moment of struggle against coercion and against discrimination. Such struggle, for Balibar, is always a "collective process", a solidarity of claims and a solidarity of effort. Such solidarity is by definition political and not primarily a moral one. This is what Balibar refers to as the "right to politics": "nobody can be properly emancipated from outside or from above, but only by his or her own (collective) activity."[52] Ideal universality comes to mean the right to politics, the right to assert collectively the desire for freedom and equality. However, such emanicpatory struggle, and the women's movement is one, are not simply transformative of a community, but of society as a whole. This is then a form of "*solidarity without creating a community*".[53] However, even where difference is the basis of struggles against discrimination, the consequence is not necessarily particularistic. In Balibar's words:

> From the point of view of *real universality*, first, because they can play a direct role in challenging the "internal exclusion" on a world scale that continuously recreates racism. From the point of view of *fictive universality*, second, because they can constitute a struggle for broadening the spectrum of pluralism, and therefore *expanding subjectivity*, or challenging the ways of life and thought which have raised above society the self-image of some historically privileged groups, under the name of "reason". From the point of view of ideal universality, finally, because discrimination between cultures...is usually also a way of reproducing intellectual difference and hierarchies, or a *de facto* privileging of those men, women, and above all children, who are more "congenial" to established standards of communication.[54]

The form of political cosmopolitanism that Balibar articulates is one that extends beyond the confines of the state, beyond the confines of what may be referred to as "methodological territorialism".[55] The form of political cosmopolitanism articulated by Balibar is one that is distinctly global in its conception of politics, not in any institutional sense, but in an active articulation of solidarity with those subjected to exclusionary practices.[56]

Conclusion

Rethinking solidarity in critical terms starts with the assumption that a positive concept, one that is constitutively built upon the idea of a collective effort, the capacity to act, the capacity to define the limits of affiliation, must retain some element of "negativity", not just that associated with resistance and non-conformity, but the idea that there is always an excess that remains un-captured by the concept.[57] This negativity applies as much to solidarity as it does to the understanding of the politics of peace that I am exploring in this chapter. What is provided above is in many ways a negative conception of solidarity; to use Balibar, solidarity without community, a mode of thinking where politics is assumed to happen with others, but one which does not lapse into reifying its own particularity as universality.

In a global context that is increasingly represented in culturally confrontational terms, when cultural diversity and the corporeal presence of the other is deemed an existential threat, any critical thinking must refocus attention on the question of difference and the modes of exclusion and suppression associated with totalising practices that view the global as their remit of operations. While liberal thought and practice have historically sought the subsumption of difference within procedural frameworks that might define a common political space, tensions remain where difference comes face to face with discourses that assume universal validity. This tension persists when we take liberal thought and practice to the global level, where moral cosmopolitanism seeks to overcome difference by a reassertion of humanity as a mode of connection despite its very human diversities.

What I have sought to argue therefore is for a form of political cosmopolitanism where solidarity is linked to an understanding of universality that is always in question, a universality that does not subsume conflict, but rather recognises the ever present condition of struggle and confrontation against all totalising practices, including those that seek cultural exclusion and domination. In a global context where the discourses of confrontation dominate, where confrontation itself is constructed as a sign of identity, and above all where confrontation is no longer defined in inter-state, but in culturalist terms, modes of exclusion become multiform and are experienced in the everyday, from the refusal of entry to the asylum seeker to the violence perpetrated against those deemed to be culturally marked, to the violence in turn of supremacist belief systems. A distinctly political rendition on cosmopolitanism sees itself confronting the exclusions and violence of all those involved in the reification of particularistic modes of identity and affiliation, whether these are expressed in the terms of a rampant neoliberalism sustained by a global war machine or in the terms of a reactionary religiosity that seeks the elimination of all whose life choices and forms of articulation are deemed unfit. If we must give a name to the form of solidarity I am calling political cosmopolitanism, then this is a name that recognises its own aporetic state, the ever-present incompleteness of its remit, the frustrating non-closure of its politics. The politics of peace understood in this sense must always be in-process and on-trial.[58]

When Hannah Arendt states, "but to the question And what is the end of peace? There is no answer...", she refers precisely to the uncapturable excess of the politics of peace that I have articulated. It is this that enables some conception of an otherwise to the present, even as we seek to capture the present, render it readable and manageable. The politics of peace I articulate here starts with an understanding of international political space as one formed in and inscribed by the discourses and institutions of modern political life and their late modern manifestations. There is continuity here, as I have indicated throughout the book, just as there is transformation in the discourses and institutions that constitute the realm of the international.

This realm of the international is, as I showed in Chapter 2, interlaced with a global matrix of war that is constituted by a complex array of interactions involving a diversity of agents that draw upon the globality of the late modern context to affect change, both locally and globally. As I stated earlier in this investigation, the wars of the contemporary era are at once both transformative of global relations as well as being subject in turn to late modernity's globalising transformations. Analysing the global matrix of war through a critical engagement with Michel Foucault's analytics of war and power, the book provides an understanding of war that exceeds its immediate battlefield sense, seeing war as a practice situated in social relations and hence intimately and constitutively related to relations of power and, ultimately, to conditions deemed to constitute "peace". As I stated earlier, while Foucault himself confined his analytics to the domestic sphere of the liberal democratic state, this investigation locates its focus in the global arena, seeking to understand the profound implications of the global matrix of war for the sphere of the international as a distinct social, political, and juridical space of interactions that is nevertheless deeply interlaced with social relations that transcend the domestic/international divide. I argue throughout the text that the violence of late modernity is not so much "new", drawing as it does from the continuities of the modern era that I highlighted above, but can be seen as transformative of the distinctions that constituted the certainties of modernity; the domestic and the international, the sovereign state and the anarchic outside, the zone of civic peace and the zone of war. War and the politics of exception upon which it relies is implicated in the realisation of such indistinctions, with profound implications for the sphere of the international and its juridical and political regulation.

The wars of the late modern era, and specifically those that articulate a global remit, can also be viewed as the apotheosis of the project of modernity in all its globalising imperatives. These wars are not only conducted by modern liberal states, but are inscribed as "liberal wars", wherein the international is no longer confined within the restrictions of sovereignty, but is defined in terms of humanity as a whole. As I argued in this chapter and throughout the text, while the claims of the "human" – conventions on human rights are but one example –

have, throughout modernity run in juxtaposition with the claims of the sovereign state, and indeed of capital, the wars of the late modern era, those conducted in the name of "rescue" as well as "pre-emptive" wars, are justified in the name of humanity at large; humanity as species being. The discourses and practices of late modern war come in this sense to acquire a distinctly cosmopolitan understanding of the global political space, calling into the investigation, an engagement with Immanuel Kant's formative treatise on "perpetual peace" and its late modern interpretation and "application" by Jurgen Habermas. As I argued in Chapter 3, where both are formative voices in liberal conceptions of the international and the universalising moment in the project of modernity, Habermas's conception of cosmopolitan law as the basis of peace seeks to override Kant's adherence to the limiting constraints of state sovereignty, actively promoting wars fought in the name of humanitarian emergency as the constitutive moments formative of the pacifying effects of cosmopolitan law. The question I highlighted in Chapter 3 relates to the location of agency and the capacity to "legislate for peace", suggesting that a focus on this places the spotlight on the relationship between peace and progress, peace and humanity, peace and war. Habermas's conception of cosmopolitan peace comes to rely on the force of law wherein law is instantiated through every act of war conducted for humanitarian purposes. In the politics of indistinction that so permeate late modernity, the agents of war, if defined in humanitarian terms, and in the Habermasian reading, are at one and same time also the agents of peace engaged in the wholesale pacification, or indeed "domestication", of the global arena.

The liberal reordering of the world and its intricate relationship to the global matrix of war was the focus of attention in Chapter 4, where the spotlight was placed on wars constructed in terms of rescue and the protection of populations. The chapter explored the global remit of these wars and their location in relation to the ongoing project of modernity, suggesting that these wars have a constitutive role in redefining, and potentially redesigning, the sphere of the international and its ordering in political and juridical terms. Read in the context of transformations that Foucault suggests in relations of power, these wars come to be expressive of biopolitical power, a mode of governmentality that locates its remit in relation to life; humanity at large. However, as Foucault indicates, this humanity is subject to dividing principles; a racial ordering wherein some are subjected to death so that others constituted within the domain of the "human" should live. In considering the implications of so-called humanitarian

wars for the international context, I drew upon Agamben's understanding of the "state of exception", suggesting that such wars lie
within a zone of indistinction, at the very limits of the juridical order
that has functioned as the regulative matrix of the sphere of the international. Humanitarian wars understood in biopolitical terms are
hence seen as lying at the threshold of law, in a zone of indistinction
that, in blurring the boundary between inside and outside, locates
those involved, the agents of war and those targeted, somehow
beyond the law, generating impunity for the former and subjection
beyond the law for the latter. The paradox of this situation is that
while populations targeted are subjected to killing and the extremes of
injury, those perpetrating the act, the "rescuers", are always hierarchically positioned, constructed in discourse as saving distant others in
the name of humanity at large.

Any future research on the wars of the late modern context must
have two inter-related elements, one focusing on the juridico-political
implications, wherein the rendering of the international in "human"
terms brings forth, as a number of authors have now argued, transformations that invoke the imperial, and the other exploring the social
and political implications, now globally manifest, wherein enemies are
no-longer coterminus with the boundaries of states but are reconstituted in terms of the very corporeality of the other. It is in this context
that the liberal project of modernity comes face to face with its postcolonial other. The redesign of the international may well be argued to
constitute the inauguration of a cosmopolitan order wherein political
community may be conceived beyond the boundaries of the sovereign
state. However, we have seen here that this project is itself imbued
with violence and exclusionary practices wherein borders shift elsewhere, in transnational spaces, carried by the other targeted, just as
sovereign power itself shifts to a global terrain, seeking the control of
societies, and at times their redesign in turn, and their aspirations
across the globe. There is then, as I showed in Chapter 5, a particularity
to the state of exception productive of subjects that are differentially
placed in relation to moral worth and moral worthiness, the right to
possess political voice and the negation of such rights. The global
matrix of war and the state of exception that enables its practices is
imbricated with racial and cultural signification, placing the spotlight
of further research on what in effect are late modern forms of colonisation. I argued in Chapter 5 that both types of war that constitute the
global matrix of war, the humanitarian and pre-emptive, must be
placed in the context of the ongoing project of modernity, for these

wars are instrumental in their programme for the wholesale transformation of societies towards a particular rendering of the rational, the modern, the civilised.

Any reconception of the cosmopolitan project must hence contain, as I have argued in this chapter, the elements for its own imminent critique, highlighting the paradoxes of the ongoing project of modernity, paradoxes that enable reflection on the consequences of modernity, the continuities generative of its violent practices as well as the ethos that drives the modern subject, an ethos that can see another moment to come, the possibility that there is an otherwise to the present. Core to an ongoing reconception of the cosmopolitan project is a distinctly political articulation, one that focuses on what I have referred to as the *politics* of peace, wherein the end of peace remains unknown, a constitutive moment of which, beyond dialogue and the recognition of difference, is the possibility of solidarity without community.

Notes

Chapter 1 Introduction: Understanding War and Violence

1 Hannah Arendt, *On Violence* (New York and London: Harcourt Brace and Co., 1970), p. 80.
2 The just war tradition has a long history in moral philosophy, a history that is deeply-rooted in Christianity, but that has distinct articulations across other religious doctrines, including Islam and Judaism as well as Buddhist and Hindu traditions. See Terry Nardin (ed.) *The Ethics of War and Peace: Religious and Secular Perspectives* (Princeton, NJ: Princeton University Press, 1996). Dominant contemporary thinkers on the just war doctrine include Michael Walzer and Jean Elshtain. See Michael Walzer, *Just and Unjust Wars: A Moral Argument with Historical Illustrations* (New York: Basic Books, 1977) and Jean Bethke Elshtain (ed.), *Just War Theory* (Oxford: Blackwell, 1992).
3 For the international law tradition, see E. de Vattel, *The Law of Nations* (New York: AMS Press, 1987), S. von Pufendorf, *The Law of Nature and Nations* (Oxford: Clarendon Press, 1934), and H. Grotius, *The Law of War and Peace* (New York: Bobbs-Merrill, 1925).
4 As Michael Howard pointed out, the assumed inevitability of war's continuing presence in the international system suggested that the sole option available was to "codify its rationale and to civilise its means." See Michael Howard, *War and the Liberal Conscience* (London: Temple Smith, 1978), p. 18.
5 The liberal internationalist tradition in international thought is framed by two formative ideas, on the "law of nations" and the "wealth of nations", the former located in sixteenth and seventeenth century treatises on international law, and the latter on the liberal economic tradition, especially articulated by Adam Smith's *The Wealth of Nations* (New York: Modern Library, 1937).
6 See especially E.H. Carr, *The Twenty Years' Crisis 1919–1939* (London: Macmillan, 1939), and Hedley Bull, *The Anarchical Society: A Study of World Order* (London: Macmillan, 1977).
7 As Hidemi Suganami rightly points out, the question of "what causes war" has historically in the discipline of International Relations and beyond been framed around three types of question: what are the enabling conditions for war, what circumstances correlate to war's occurrence, and what are the causes of a particular war. See Hidemi Suganami, *On the Causes of War* (Oxford: Clarendon Press, 1996).
8 As elaborated by Kenneth Waltz, in his *Theory of International Politics* (Reading, MA: Addison-Wesley, 1979).
9 For a discussion of the debate between correlation and causation, the latter conceptualised in constitutive terms, see David Dessler, "Beyond Correlations: Towards a Causal Theory of War", *International Studies Quarterly*, Vol. 35 (1991), pp. 337–55.

10 Clausewitz's *On War* is here the defining text, though recent rationalist approaches to war rely variously on game theory and microeconomic theory. See Carl von Clausewitz, *On War*, edited and translated by M. Howard and P. Paret (Princeton, NJ: Princeton University Press, 1976). For rationalist approaches in International Relations, see Michael Nicholson, *Rationality and the Analysis of Conflict* (Cambridge: Cambridge University Press, 1992) and B. Bueno de Mesquita, *The War Trap* (New Haven, CT: Yale University Press, 1981).

11 Habermas, *Knowledge and Human Interests* (Boston: Beacon Press, 1972), p. 308.

12 *Ibid.*, p. 308.

13 *Ibid.*, p. 309.

14 For an excellent text on debates within the philosophy of the social sciences, see Martin Hollis's *The Philosophy of Social Science: An Introduction* (Cambridge: Cambridge University Press, 1994). For the application of these debates in politics and international relations, see Martin Hollis and Steve Smith, *Explaining and Understanding International Relations* (Oxford: Clarendon Press, 1990) and David Marsh and Gerry Stoker (eds), *Theory and Methods in Political Science* (London and New York: Palgrave Macmillan, 2002).

15 For this debate in International Relations, see Hollis and Smith, *Explaining and Understanding International Relations*, *op. cit.*, and Alexander Wendt, "On Constitution and Causation in International Relations", *Review of International Studies*, Vol. 24, special issue (1998), pp. 101–17.

16 Habermas, *op. cit.*, p. 310.

17 James Der Derian, "9/11: Before, After and In Between", Craig Calhoun, Paul Price and Ashley Timmer (eds), *Understanding September 11* (New York: The New Press, 2002), p. 178.

18 Michel Foucault, "Truth and Power", in *Power/Knowledge*, edited by Colin Gordon (New York and London: Prentice Hall, 1980), p. 117.

19 See Michel Foucault, "What is Enlightenment", in Michel Foucault, *Ethics: Subjectivity and Truth*, Vol. 1 of The Essential Works of Foucault, edited by Paul Rabinow (New York: The New Press, 1997), p. 319. For Deleuze's interpretation of Foucault's triptych, power, knowledge, subjectivity, see Gilles Deleuze, *Foucault*, translated by Sean Hand (Minneapolis and London: University of Minnesota Press, 1988). For an analysis of the implications of Foucault's understanding of critique in the context of war, see Vivienne Jabri, "Critical Thought and Political Agency in Time of War", *International Relations*, Vol. 19, No. 1 (2005), pp. 70–8.

20 Andrew Linklater, *The Transformation of Political Community* (Cambridge: Polity Press, 1998).

21 Michel Foucault's corpus is centrally concerned with war as "analyser" of social relations. See especially, Michel Foucault, *Discipline and Punish*, translated by Alan Sheridan (London: Penguin, 1977); *The Will to Knowledge, History of Sexuality Vol. 1*, translated by Robert Hurley (London: Penguin, 1998); and *Society Must Be Defended*, translated by David Macey (London: Allen Lane, 2003). See also, Michael Mann, *The Sources of Social Power*, Vol. II (Cambridge: Cambridge University Press, 1993).

22 See Giorgio Agamben's two formative texts on the 'state of exception': Agamben, G. *Homo Sacer: Sovereign Power and Bare Life*, trans. D. Heller Roazen

(Stanford, CA: Stanford University Press, 1995) and *The State of Exception* (Chicago, Ill, and London: Chicago University Press, 2005). I will return to Agamben's reading of the state of exception later in this investigation.

23 The concept of a "global matrix of war" used here is drawn from an earlier investigation. See Vivienne Jabri, "War, Security and Liberal State", *Security Dialogue*, Vol. 37, No. 1 (2006), pp. 47–64.

24 Hans Joas, *War and Modernity* (Cambridge: Polity, 2003), p. 10.

25 Hannah Arendt, *On Violence, op. cit.*, p. 76.

26 Elaine Scarry, *The Body in Pain: The Making and Unmaking of the World* (Oxford and New York: Oxford University Press, 1985), p. 63.

27 *Ibid.*, p. 66.

28 There is much written in the recent past on the so-called "western way of war", defined variously as "risk-transfer warfare" and "humane warfare". See, respectively, Martin Shaw, "Risk-transfer war, the militarism of small of small massacres and the historic legitimacy of war", *International Relations*, Vol. 17, No. 3 (2002), pp. 343–60, and Christopher Coker, *Humane Warfare* (London and New York: Routledge, 2001).

29 That war is constitutive of full individuality is an ontological commitment that is manifestly present in Hegel's reflections on war and the state. Clausewitz's ideas on the constitutive role of war in the formation of a distinctly masculine subjectivity in individual and nation directly reflects Hegelian thought. For a discussion of the ontological commitments present in Clausewitz, see Daniel Pick, *War Machine: The Rationalisation of Slaughter in the Modern Age* (New Haven, CT, and London: Yale University Press, 1993). For a discussion of Hegel's understanding of the constitutive role of war, specifically in his *Elements of the Philosophy of Right*, trans. H.B. Nisbet (Cambridge: Cambridge University Press, 1991), see Vivienne Jabri, *Discourses on Violence* (Manchester: Manchester University Press, 1996), pp. 41–50.

30 Walter Benjamin draws on Sorel, whose *Reflections on Violence* was first published in Italian in 1906, in developing his argument for the constitutive role of violence in his *Critique of Violence*, published in 1921, See Walter Benjamin, "Critique of Violence", in *Selected Writings*, Vol. 1: 1913–1926, edited by Marcus Bullock and Michael W. Jennings (Cambridge MA, and London: Harvard University Press, 1996). See also Georges Sorel, *Reflections on Violence*, edited by Jeremy Jennings (Cambridge: Cambridge University Press, 1999). For Fanon's understanding of violence and the colonial subject, see his *The Wretched of the Earth*, trans. Constance Farrington (Harmondsworth: Penguin Books, 1967).

31 See Jabri, *Discourses on Violence, op. cit.*, pp. 119–44. See also Iver B. Neumann, *Uses of the Other: The "East" in European Identity Formation* (Manchester: Manchester University Press, 1999).

32 Arendt, *On Violence, op. cit.*, p. 51.

33 Vivienne Jabri, *Discourses on Violence*, pp. 104–10.

34 M. Weber, *Economy and Society*, Vol. 1 (Berkeley: University of California Press, 1978), p. 56.

35 Kenneth Waltz is foremost in locating war in the international system of states. See his *Theory of International Politics, op. cit.* For a neorealist investigation of war and the dynamics of change in the international system, see

Robert Gilpin, *War and Change in World Politics* (Cambridge: Cambridge University Press, 1981).

36 Michael Mann, *The Sources of Social Power, op. cit.*

37 Charles Tilly, *Coercion, Capital, and European States AD990–1990* (Oxford: Blackwell, 1990).

38 Anthony Giddens, *The Nation-State and Violence* (Cambridge: Polity, 1985), p. 13. Giddens's understanding of the dynamics of surveillance and pacification draw on Michel Foucault's understanding of technologies of power and their workings in institutional settings, from the military to the asylum. See Michel Foucault, *Discipline and Punish, op. cit.*

39 Giddens, 1985, *op. cit.*, p. 121.

40 Rob Walker, *Inside/Outside: International Relations as Political Theory* (Cambridge: Cambridge University Press, 1993), p. 155.

41 According to Hardt and Negri, controversially, this relocation of juridical power suggests the emergence of "Empire". See Michael Hardt and Antonio Negri, *Empire* (Cambridge, MA, and London: Harvard University Press, 2000).

42 Johan Galtung, "Violence, Peace, and Peace Research", *Journal of Peace Research*, Vol. 6, No. 3 (1969), pp. 167–91.

43 See especially, Judith Butler, *Excitable Speech: A Politics of the Performative* (London and New York: Routledge, 1997).

44 The United Kingdom legislation against terrorism, especially the recent Prevention of Terrorism Act (2005), is clearly conceived in terms of both domestic and international terrorism. As stated by the Home Office, the Act targets both UK and non-UK nationals suspected of terrorist activity, whether such activity is domestic or international. See www.homeoffice.gov.uk/security/terrorism-and-the-law/.

45 Judith Butler, "Explanation and Exonation", *Theory and Event*, Vol. 5, No. 4 (2002).

46 As highlighted by Butler in her critique of instrumental conceptions of agency and their application to the first Gulf War. See Judith Butler, "Contingent Foundations", in Seyla Benhabib, *et al, Feminist Contentions: A Philosophical Exchange* (New York and London: Routledge, 1995), pp. 42–5. For the parallels between rationalist and just war approaches, see Vivienne Jabri, "Critical Thought and Political Agency in Time of War", *International Relations*, Vol. 19, No. 1 (2005), p. 70. For the complicities of rationalist approaches in rendering invisible forms of violence and exclusion in global politics, see Steve Smith's powerful presidential address to the International Studies Association, reproduced as "Singing Our World Into Existence: International Relations Theory and September 11th", *International Studies Quarterly*, Vol. 48, No. 3 (2004), pp. 491–515.

47 Michel Foucault, *The Use of Pleasure*, Vol. 2 of *The History of Sexuality*, trans. Robert Hurley (London: Penguin Books, 1992), p. 6.

48 Jabri, *op. cit.*, 2005.

49 David Campbell, *Politics Without Principle* (Boulder CO and London: Lynne Rienner Publishers, 1993), p. 7.

50 David Campbell, *National Deconstruction: Violence, Identity and Justice in Bosnia* (Minneapolis and London: University of Minnesota Press, 1998).

51 Vivienne Jabri, "Shock and Awe: Power and the Resistance of Art", *Millennium: Journal of International Studies*, Vol. 34, No. 3 (2006), pp. 819–39.

52   The Arabic language network, *Al Jazeera*, was targeted during the US aerial bombardment of both Kabul (2001) and Baghdad (2003).
53   The term "structuration" derives from Anthony Giddens's theory of structuration, which suggests the duality of agency and structure, the mutually constitutive relationship between action and the continuities of social life. I use this term in analysing the ways in which war is structured in social and political life. See Anthony Giddens, *The Constitution of Society* (Cambridge: Polity Press, 1984). For a structurationist analysis of violent conflict, see Vivienne Jabri, *Discourses on Violence, op. cit.*
54   Howard Caygill, "Violence, Civility and the Predicaments of Philosophy", in David Campbell and Michael Dillon (eds), *The Political Subject of Violence* (Manchester: Manchester University Press, 1993).
55   Stephen Toulmin, *Cosmopolis: The Hidden Agenda of Modernity* (Chicago, Ill.: The University of Chicago Press, 1990), p. 71.
56   Linklater, *The Tranformation of Political Community, op. cit.*, p. 146.
57   *Ibid.*, pp. 146–7.
58   *Ibid.*, p. 149.
59   *Ibid.*, p. 175.
60   David Slater, *Geopolitics and the Postcolonial: Rethinking North-South Relations* (Oxford: Blackwell, 2004), p. 10.
61   Weber, *Economy and Society*, p. 480, quoted in David Slater, *ibid.*, p. 10.
62   Slater points in particular to Zizek and Castoriadis in this context. See especially, Slavoj Zizek, "A Leftist Plea for 'Eurocentrism'", *Critical Inquiry*, Summer 1998, pp. 988–1009.
63   Slater, p. 11.
64   *Ibid.*
65   See Enrique Dussel, *The Underside of Modernity* (New York: Humanity Books, 1998).

Chapter 2   The Politics of Global War

1   Simon Armitage, *Killing Time* (London: Faber and Faber, 1999), p. 4.
2   Under UN Security Council Resolution 1483 (22 May 2003) the $6 billion funds from the UN Oil for Food Programme were placed under the control of the US-led Coalition Provisional Authority, to be spent "for the benefit of the Iraqi people". For a full analysis into how much of this money simply "disappeared", see Ed Harriman, "Where Has all the Money Gone?", *London Review of Books*, Vol. 27, No. 13, 7 July 2005.
3   The Congo alone claims 1,200 lives per day, according to a recent UN report, see Simon Tisdall, *The Guardian* 16/2/06.
4   Michael Walzer, *Just and Unjust Wars* (New York: Basic Books, 1977).
5   This reluctance to intervene in Africa's wars was especially illustrated in the case of the Rwanda genocide. See Michael Barnett, *Eyewitness to a Genocide: The United Nations and Rwanda* (Ithaca and London: Cornell University Press, 2002).
6   *Ibid.*, p. 26.
7   There is a wide literature on "peacebuilding", some instrumental, focused on the institutional requisites of programmes geared towards establishing

the conditions for peace in a post-conflict situation, others reflective, and hence critical, focusing on the political significance of such programmes. For an excellent analysis of peacebuilding as a "liberal peace" project, see Oliver Richmond, *The Transformation of Peace* (London and New York: Palgrave, 2005). See also, Roland Paris, "International Peacebuilding and the 'Mission Civilisatrice'", *Review of International Studies*, Vol. 28, No. 4 (2002) and Roland Paris, *At War's End* (Cambridge: Cambridge University Press, 2004).

8 A triumphalism that finds its most consistent articulation in Francis Fukuyama, *The End of History and the Last Man* (London: Penguin, 1993).

9 No-where is this call for a greater transformative role for international intervention more clearly stated than in the former United Nations Secretary General, Boutros Boutros-Ghali's document, "An Agenda for Peace: preventive Diplomacy, Peacemaking and Peacekeeping" (New York: United Nations, 1992).

10 David Held, *et al* (eds), *Global Transformations: Politics, Economics and Culture* (Cambridge: Polity Press, 1999).

11 Hay, C. and D. Marsh (eds), *Demystifying Globalisation* (Basingstoke: Macmillan, 2000).

12 Paul Hirst and Graham Thompson, *Globalisation in Question* (Cambridge: Polity Press, 1999), p. 15.

13 Michel Foucault, *The Archaeology of Knowledge*, trans. A.M. Sheridan Smith (London and New York: Routledge, 1997), p. 167.

14 *Ibid.*, p. 194.

15 Zygmunt Bauman, *Globalisation: The Human Consequences* (Cambridge: Polity Press, 1998), p. 18.

16 Especially significant readings of late modern transformation in social theoretical terms are Manuel Castells, *The Rise of the Network Society*, Volumes 1 and 2 (Oxford: Blackwell, 2000), Anthony Giddens, *The Consequences of Modernity* (Cambridge: Polity Press, 1990), and Ulrich Beck, *The Reinvention of Politics: Rethinking Modernity in the Global Social Order* (Cambridge: Polity Press, 1997).

17 Rob Walker, "Lines of Insecurity: International, Imperial, Exceptional", *Security Dialogue*, Vol. 37, No. 1 (2006), p. 67. Hardt and Negri point to the reinscription of political authority in reference to the emergence of what they refer to as Empire. See *Empire* (Cambridge: Harvard University Press, 2000).

18 Vivienne Jabri, "Feminist Ethics and Hegemonic Global Politics", *Alternatives*, Vol. 29, No. 3 (2004).

19 Hardt and Negri, *Empire, op. cit.*, p. 9.

20 Michel Foucault, *Archaeology of Knowledge, op. cit.*, p. 194.

21 This is what Foucault refers to as the "political economy of truth". See his "Truth and Power", in *Power/Knowledge*, edited by Colin Gordon (New York and London: Prentice Hall, 1980), p. 131.

22 Robert Jackson, borrowing from Harold Laski, refers to sovereignty as the "basic element of the grammar of politics", defining of the modern era. See Robert Jackson, "Sovereignty in World Politics: A Glance at the Conceptual and Historical Landscape", *Political Studies*, Vol. 47 (1999), p. 431. However, as pointed out by Jens Bartelsen, "sovereignty is no longer empirically or

transcendentally given, but something contingent upon historical forces...". See Jens Bartelsen, *A Genealogy of Sovereignty* (Cambridge: Cambridge University Press, 1995), p. 36.

23　See discussion in Chapter 1. This representation of the historical evolution of the modern state derives especially from Anthony Giddens, *The Nation-State and Violence* (Cambridge: Polity Press, 1985).

24　For the view that "sovereignty" acts as a framing device for understanding the social and political world, see Neil Walker, "Late Sovereignty in the European Union", in Neil Walker (ed.), *Sovereignty in Transition* (Oxford: Hart, 2003), pp. 3–32.

25　That the state can no longer be conceived as holding the monopoly over the provision of security is illustrated by the workings of international security firms. See, for example, Anna Leander, "Privatizing the Politics of Protection: Military Companies and the Definition of Security Concerns", in Jef Huysmans, *et al* (eds), *The Politics of Protection* (London and New York: Routledge, 2006).

26　For this understanding of globalisation, see Anthony Giddens, *The Consequences of Modernity* (Cambridge: Polity Press, 1990).

27　See Jurgen Habermas, *The Past as Future*, interviewed by Michael Haller, translated and edited by Max Pensky (Cambridge: Polity Press, 1994), pp. 5–32. Mary Kaldor's definition of "new wars" focuses attention on the indistinction between war and criminality within the enabling conditions of globalised social relations. See her *New and Old Wars: Organised Violence in a Global Era* (Cambridge: Polity Press, 1999).

28　Mary Kaldor, "Beyond Militarism, Arms Races, and Arms Control", in Craig Calhoun *et al* (eds), *Understanding September 11* (New York: The New Press, 2002), p. 164.

29　That Jihadi violence can be read as emergent from conflicting Islamic identities in a globalised context, see Olivier Roy, *Globalised Islam: The Search for a New Ummah* (London: Hurst, 2004).

30　The association of the late or postmodern with fragmentation and uncertainty is especially made by Zygmunt Bauman. See his *Postmodern Ethics* (Oxford: Blackwell, 1993). Other social theorists stress uncertainty as the defining feature of the late modern context, including Anthony Giddens. See his *Modernity and Self-identity: Self and Society in the Late Modern Age* (Cambridge: Polity Press, 1991).

31　James Der Derian, "9/11: Before, After and In Between", in Craig Calhoun, *et al* (eds), *Understanding September 11* (New York: The New Press, 2002), p. 180.

32　*Ibid.*

33　All quotations in Der Derian, *ibid.*, pp. 184–5.

34　For an analysis of the global remit of the Bush Administration's wars, see Seymour Hersh, *Chain of Command* (London: Penguin, 2004). For an analysis of the global remit expressed by Osama Bin Laden, see Bruce Lawrence (ed.) *Messages to the World: The Statements of Osama Bin Laden*, trans. James Howarth (London: Verso, 2005).

35　See Kenneth Waltz, *Man, the State and War: A Theoretical Analysis* (New York: Columbia University Press, 1954), and his *Theory of International Politics* (Reading, Mass, and London: Addison-Wesley, 1979).

36 Kenneth Waltz, "The Continuity of International Politics", Chapter 31 in Ken Booth and Tim Dunne (eds) *Worlds in Collision* (London: Palgrave, 2002).

37 Barnett and Duvall, "Power in International Politics", *International Organisation*, Vol. 59, Winter 2005, p. 40.

38 Barnett and Duvall, *ibid.*, p. 64. See also Andrew Bacevitch, *American Empire: The Realities and Consequences of U.S. Diplomacy* (Cambridge, MA: Harvard, 2002).

39 Examples here include constituencies within both camps in the Israeli-Palestinian conflict, diaspora groups connected with factions in the former Yugoslavia, and exiled individuals and groups mobilising US support in opposition to the Baath regime in Iraq or the theocratic regime in Iran. While all such constituencies seek to mobilise the support of the United States, they clearly differ in their mobilising capacities.

40 Michael Hardt and Antonio Negri, *Multitude* (London: Hamish Hamilton, 2005), p. 3.

41 *Ibid.*, p. 4.

42 A concept that Hardt and Negri derive from Agamben, referring to "the temporary suspension of the constitution and the rule of law". Hardt and Negri, *ibid.*, p. 7. See Giorgio Agamben, *Homo Sacer: Sovereign Power and Bare Life*, trans. Daniel Heller-Raozen (Stanford, CA: Stanford University Press, 1995).

43 Hardt and Negri, *Multitude, ibid.*, p. 9.

44 *Ibid.*, p. 16.

45 *Ibid.*, p. 21.

46 A concept that Hardt and Negri derive from Michel Foucault, suggesting power directed at the life of populations, the "government" of all aspects of the life of the population.

47 *Ibid.*, p. 23.

48 For an understanding of the global matrix of war from which this Foucaultian analysis is drawn, see Vivienne Jabri, "War, Security and the Liberal State", *Security Dialogue*, Vol. 37, No. 1 (2006), pp. 47–64.

49 Michel Foucault, *Society Must Be Defended*, trans. David Macey (London: Allen Lane, 2003), pp. 49–62.

50 For Foucault, the "distant roar of battle" permeates what he refers to as the "carceral" society. See his *Discipline and Punish*, trans. Alan Sheridan (London: Penguin, 1977), p. 308.

51 Foucault, *Society Must Be Defended, op. cit.*, p. 242.

52 *Ibid.*, p. 243.

53 *Ibid.*, p. 245.

54 *Ibid.*, p. 249.

55 Michel Foucault, *The Will to Knowledge, History of Sexuality*, Vol. 1, trans. Robert Hurley (London: Penguin, 1978), p. 137.

56 Stuart Elden, "The War of Races and the Constitution of the State: Foucault's 'il faut defender la societe' and the Politics of Calculation", *Boundary*, Vol. 2, p. 151.

57 Paul Gilroy, *After Empire: Melancholia or Convivial Culture* (London and New York: Routledge, 2004), p. 47.

58 The crucial difference, however, between local warlords engaged in the drive for personal or even communal gain and the global clandestine

organisation having a self-understanding that is global, is that the latter articulates a programme that is distinctly global in its definition of political community and provides a distinct rendition on the modalities of government it seeks for this community.

59 Vivienne Jabri, "War, Security and the Liberal State", *op. cit.*, p. 54.
60 Giddens, *Modernity and Self-Identity, op. cit.*
61 Mary Kaldor, "Beyond Militarism, Arms Races, and Arms Control", *op. cit.*, p. 176.
62 See Paul Gilroy, *op. cit.* and Gayatry Chakravorty Spivak, *A Critique of Postcolonial Reason: Toward a History of the Vanishing Present* (Cambridge, MA, and London: Harvard University Press, 1999), pp. 248–9.
63 Derek Gregory, *The Colonial Present* (Oxford: Blackwell, 2004), p. 7.
64 *Ibid.*, p. 8.
65 *Ibid.*, p. 11.
66 *Ibid.*, p. 13.
67 Rob Walker, *Inside/Outside: International Relations as Political Theory* (Cambridge: Cambridge University Press, 1993), p. 78.

Chapter 3 Late Modernity, War and Peace

1 Theodor W. Adorno, "Progress", in *Critical Models: Interventions and Catchwords*, translated by Henry W. Pickford (New York: Columbia University Press, 1998), p. 145.
2 On an analysis of Clausewitz's association of war with mature (male) subjectivity, see Daniel Pick, *War Machine: The Rationalisation of Slaughter in the Modern Age* (New Haven, CT, and London: Yale University Press, 1993), p. 31. For a full discussion of the constitutive role of war in Clausewitz and Hegel, see Vivienne Jabri, *Discourses On Violence* (Manchester: Manchester University Press, 1996), pp. 41–50.
3 Immanuel Kant, "Perpetual Peace: A Philosophical Sketch", in Kant, *Political Writings*, edited by Hans Reiss, trans. H.B. Nisbet (Cambridge: Cambridge University Press, 1970).
4 See Michael Doyle, *Ways of War and Peace* (New York: Norton, 1997) for the Kantian underpinnings of liberal conceptions of peace in International Relations. For a critical interrogation of the "liberal democratic peace" project and its conceptions of international order, see Nicholas Rengger, *International Relations, Political Theory and the Problem of Order* (London and New York: Routledge, 2000), pp. 112–31.
5 Vivienne Jabri, *Discourses on Violence, op. cit.*, 145.
6 Walter Benjamin, "Theses on the Philosophy of History", in *Illuminations*, edited with an introduction by Hannah Arendt, translated by Harry Zorn (London: Pimlico, 1999), p. 252.
7 Andrew Linklater, *The Transformation of Political Community* (Cambridge: Polity Press, 1998).
8 Michel Foucault, "What is Enlightenment", in Paul Rabinow (ed.), *The Foucault Reader* (Penguin, London: 1984), p. 39.
9 Kant, *Perpetual Peace, op. cit.*, p. 97.
10 *Ibid.*, p. 98.
11 *Ibid.*, p. 98.

12 *Ibid.*, p. 100.
13 James Bohman and Matthias Lutz-Bachmann, "Introduction", in J. Bohman and M. Lutz-Bachmann (eds), *Perpetual Peace: Essays on Kant's Cosmopolitan Ideal* (Cambridge, MA, and London: The MIT Press, 1997), p. 4.
14 Kant, *Political Writings, op. cit.*, p. 103.
15 *Ibid.*, p. 108.
16 *Ibid.*, p. 108.
17 Immanuel Kant, "Idea for a Universal History with a Cosmopolitan Purpose", in Kant, *Political Writings, op. cit.*, p. 45.
18 Jurgen Habermas, "Interpreting the Fall of a Monument", *German Law Journal*, Vol. 4, No. 7, July 2003, p. 2; accessed at http://www.german-lawjournal.com, 6/2/06.
19 *Ibid.*
20 *Ibid.*
21 *Ibid.*, p. 4.
22 *Ibid.*, p. 4.
23 *Ibid.*, p. 6.
24 *Ibid.*, p. 6.
25 *Ibid.*, p. 7.
26 Jurgen Habermas, *The Inclusion of the Other: Studies in Political Theory*, edited by Ciaran Cronin and Pablo de Greiff (Cambridge, Mass: MIT Press, 1998), p. 179.
27 *Ibid.*, p. 181
28 *Ibid.*, p. 183.
29 Jurgen Habermas, *The Past as Future*, translated and edited by Max Pensky and Peter Hohendahl (Cambridge: Polity Press, 1994), p. 21.
30 *Ibid.*, p. 22.
31 Habermas, "Kant's Idea of Perpetual Peace, with the Benefit of Two Hundred Years' Hindsight", in J. Bohman and M. Lutz-Bachmann (eds), *op. cit.*, p. 116.
32 *Ibid.*, p. 116.
33 *Ibid.*, p. 116, quoting Kant, *Perpetual Peace, op. cit.*, p. 92.
34 Habermas, *ibid.*, p. 116.
35 *Ibid.*, p. 117.
36 *Ibid.*, p. 117.
37 *Ibid.*, p. 118.
38 *Ibid.*, p. 118.
39 *Ibid.*, p. 119.
40 *Ibid.*, p. 119.
41 *Ibid.*, p. 129.
42 *Ibid.*, p. 130.
43 Habermas, *Past as Future, op. cit.*, p. 11.
44 *Ibid.*, p. 21.
45 *Ibid.*, p. 20.
46 See Vivienne Jabri, *Discourses on Violence*, chapter 6.
47 According to Schmitt, the "sovereign" is "he who decides the exception", the moment of emergency wherein the law is suspended. See Carl Schmitt, *Political Theology*, trans. George Schwab (Cambridge, MA, and London: The MIT Press, 1985).

48 Hans Joas, *War and Modernity*, trans. Rodney Livingstone (Cambridge: Polity Press, 2003), p. 153. Schmitt's *The Concept of the Political*, published in 1932, remains his most influential text, used extensively in contemporary scholarship on emergency politics.

49 Joas, *ibid.*, p. 154.

50 *Ibid.*

51 Schmitt, *The Concept of the Political*, quoted in Joas, *op. cit.*

52 Herbert Marcuse, "The Struggle Against Liberalism in the Totalitarian View of the State", in Herbert Marcuse, *Negations: Essays in Critical Theory* (London: Free Association Books, 1988).

53 Theodor Adorno and Max Horkheimer, *Dialectic of Enlightenment* (London and New York: Verso, 1979), p. 5.

54 *Ibid.*, pp. 6–7.

55 *Ibid.*, p. 9.

56 *Ibid.*, p. 10.

57 *Ibid.*, p. 16.

58 Thomas McCarthy, "Introduction", in Jurgen Habermas, *The Philosophical Discourse of Modernity*, trans. Frederick Lawrence (Cambridge: Polity Press, 1987), pp. xvi–xvii.

59 Habermas, *The Philosophical Discourse of Modernity*, *op. cit.*, p. 113.

60 *Ibid.*, p. 114.

61 Zygmunt Bauman, *Modernity and the Holocaust* (Cambridge: Polity Press, 1989), p. 7.

62 Michael Mann, *The Dark Side of Democracy: Explaining Ethnic Cleansing* (Cambridge: Cambridge University Press, 2005).

63 Habermas, *Past as Future*, *op. cit.*, pp. 11 and 20–1 respectively.

64 Vivienne Jabri, *Discourses on Violence*, *op. cit.*, chapter 6.

65 Habermas, 'Interpreting the Fall of a Monument', *op. cit.*

66 Habermas, *Inclusion of the Other*, *op. cit.*, p. 178.

67 Hannah Arendt, *Men in Dark Times* (New York and London: Harcourt, Brace and Company, 1968), p. 92.

Chapter 4   War, the International, the Human

1 C.P. Cavafy, *Collected Poems*, trans. Edmund Keeley and Philip Sherrard (London: Chatto and Windus, 1998), p. 14.

2 See, for example, Lawrence Freedman, "The Age of Liberal Wars", *Review of International Studies*, Vol. 31 (2005), pp. 93–108. Freedman suggests that while the wars of the past were conducted in the name of national and international security, both invoking the state as the primary referent in international politics, the wars of the twenty-first century, specifically wars of intervention conducted by the West, are concerned with "human security".

3 Carl Schmitt, quoted in Hans Joas, *War and Modernity*, trans. Rodney Livingstone (Cambridge: Polity Press, 2003), p. 39.

4 Joas, *ibid.*, p. 39.

5 *Ibid.*

6 For a powerful critique of this age-old dualism, realism versus liberalism, see Michael Williams, *The Realist Tradition and the Limits of International*

Relations (Cambridge: Cambridge University Press, 2005), especially chapters 3 and 4.

7   The Geneva Conventions provide the basis of the protection of civilians in time of war and in periods of occupation. The Nuremberg and Tokyo Trials set the framework for war crimes, including "crimes against peace", "war crimes", and "crimes against humanity". See Geoffrey Best, *War and Law* (Oxford: Oxford University Press, 1994).

8   See Philippe Sands, *Lawless World: America and the Making and Breaking of Global Rules* (London: Allen Lane, 2005).

9   See Rob Walker, "International Relations and the Concept of the Political", in Ken Booth and Steve Smith (eds), *International Relations Theory Today* (Cambridge: Polity Press, 1995).

10 For debates around humanitarian intervention, see Andrew Williams, *Liberalism and War* (London and New York: Routledge, 2006). See also Nicholas Wheeler, *Saving Strangers: Humanitarian Intervention in International Society* (Oxford: Oxford University Press, 2000).

11 Danilo Zolo, *Invoking Humanity: war, law, and global order* (London: Continuum, 2002), p. 38.

12 *Ibid.*, p. 39.

13 The term "legal pacifism", is used by Habermas in his support for the NATO action in Kosovo to refer to this action as a "pacifying mission which made use of arms, but did so with the consensus of the international community, albeit without a mandate from the United Nations". Quoted in Zolo, *ibid.*, p. 79. As Zolo rightly points out, Habermas is here relying more on Kelsen's just war understanding of "peace through law" than on Kant, for the latter is distinctly opposed to the claim that any one state can determine the conditions for just cause. See Hans Kelsen, *The Law of the United Nations* (New York: Praeger, 1950).

14 Zolo, *ibid.*, p. 88.

15 Michael Dillon, "Criminalising Social and Political Violence Internationally", *Millennium*, Vol. 27, No. 3 (1998), pp. 543–69.

16 *Ibid.*, pp. 551–2.

17 *Ibid.*, p. 563.

18 See Mike Crang and Nigel Thrift, "Introduction", in Mike Crang and Nigel Thrift (eds), *Thinking Space* (London and New York: Routledge, 2000), for a discussion of the spatiality of knowledge and its implications for self-other relations.

19 Anthony Giddens, *Modernity and Self Identity: Self and Society in the Late Modern Age* (Cambridge: Polity, 1991), pp. 21–2.

20 See, for example, Thomas Franck, "Who Killed Article 2 (4)? Or: Changing Norms Governing the Use of Force by States", *American Journal of International Law*, Vol. 64 (1970).

21 For the advocacy of the view that "If power is used to do justice, law will follow", see M.J. Glennon, "The New Interventionism: The Search for a Just International Law", *Foreign Affairs*, Vol. 78, No. 3 (1999).

22 Richard Falk, "Legality and legitimacy: the quest for principled flexibility and restraint", *Review of International Studies*, Vol. 31 (2005), p. 33.

23 Boutros Boutros-Ghali's "An Agenda for Peace" focuses on the concept of "human security", suggesting that the role of the United Nations, in

particular, must extend beyond state security and towards the human. Highlighting the fact that states are often the source of insecurity, effective action towards peace must incorporate the transformation of domestic political and legal formations towards the rule of law. Kofi Annan's "In Larger Freedom" is primarily concerned with defining a form of reconciliation between the principle of state sovereignty and the legitimacy of interventions in situation of extreme emergency, underwritten by the Security Council. See his "In Larger Freedom: Towards Development, Security and Human Rights for All", *Report of the Secretary-General*, A/59/2005, 21 March 2005.

24 Martin Shaw, *War and Genocide* (Cambridge: Polity, 2003), p. 60.
25 *Ibid.*, p. 60.
26 Neil Walker, "Sovereignty, International Security, and the Regulation of Armed Conflict: the Possibilities of Political Agency", in Jef Huysmans, Andrew Dobson, and Raia Prokhovnik (eds) *The Politics of Protection* (London and New York: Routledge, 2006), p. 155.
27 Paul Hirst and Graham Thompson, *Globalisation in Question* (Cambridge: Polity Press, 1999).
28 See Jef Huysmans, "Discussing Sovereignty and Transnational Politics", in Neil Walker (ed.), *Sovereignty in Transition* (Oxford: Hart, 2003), pp. 209–28.
29 See Enrique Dussel, *The Underside of Modernity* (New York: Humanity Books, 1998).
30 E.H. Carr, *Nationalism and After* (London: Macmillan, 1945).
31 Andrew Linklater, *The Transformation of Political Community* (Cambridge: Polity Press, 1998), p. 159.
32 *Ibid.*, p. 160.
33 *Ibid.*, p. 161.
34 *Ibid.*, p. 167.
35 *Ibid.*, p. 169.
36 *Ibid.*, p. 171.
37 *Ibid.*, p. 175.
38 David Held, *Global Covenant: The Social Democratic Alternative to the Washington Consensus* (Cambridge: Polity Press, 2004).
39 *Ibid.*, p. 171.
40 Neil Walker, "Sovereignty, International Security and the Regulation of Armed Conflict: The Possibilities of Political Agency", *op. cit.*, pp. 168–72.
41 David Held, *Global Covenant, op. cit.*
42 Linklater, *op. cit.*, p. 174.
43 Andrew M. Moravcsik, *Liberalism and International Relations Theory* (Centre for International Affairs, Harvard University, Working Paper No. 92-6, 1992) and A.M. Moravcsik, "Taking Preferences Seriously: A Liberal Theory of International Politics", *International Organisation*, Vol. 51 (1997).
44 Anne-Marie Slaughter, "International Law in a World of Liberal States", *European Journal of International Law*, Vol. 6 (1995), p. 6.
45 *Ibid.*, p. 7.
46 *Ibid.*, p. 7. One of the most prominent scholars in this area is Michael Doyle. See his *Ways of War and Peace* (New York: Norton, 1997).
47 Slaughter, *Ibid.*, p. 9. Where peace is defined in terms of conflict resolution through non-military means, liberal democracy suggests "some form of representative government secured by the separation of powers, constitutional

guarantees of civil and political rights, juridical equality, and a functioning judicial system dedicated to the rule of law."

48 If we look to the cosmopolitanism elaborated by Andrew Linklater or David Held, we see similarities with liberal international thought on the requirement to move beyond the sovereignty of states as the regulative principle of international life as well as the focus on constitutionalism as a force for peace and respect for human rights domestically and internationally. While both Linklater and Held derive their cosmopolitanism mainly from Marxism and Frankfurt School critical theory, especially that articulated by Jurgen Habermas in the contemporary period, Slaughter derives her liberal theory primarily from liberal international relations thought.

49 A conception often associated with Hedley Bull. See his *The Anarchical Society: A Study of Order in World Politics* (London: Macmillan, 1977).

50 Christian Reus-Smit, "Liberal Hierarchy and the License to Use Force", *Review of International Studies*, Vol. 31, Special Issue, December (2005), pp. 71–92.

51 See Mary Kaldor, *New and Old Wars: Organised Violence in a Global Era* (Cambridge: Polity Press, 1999), pp. 91–2.

52 Robert Jackson defines "quasi-states" or "failed states" in terms of governance structures. "the state jurisdiction and its government may be free while the citizens or subjects may not be free. Often they are not free." See his "Sovereignty in World Politics: A Glance at the Conceptual and Historical Landscape", *Political Studies*, Vol. 47, No. 3 (1999), p. 455. For Jackson's full conceptualisation of the failed state, see his *Quasi-States: Sovereignty, International Relations and the Third World* (Cambridge: Cambridge University Press, 1990).

53 Francis Fukuyama, *State Building: Governance and World Order in the Twenty-First Century* (London: Profile Books, 2004), p. 125.

54 For "solidarist" conceptions of intervention, see Nicholas Wheeler, *Saving Strangers, op. cit.*

55 On the state as "protection racket" see Charles Tilly, "War Making and State Making as Organised Crime", in P.B. Evans, D. Rueschemeyer and T. Skocpol (eds), *Bringing the State Back In* (Cambridge: Cambridge University Press, 1985), pp. 169–91. On the concept of "protection" in feminist thought, see Carol Pateman, *The Sexual Contract* (Cambridge: Polity Press, 1988).

56 For an investigation into the politics of the "protector/protected" dualism in the context of the politics of emergency, see Vivienne Jabri, "The limits of agency in times of emergency", in Jef Huysmans *et al*, *The Politics of Protection* (London and New York: Routledge, 2006), pp. 136–53.

57 Fukuyama, *State Building, op. cit.*

58 Michael Hardt and Antonio Negri, *Empire* (Cambridge, MA, and London: Harvard University Press, 2000).

59 David Campbell, *Politics Without Principle: Sovereignty, Ethics, and the Narratives of the Gulf War* (Boulder, CO, and London: Lynne Rienner Publishers, 1993).

60 For a discussion of the language of war, see Vivienne Jabri, *Discourses on Violence: Conflict Analysis Reconsidered* (Manchester: Manchester University Press, 1996), chapter 4.

61 For Judith Butler, this represented a championing of a "masculinized Western subject whose will immediately translates into a deed." See Judith Butler, "Contingent Foundations", in Benhabib *et al*, *Feminist Contentions* (London and New York: Routledge, 1995), p. 43.

62 The idea of "short, sharp, shock" emerged during the Thatcher era as a policy in the treatment of "young offenders" within the criminal justice system of the United Kingdom. The notion of "shock therapy" has been used in the context of development policy, and the term "shock and awe" as military strategy was used in the more recent invasion of Iraq in March 2003. See Vivienne Jabri, "Shock and Awe: Power and the Resistance of Art", *Millennium: Journal of International Studies*, Vol. 34, No. 3 (2006), pp. 819–39.

63 Tony Blair, "A New Generation Draws the Line", *Newsweek*, April 19th 1999. For a discussion of the genesis of this speech, see John Kampfner, *Blair's Wars* (London: Free Press, 2004), p. 52.

64 Alexandra Gheciu, "Civilising the Balkans, protecting Europe", in Jef Huysmans *et al*, *Politics of Protection, op. cit.*, p. 115.

65 For a critical evaluation of the concept of peace as governance, see Oliver Richmond, *The Transformation of Peace* (London and New York: Palgrave, 2005).

66 Michel Foucault, "Governmentality", in Michel Foucault, *Power, The Essential Works*, Vol. 3, edited by James D. Faubion, trans., Robert Hurley and others (London: Allen Lane, 2001), p. 220.

67 Richmond, *op. cit.*, p. 216.

68 Jean Elshtain, "International Justice as Equal Regard and the Use of Force", *Ethics and International Affairs*, Vol. 17, No. 2 (2003).

69 Richard Falk, "Legality and Legitimacy: the quest for principled flexibility and restraint", *Review of International Studies*, Vol. 31, Special Issue, December 2005, p. 34.

70 *Ibid.*, p. 50.

71 *Ibid.*, p. 37. Falk here refers to the *Kosovo Report*, Independent International Commission on Kosovo (Oxford: Oxford University Press, 2000) which highlighted the legitimacy for the use of force on the basis of the humanitarian emergency.

72 As Jean L. Cohen argues in reference to Hardt and Negri, and in seeking to make the case against cosmopolitan right trumping sovereign equality, "If one shifts to a political perspective, the sovereignty-based model of international law appears to be ceding not to cosmopolitan justice but to a different bid to restructure the world order: the project of empire." See Jean L. Cohen, "Whose Sovereignty? Empire Versus International Law", *Ethics and International Affairs*, Vol. 18, No. 3 (2004), p. 2.

73 Falk, *op. cit.*, p. 35.

74 For Agamben, "the state of exception has today reached its maximum worldwide deployment." See Giorgio Agamben, *State of Exception*, trans. Kevin Attell (Chicago and London: University of Chicago Press, 2005), p. 87.

75 See in particular, Allen Buchanan and Robert Keohane, "The Preventive Use of Force: A Cosmopolitan Institutional Proposal", *Ethics and International Affairs*, Vol. 18, No. 1 (2004), pp. 1–22.

76 See Martti Koskenniemi, "The Lady Doth Protest Too Much: Kosovo and the Turn to Ethics in International Law", *Modern Law Review*, Vol. 65, No. 2 (2002).

77 Agamben, *State of Exception, op. cit.*, p. 4.

78 *Ibid.*, p. 23.

79 Michael Dillon, "Cared to Death: The Biopoliticised Time of Your Life", *Foucault Studies*, No. 2 (2005), pp. 37–46. For another reading of invocations of security in relation to development, see Mark Duffield, *Global Governance and the New Wars: The Merging of Development and Security* (London: Zed Books, 2001).

80 All quotations from Sara Ahmed in her "Collective Feelings Or, The Impressions Left by Others", *Theory, Culture & Society*, Vol. 21, No. 2 (2004), pp. 25–42.

81 Michel Foucault, *The Will to Knowledge, History of Sexuality*, Vol. 1 (London: Penguin, 1998), p. 141.

82 Hardt and Negri, *Empire, op. cit.*, p. 33.

83 Giorgio Agamben, *Remnants of Auschwitz: The Witness and the Archive* (New York, NY: Zone Books, 1999).

84 *Ibid.*, p. 83.

85 *Ibid.*

86 *Ibid.*

87 Michel Foucault, *Society Must Be Defended*, trans. David Macey (London: Allen Lane, 2003).

88 *Ibid.*

89 *Ibid.*, p. 85.

90 Giorgio Agamben, *Homo Sacer: Sovereign Power and Bare Life*, trans. Daniel Heller-Roazen (Stanford, CA: Stanford University Press, 1998), p. 6.

91 Michel Foucault, *History of Sexuality, op. cit.*, p. 137.

92 Mitchell Dean, *Governmentality: Power and Rule in Modern Society* (London and New York, Sage, 1999), p. 132.

Chapter 5 War and the Politics of Cultural Difference

1 Raymond Williams, *Culture and Materialism* (London and New York: Verso, 2005), p. 38.

2 For investigations into the ways in which immigration controls in the European context are increasingly constructed in terms of combating terrorism, see chapters by Anastassia Tsoukala, "Looking at Migrants as Enemies", Laurent Bonelli, "The Control of the Enemy Within? Police Intelligence in the French Suburbs (*banlieues*) and its Relevance for Globalisation", and Ayse Ceyhan, "Policing by Dossier: Identification and Surveillance in an Era of Uncertainty and Fear", all in Didier Bigo and Elspeth Guild (eds), *Controlling Frontiers: Free Movement Into and Within Europe* (Ashgate Aldershot: 2005). On the specific anti-terrorism measures incorporated within UK domestic legislation and their implications for the liberal multicultural state, see Vivienne Jabri, "War, Security and the Liberal State", *Security Dialogue*, Vol. 37, No. 1 (2006), pp. 47–64.

3 Samuel P. Huntington, *The Clash of Civilizations and the Remaking of World Order* (New York: Simon and Schuster, 1996). For a powerful critique of

Huntington's civilisational division of the world, see Stephen Chan, *Out of Evil: New International Politics and Old Doctrines of War* (London: I.B. Tauris, 2005).

4   For such culturally essentialist discourses surrounding representations of the Middle East, see Edward Said, "Orientalism reconsidered", in Edward Said, *Reflections on Exile and Other Essays* (Cambridge, MA, and London: Harvard University Press, 2000). See also his "A Window on the World", *The Guardian*, 2nd August 2003, quoted in Chan, *Out of Evil*, *op. cit.*, p. 32.

5   I am grateful to James Der Derian for pointing this out to me.

6   See especially Arjun Appaduri, *Modernity at Large: Cultural Dimensions of Globalisation* (Minneapolis: University of Minnesota Press, 1996). Appaduri refers to "transnational cultural movements" and highlights their political implications. For an investigation into the politics of transnational movements in relation to Islamic groups, see Peter Mandaville, *Transnational Muslim Politics: Reimagining the Umma* (London and New York: Routledge, 2003).

7   Paul Gilroy, *After Empire: Melancholia or Convivial Culture* (London and New York: Routledge, 2004), p. 39.

8   Cultural identity constitutes both a relation to oneself as well as relations with others. Both are clearly interconnected. On cultural identity as an element in the articulations of self, see Homi Bhabha, *The Location of Culture* (London and New York: Routledge, 1994). For cultural difference as constitutive of relations with others, and specifically relations articulated in a politics of representation, see Edward Said, "The World, the Text, and the Critic", in Edward Said, *Power, Politics and Culture: Interviews with Edward Said*, edited by Gauri Viswanathan (London: Bloomsbury, 2004).

9   See Vivienne Jabri, "Explorations of Difference in Normative International Relations", in Vivienne Jabri and Eleanor O'Gorman (eds) *Women, Culture and International Relations* (Boulder, CO, and London: Lynne Rienner, 1999).

10   Homi Bhabha, *The Location of Culture, op. cit.*

11   For a discussion of Julia Kristeva's notion of the subject "in process", see "A conversation with Julia Kristeva", interview conducted by Ina Lipkowitz and Andrea Loselle in Ross M. Guberman (ed.), *Julia Kristeva Interviews* (New York: Columbia University Press, 1996), p. 26. For a discussion of this concept in the context of International Relations, see Vivienne Jabri, "Restyling the Subject of Responsibility in International Relations", *Millennium*, Vol. 27, No. 3 (1998), pp. 591–612.

12   Stuart Hall, "Introduction: Who Needs Identity", in Stuart Hall and Paul du Gay (eds), *Questions of Cultural Identity* (London and New York: Sage, 1996).

13   Nicolas Rose explores the implications of the "multiplication of the forms of political subjectivity" for efforts at the creation of a single "governmental" space. See his *Powers of Freedom: Reframing Political Thought* (Cambridge: Cambridge University Press, 1999), pp. 167–96.

14   Stuart Hall, *op. cit.*, p. 4.

15   Zygmunt Bauman, *Globalisation: The Human Consequences* (Cambridge: Polity Press, 1998), p. 13.

16   *Ibid.*, p. 17.

17   Homi Bhabha, *The Location of Culture, op. cit.*

18 On the "politics of representation", see David Campbell, *National Deconstruction: Violence, Identity and Justice in Bosnia* (Minneapolis: University of Minnesota Press, 1998).

19 Michel Foucault, "Truth and Power", interview with Alessandro Fontana and Pasquale Pasquino, in Michel Foucault, *Power/Knowledge*, edited by Colin Gordon (Edinburgh: Harvester Wheatsheaf, 1980), p. 114.

20 For the historically tense relationship between the discipline of International Relations and cultural difference, see Naeem Inayatullah and David Blaney, *International Relations and the Problem of Difference* (London and New York: Routledge, 2004). See also Stephen Chan, Peter Mandaville and Roland Bleiker, *The Zen of International Relations: IR Theory from East to West* (London: Palgrave, 2001).

21 Foucault, *Power/Knowledge, op. cit.*

22 *Ibid.*

23 Negib Mahfouz's *Cairo Trilogy* precisely portrays this social and political struggle that has its origins in the colonial period.

24 Inayatullah and Blaney, *op. cit.*, p. 117.

25 Edward Said, "The Arab-American War: The Politics of Information", in *The Politics of Dispossession* (London: Chatto and Windus, 1994), p. 298.

26 *Ibid.*

27 Julia Kristeva, *Powers of Horror* (New York: Columbia University Press, 1982), p. 4.

28 *Ibid.*, p. 1.

29 Gayatry Chakravorty Spivak, *A Critique of Postcolonial Reason: Toward a History of the Vanishing Present* (Cambridge, Mass, and London: Harvard University Press, 1999), p. 277.

30 Edward Said, "In the Shadow of the West", in Said, *Power, Politics, and Culture, op. cit.*, p. 40.

31 Edward Said, *Orientalism: Western Conceptions of the Orient* (London: Penguin, 1978), p. 291.

32 That particular conceptions of the "Arab" fed into the formulation of techniques of interrogation and torture, as now evident in relation to practices at Guantanamo and Abu Ghraib, is recorded by Seymour Hersh in his *Chain of Command: The Road from 9/11 to Abu Ghraib* (London: Allen Lane, 2004).

33 See Judith Butler, *Excitable Speech: The Politics of the Performative* (London and New York: Routledge, 1997).

34 Of particular interest here is a speech delivered by the British Chancellor of the Exchequer, Gordon Brown, wherein he appeared to suggest that British colonial rule in Africa could be read as a progressive force. The historian, Niall Furgesson has made similar claims. See Niall Ferguson, *Empire: How Britain Made the Modern World* (London: Penguin, 2004). For a more recent call for a "progressive" reading of British imperialism and the long history of "liberal imperialism", see Geoffrey Wheatcroft, "They should come out as imperialist and proud of it", *The Guardian*, May 10, 2006.

35 See especially Caroline Elkins, *Britain's Gulag: The Brutal End of Empire in Kenya* (London: Pimlico, 2005).

36 Of interest in this context is Charles Krauthammer, who in the Irving Kristol lecture to the American Enterprise Institute in Washington, declared "We will support democracy everywhere, but we will commit blood and

treasure only in places where there is strategic necessity – meaning, places central to the larger war against the existential enemy, the enemy that poses a global mortal threat to freedom", an enemy that Krauthammer identifies as "Arab-Islamic totalitarianism". Quoted by Louis Menand, *The New Yorker*, March 27th 2006. For an in-depth analysis of the neoconservative project in the United States, and its major outlet, *The National Interest*, see Michael C. Williams, "What is the National Interest? The Neoconservative Challenge in IR Theory", *European Journal of International Relations*, Vol. 11, No. 3 (2005), pp. 307–38.

37 For a discussion of "shock and awe", and the display of the excess of power, see Vivienne Jabri, "Shock and Awe: Power and the Resistance of Art", *Millennium*, 2006.

38 See Michel Foucault, *Abnormal, Lectures at the College de France 1974–1975*, edited by Valerio Marchetti and Antonella Salomoni, translated by Graham Burchell (New York: Picador, 2003), pp. 82–3.

39 As pointed out by Paul Gilroy, " 'Race' has to be socially and politically constructed and elaborate ideological work is done to secure and maintain the different forms of 'racialization' which have characterised capitalist development." See Paul Gilroy, *There Ain't No Black in the Union Jack* (London and New York: Routledge, 1987).

40 Linda Alcoff, "Towards a Phenomenology of Racial Embodiment", *Radical Philosophy*, 95 (1998), pp. 15–26.

41 Gilroy, *After Empire, op. cit.*, p. 42.

42 On injury directed against the body of the other, see Judith Butler, *Precarious Life: The Powers of Mourning and Violence* (London and New York: Verso, 2004), pp. 19–49.

43 Vivienne Jabri, "War, Security and the Liberal State", *op. cit.*

44 An example here is William Shawcross, "It's No Time to Quit Iraq: We're Winning", *Sunday Times*, 21st May 2006.

45 "Questions on Geography", in Michel Foucault, *Power/Knowledge, op. cit.*, p. 63.

46 Gayatry Chakravorty Spivak, *A Critique of Postcolonial Reason: Toward a History of the Vanishing Present* (Cambridge, MA, and London: Harvard University Press, 1999), p. 279.

47 Foucault's engagement with the non-west is explored in Vivienne Jabri, "The Social, the International, and the Racial in Michel Foucault's Analytics of War and their Application to the Present", paper presented at the conference of the International Studies Association, San Diego, March 2006.

48 Michel Foucault, "Questions on Geography'", in *Power/Knowledge, op. cit.*, p. 77.

49 Laclau refers to the "universal" as an "empty place": "universality can only be a particularity which defines itself in terms of a limitless exclusion." See Ernesto Laclau, "Universalism, Particularism and the Question of Identity", in Ernesto Laclau, *Emancipation(s)* (London and New York: Verso, 1996), p. 22.

50 See Martha Nussbaum's "Patriotism and Cosmopolitanism", in M. Nussbaum (ed.), *For Love of Country: Debating the Limits of Patriotism* (Boston, Mass: Beacon Press, 1966). For a critical evaluation of Nussbaum's distinctly feminist humanism, see Vivienne Jabri, "Feminist Ethics and Hegemonic Global Politics", *Alternatives*, Vol. 29, No. 3 (2004), pp. 265–84.

51 Sara Ahmed, "Collective Feelings Or the Impressions Left By Others", *Theory Culture & Society*, Vol. 21, No. 2 (2004), p. 36.

52 Tony Blair, "Not a Clash Between Civilisations, But a Clash About Civilisation", The Foreign Policy Centre, 21st March 2006. Accessed on 12/4/06 at www.fpc.org.uk/events/past/231.

53 *Ibid.*

54 *Ibid.*

55 Stephen Toulmin, *Cosmopolis: The Hidden Agenda of Modernity* (Chicago, Ill: University of Chicago Press, 1990), p. 75.

56 *Ibid.*

57 *Ibid.*

58 David Slater, *Geopolitics and the Postcolonial* (Oxford: Blackwell, 2004), p. 20.

Chapter 6   Beyond War and By Way of a Conclusion: Solidarity, the Politics of Peace and Political Cosmopolitanism

1 Jacques Derrida interviewed by Giovanna Borradori in her *Philosophy in a Time of Terror: Dialogues with Jurgen Habermas and Jacques Derrida* (Chicago, Ill, and London: University of Chicago Press, 2003), p. 131.

2 Here, the names of John Burton and Johan Galtung come to mind. See especially John Burton, *Deviance, Terrorism and War* (Oxford: Martin Robertson, 1979) and Johan Galtung, *Essays in Peace Research* (Copenhagen: Christian Ejlers, 1975).

3 Oliver Richmond, *The Transformation of Peace* (London and New York: Palgrave, 2005).

4 For an excellent exploration of order as a primary construct in the genealogy of discourse in International Relations, see Nicholas Rengger, *International Relations, Political Theory and the Problem of Order: Beyond International Relations Theory?* (London and New York: Routledge, 2000).

5 E.H. Carr and Hedley Bull are primary voices here. See especially, Hedley Bull, *The Anarchical Society* (London: Macmillan, 1977) and E.H. Carr, *The Twenty Years' Crisis 1919–1939* (London: Macmillan, 1939).

6 Christine Sylvester, *Feminist Theory and International Relations in a Postmodern Era* (Cambridge: Cambridge University Press, 1994).

7 Rob Walker, *Inside/Outside: International Relations as Political Theory* (Cambridge: Cambridge University Press, 1993).

8 For an excellent investigation into the modern legacy's rationalising imperatives in colonialism, see Nicholas Higgins, *Understanding the Chiapas Rebellion: Modernist Visions and the Invisible Indian* (Austin, TX: University of Texas Press, 2004).

9 Two publications that capture the debate on globalisation and the role of the state include David Held *et al*, *Global Transformations: Politics, Economics and Culture* (Cambridge: Polity Press, 1999) and Paul Hirst and Graham Thompson, *Globalisation in Question* (Cambridge: Polity Press, 1999).

10 For a prescient exploration of late modern identities see Zygmunt Bauman's *Identity* (Cambridge: Polity Press, 2004).

11 For such different interpretations of the consequences of late modern glob-
alisation, see Mary Kaldor, *Global Civil Society: An Answer to War*
(Cambridge: Polity Press, 2003), John Keane, *Global Civil Society?*
(Cambridge: Cambridge University Press, 2003), and Saskia Sassen,
Globalisation and Its Discontents (New York: The New Press, 1999).

12 Of specific interest here are Theodor Adorno and Max Horkheimer's
Dialectic of Enlightenment (London and New York: Verso, 1997) and Michel
Foucault's *Discipline and Punish* (London: Penguin, 1991).

13 See chapters by Michael Dillon and Rob Walker in David Campbell and
Michael Dillon (eds) *The Political Subject of Violence* (Manchester University
Press, 1993). See also Christopher Coker, "Savage Wars of Peace: The West
Encounters the Non-Western World" in his *War and the Twentieth Century*
(London, 1994).

14 Rob Walker, *Inside/Outside, op. cit.*

15 As formulated by Anthony Giddens in *Modernity and Self Identity*
(Cambridge: Polity Press, 1991).

16 For a rich exposition of the interplay between technological innovation and
the dispersal of power, see Manuel Castells, *The Rise of the Network Society*,
Vol. 1 *The Information Age, Economy, Society and Culture* (Oxford: Blackwell
Publishers, 2000).

17 Edward Said's renditions on representations of the cultural other are espe-
cially important in this context. See his *Orientalism* (London: Penguin
Books, 1978, 2003) and *Culture and Imperialism* (London: Chatto and
Windus, 1993). See also Gayatry Spivak's *A Critique of Postcolonial Reason*
(Cambridge, MA, and London: Harvard University Press, 1999), for her
exploration of representations of modernity's "other".

18 When the Kosovan population, for example, was subjected for years to the
most extreme condition of exclusion from all social institutions, their non-
violent resistance, along with that of human rights organisations in
Belgrade, drew no significant official support from Western government,
and specifically those that later came to be involved in the "rescue" of the
Kosovars through war.

19 Hannah Arendt, *The Human Condition* (Chicago, Ill, and London: University
of Chicago Press, 1998), p. 198.

20 See especially Rob Walker, *One World Many Worlds: Struggles for a Just World
Peace* (Boulder, CO, and London: Lynne Rienner and Zed, 1988).

21 My exploration of the concept of "solidarity" in this chapter derives from
earlier papers presented to the "Solidarity" Workshop funded by the British
International Studies Association and convened by Martin Weber, formerly
of the Universities of Aberdeen and Oxford Brooks, now of the University
of Queensland. I am grateful to Martin Weber for his comments on an
earlier paper, "Solidarity and Spheres of Culture", presented at Oxford
Brooks in 2005.

22 For Chantal Mouffe, any conception of pluralism that misses "the dimen-
sion of the *political*", negates relations of power and antagonism, relations
that what she calls "radical democratic politics" must take into account.
See Chantal Mouffe, "Democracy, Power, and the 'Political' ", in Seyla
Benhabib (ed.), *Democracy and Difference: Contesting the Boundaries of the
Political* (Princeton, NJ: Princeton University Press, 1996), p. 247. Arash

Abizadeh arguing against Schmittian inspired conceptions of the political, suggests that such particularistic conceptions of solidarity, those that assume an "us" versus "them" scenario, derive from a "reification" of sovereignty and nationalist doctrines on community. See his "Does Collective Identity Presuppose an Other? On the Alleged Incoherence of Global Solidarity", *American Political Science Review*, Vol. 99, No. 1, 2005, pp. 45–60.

23 This distinctly Schumpeterian idea, that liberal democracy is ultimately about the procedural regulation of conflict, runs through liberal thought. See Mouffe, "Democracy, Power, and the 'Political'", *op. cit.*

24 Jurgen Habermas, "Three Normative Models of Democracy", in Seyla Benhabib (ed.) *Democracy and Difference* (Princeton, NJ: Princeton University Press, 1996), p. 21. Clearly, the republican view of the liberal democratic state places greater emphasis on the idea of liberty as a distinctly cultural formation the protections for which are formally enshrined in a constitution. See Quentin Skinner, *Liberty Before Liberalism* (Cambridge: Cambridge University Press, 1988).

25 The European Union is hence clearly an important location wherein the formative assumption has been that the establishment of governmental institutions beyond the state can, ultimately, be generative of a European social consensus, a European political community.

26 The ideal of individual autonomy is present in the writings of Kant, Rousseau and Mill and is reflected in contemporary renditions on liberal thought. See, for example, Joseph Raz, *The Morality of Freedom* (Cambridge: Cambridge University Press, 1988), and Stanley Benn, *A Theory of Freedom* (Cambridge: Cambridge University Press, 1988).

27 For a powerful critique of "toleration" as the linchpin of liberal thought and an argument for "modus vivendi" within the actuality of pluralist societies, see John Gray, "Pluralism and Toleration in Contemporary Political Philosophy", *Political Studies*, Vol. 48 (2000), pp. 323–33.

28 Raymond Guess, "Liberalism and Its Discontents", *Political Theory*, Vol. 30, No. 3, 2002, p. 326.

29 For a prescient critique of a "European political culture", see Dorte Andersen, "The Paradox of 'the people' – Cultural identity and European integration", *Radical Philosophy*, May–June 2003.

30 Habermas and Derrida reiterate the desire for a return of Europe's Enlightenment values in Giovanna Borradori, *Philosophy in a Time of Terror: Dialogues with Jurgen Habermas and Jacques Derrida*, *op. cit.*

31 The Preamble to the European Constitution refers to the "cultural, religious, and humanist inheritance of Europe, from which have developed the universal values of the inviolable and inalienable rights of the human person, freedom, democracy, equality, and the rule of law...". See Treaty Establishing a Constitution for Europe, *Official Journal of the European Union*, C310, Vol. 47, 16122004. http://europa.eu.int/eur-lex/lex.JOHtml.do?uri= OJ:C:2004:310:SOM:EN:HTML. Accessed 17th August 2005.

32 See John Rawls, *Political Liberalism* (New York, NY: Columbia University Press, 1993).

33 Walker, *One World Many Worlds*, *op. cit.*, p. 102.

34 All quotations from Walker, *ibid.*

35 This conception of cosmopolitanism is perhaps best articulated in David Held's *Democracy and the Global Order: From the Modern State to Cosmopolitan Governance* (Stanford, CA: Stanford University Press, 1995). Andrew Linklater's conception of a post-Westphalian political community also exemplifies a more dialogically based conception of the cosmopolitan ethos. See his *Tranformation of Political Community* (Cambridge: Polity Press, 1998).

36 Fred Dallmayr, "Cosmopolitanism: Moral and Political", *Political Theory*, Vol. 31, No. 3, 2003, p. 427.

37 Dallmayr makes this crucial distinction between "moral" and "political" cosmopolitanism. See his "Cosmopolitanism: Moral and Political", *ibid*.

38 Bonnie Honig, "Difference, Dilemmas, and the Politics of Home", in Seyla Benhabib (ed.), *Democracy and Difference: Contesting Boundaries of the Political* (Princeton, NJ: Princeton University Press, 1996), p. 258.

39 Ash Amin, "Multi-ethnicity and the Idea of Europe", *Theory, Culture & Society*, Vol. 21, No. 2, 2004, pp. 1–2.

40 Ash Amin, *ibid*., p. 2.

41 Ash Amin, *ibid*., p. 2.

42 Etienne Balibar, *Politics and the Other Scene* (London: Verso, 2002), p. 148.

43 Balibar, *ibid*., p. 149.

44 Balibar, *ibid*., p. 171.

45 Michel Foucault, "Governmentality", in Michel Foucault, *Power, The Essential Works*, Vol. 3, ed. James D. Faubion (London: Allen Lane, 2001).

46 Manuel Castells, *The Power of Identity* (Oxford: Blackwell Publishers, 2003).

47 Balibar, *op. cit*., p. 161.

48 See debate in Joshua Cohen, Matthew Howard, and Martha Nussbaum (eds) *Is Multiculturalism Bad for Women* (Princeton, NJ: Princeton University Press, 1999).

49 Balibar, *op. cit*., pp. 163–4.

50 See Jacques Derrida's *Spectres of Marx* (London: Routledge, 1994).

51 Balibar, *op. cit*., p. 165.

52 Balibar, p. 167.

53 Balibar, p. 168.

54 Balibar, p. 170.

55 I am grateful to Martin Weber for pointing me to the concept of "methodological territorialism".

56 See Balibar's "Difference, Otherness, Exclusion", *Parallax*, Vol. 11, No. 1 (2005), pp. 19–34. I am grateful to Claudia Aradau for pointing me to this article.

57 For an excellent exploration of philosophies of negativity, see Diana Coole, *Negativity and Politics* (London: Routledge, 2000).

58 Terms I borrow once again from Julia Kristeva.

Bibliography

Abizadeh, Arash, "Does Collective Identity Presuppose an Other? On the Alleged Incoherence of Global Solidarity", *American Political Science Review*, Vol. 99, No. 1, 2005, pp. 45–60.

Adorno, Theodor W., *Critical Models: Interventions and Catchwords*, translated by Henry W. Pickford (New York: Columbia University Press, 1998).

Adorno, Theodor and Max Horkheimer, *Dialectic of Enlightenment* (London and New York: Verso, 1979).

Agamben, Giorgio, *Homo Sacer: Sovereign Power and Bare Life*, trans. D. Heller-Roazen (Stanford, CA: Stanford University Press, 1995).

Agamben, Giorgio, *Remnants of Auschwitz: The Witness and the Archive* (New York, NY: Zone Books, 1999).

Agamben, Giorgio, *State of Exception* (Chicago, Ill, and London: Chicago University Press, 2005).

Ahmed, Sara, "Collective Feelings Or, The Impressions Left by Others", *Theory, Culture & Society*, Vol. 21, No. 2 (2004), pp. 25–42.

Alcoff, Linda, "Towards a Phenomenology of Racial Embodiment", *Radical Philosophy*, 95 (1998).

Amin, Ash, "Multi-ethnicity and the Idea of Europe", *Theory, Culture & Society*, Vol. 21, No. 2 (2004).

Andersen, Dorte, "The Paradox of 'the people' – Cultural identity and European integration", *Radical Philosophy*, May–June 2003.

Annan, Kofi, "In Larger Freedom: Towards Development, Security and Human Rights for All", *Report of the Secretary-General*, A/59/2005, 21 March 2005.

Appaduri, Arjun, *Modernity at Large: Cultural Dimensions of Globalisation* (Minneapolis: University of Minnesota Press, 1996).

Arendt, Hannah, *The Human Condition* (Chicago, Ill, and London: University of Chicago Press, 1998).

Arendt, Hannah, *On Violence* (New York and London: Harcourt Brace and Co., 1970).

Arendt, Hannah, *Men in Dark Times* (New York and London: Harcourt, Brace and Company, 1968).

Armitage, Simon, *Killing Time* (London: Faber and Faber, 1999).

Bacevitch, Andrew, *American Empire: The Realities and Consequences of U.S. Diplomacy* (Cambridge, MA: Harvard, 2002).

Balibar, Etienne, *Politics and the Other Scene* (London: Verso, 2002).

Balibar, Etienne, "Difference, Otherness, Exclusion", *Parallax*, Vol. 11, No. 1 (2005).

Barnett, Michael, *Eyewitness to a Genocide: The United Nations and Rwanda* (Ithaca and London: Cornell University Press, 2002).

Barnett, Michael and Raymond Duvall, "Power in International Politics", *International Organisation*, Vol. 59, Winter (2005).

Bartelsen, Jens, *A Genealogy of Sovereignty* (Cambridge: Cambridge University Press, 1995).

Bauman, Zygmunt, *Modernity and the Holocaust* (Cambridge: Polity Press, 1989).

Bauman, Zygmunt, *Postmodern Ethics* (Oxford: Blackwell, 1993).

Bauman, Zygmunt, *Globalisation: The Human Consequences* (Cambridge: Polity Press, 1998).

Bauman, Zygmunt, *Identity* (Cambridge: Polity Press, 2004).

Beck, Ulrich, *The Reinvention of Politics: Rethinking Modernity in the Global Social Order* (Cambridge: Polity Press, 1997).

Benjamin, Walter "Critique of Violence", in *Selected Writings*, Vol. 1: 1913–1926, edited by Marcus Bullock and Michael W. Jennings (Cambridge MA, and London: Harvard University Press, 1996).

Benjamin, Walter, "Theses on the Philosophy of History", in *Illuminations*, edited with an introduction by Hannah Arendt, translated by Harry Zorn (London: Pimlico, 1999).

Benn, Stanley, *A Theory of Freedom* (Cambridge: Cambridge University Press, 1988).

Best, Geoffrey, *War and Law* (Oxford: Oxford University Press, 1994).

Bhabha, Homi, *The Location of Culture* (London and New York: Routledge, 1994).

Bigo, Didier and Elspeth Guild (eds), *Controlling Frontiers: Free Movement Into and Within Europe* (Aldershot: Ashgate, 2005).

Blair, Tony, "A New Generation Draws the Line", *Newsweek*, April 19th 1999.

Blair, Tony, "Not a Clash Between Civilisations, But a Clash About Civilisation", The Foreign Policy Centre, 21st March 2006.

Bohman, James and Matthias Lutz-Bachmann, "Introduction", in J. Bohman and M. Lutz-Bachmann (eds), *Perpetual Peace: Essays on Kant's Cosmopolitan Ideal* (Cambridge, MA, and London: The MIT Press, 1997).

Bonelli, Laurent, "The Control of the Enemy Within? Police Intelligence in the French Suburbs (banlieues) and its Relevance for Globalisation", in Didier Bigo and Elspeth Guild (eds), *Controlling Frontiers: Free Movement Into and Within Europe* (Aldershot: Ashgate, 2005).

Borradori, Giovanna, *Philosophy in a Time of Terror: Dialogues with Jurgen Habermas and Jacques Derrida* (Chicago, Ill, and London: University of Chicago Press, 2003).

Boutros-Ghali, Boutros, "An Agenda for Peace: preventive Diplomacy, Peacemaking and Peacekeeping" (New York: United Nations, 1992).

Buchanan, Allen, and Robert Keohane, "The Preventive Use of Force: A Cosmopolitan Institutional Proposal", *Ethics and International Affairs*, Vol. 18, No. 1 (2004).

Bull, Hedley, *The Anarchical Society: A Study of World Order* (London: Macmillan, 1977).

Burton, John, *Deviance, Terrorism and War* (Oxford: Martin Robertson, 1979).

Butler, Judith, "Contingent Foundations", in Seyla Benhabib, *et al*, *Feminist Contentions: A Philosophical Exchange* (London and New York: Routledge, 1995).

Butler, Judith, *Excitable Speech: A Politics of the Performative* (London and New York: Routledge, 1997).

Butler, Judith "Explanation and Exonation", *Theory and Event*, Vol. 5, No. 4 (2002).

Butler, Judith, *Precarious Life: The Powers of Mourning and Violence* (London and New York: Verso, 2004).

Campbell, David, *Politics Without Principle* (Boulder, CO, and London: Lynne Rienner Publishers, 1993).

Campbell, David, *National Deconstruction: Violence, Identity and Justice in Bosnia* (Minneapolis and London: University of Minnesota Press, 1998).

Campbell, David and Michael Dillon (eds) *The Political Subject of Violence* (Manchester University Press, 1993).

Carr, E.H., *The Twenty Years' Crisis 1919–1939* (London: Macmillan, 1939).

Carr, E.H., *Nationalism and After* (London: Macmillan, 1945).

Castells, Manuel, *The Rise of the Network Society*, Vol. 1 *The Information Age, Economy, Society and Culture* (Oxford: Blackwell Publishers, 2000).

Castells, Manuel, *The Power of Identity* (Oxford: Blackwell Publishers, 2003).

Cavafy, C.P., *Collected Poems*, trans. Edmund Keeley and Philip Sherrard (London: Chatto and Windus, 1998).

Caygill, Howard, "Violence, Civility and the Predicaments of Philosophy", in David Campbell and Michael Dillon (eds), *The Political Subject of Violence* (Manchester: Manchester University Press, 1993).

Ceyhan, Ayse, "Policing by Dossier: Identification and Surveillance in an Era of Uncertainty and Fear", in Didier Bigo and Elspeth Guild (eds), *Controlling Frontiers: Free Movement Into and Within Europe* (Ashgate Aldershot: 2005).

Clausewitz, Carl von, *On War*, edited and translated by M. Howard and P. Paret (Princeton, NJ: Princeton University Press, 1976).

Chan, Stephen, Peter Mandaville and Roland Bleiker, *The Zen of International Relations: IR Theory from East to West* (London: Palgrave, 2001).

Chan, Stephen, *Out of Evil: New International Politics and Old Doctrines of War* (London: I.B. Tauris, 2005).

Cohen, Joshua, Matthew Howard, and Martha Nussbaum (eds) *Is Multiculturalism Bad for Women* (Princeton, NJ: Princeton University Press, 1999).

Coker, Christopher, *War and the Twentieth Century* (London, 1994).

Coker, Christopher, *Humane Warfare* (London and New York: Routledge, 2001).

Cohen, Jean L., "Whose Sovereignty? Empire Versus International Law", *Ethics and International Affairs*, Vol. 18, No. 3 (2004).

Coole, Diana, *Negativity and Politics* (London: Routledge, 2000).

Crang, Mike and Nigel Thrift, "Introduction", in Mike Crang and Nigel Thrift (eds), *Thinking Space* (London and New York: Routledge, 2000).

Dallmayr, Fred, "Cosmopolitanism: Moral and Political", *Political Theory*, Vol. 31, No. 3 (2003).

Dean, Mitchell, *Governmentality: Power and Rule in Modern Society* (London and New York, Sage, 1999).

Deleuze, Gilles, *Foucault*, translated by Sean Hand (Minneapolis and London: University of Minnesota Press, 1988).

Der Derian, James, "9/11: Before, After and In Between", in Craig Calhoun, Paul Price and Ashley Timmer (eds), *Understanding September 11* (New York: The New Press, 2002).

Derrida, Jacques, *Spectres of Marx* (London: Routledge, 1994).

Dessler, David, "Beyond Correlations: Towards a Causal Theory of War", *International Studies Quarterly*, Vol. 35 (1991), pp. 337–55.

Dillon, Michael, "Criminalising Social and Political Violence Internationally", *Millennium*, Vol. 27, No. 3 (1998), pp. 543–69.

Dillon, Michael, "Cared to Death: The Biopoliticised Time of Your Life", *Foucault Studies*, No. 2 (2005).

Doyle, Michael, *Ways of War and Peace* (New York: Norton, 1997).

Duffield, Mark, *Global Governance and the New Wars: The Merging of Development and Security* (London: Zed Books, 2001).

Dussel, Enrique, *The Underside of Modernity* (New York: Humanity Books, 1998).

Elden, Stuart, "The War of Races and the Constitution of the State: Foucault's 'il faut defender la societe' and the Politics of Calculation", *Boundary*, Vol. 2, p. 151.

Elkins, Caroline, *Britain's Gulag: The Brutal End of Empire in Kenya* (London: Pimlico, 2005).

Elshtain, Jean Bethke (ed.), *Just War Theory* (Oxford: Blackwell, 1992).

Elshtain, Jean Bethke, "International Justice as Equal Regard and the Use of Force", *Ethics and International Affairs*, Vol. 17, No. 2 (2003).

Falk, Richard, "Legality and legitimacy: the quest for principled flexibility and restraint", *Review of International Studies*, Vol. 31 (2005).

Fanon, Frantz, *The Wretched of the Earth*, trans. Constance Farrington (Harmondsworth: Penguin Books, 1967).

Ferguson, Niall, *Empire: How Britain Made the Modern World* (London: Penguin, 2004).

Foucault, Michel, *The Archaeology of Knowledge*, trans. A.M. Sheridan Smith (London and New York: Routledge, 1997).

Foucault, Michel, *Discipline and Punish*, translated by Alan Sheridan (London: Penguin, 1977).

Foucault, Michel, *The Will to Knowledge, History of Sexuality*, Vol. 1, translated by Robert Hurley (London: Penguin, 1978).

Foucault, Michel, *The Use of Pleasure*, Vol. 2 of *The History of Sexuality*, trans. Robert Hurley (London: Penguin Books, 1992).

Foucault, Michel, *Society Must Be Defended*, translated by David Macey (London: Allen Lane, 2003).

Foucault, Michel, "Truth and Power", in *Power/Knowledge*, edited by Colin Gordon (New York and London: Prentice Hall, 1980).

Foucault, Michel, "Questions on Geography", in Michel Foucault, *Power/Knowledge*, edited by Colin Gordon (New York and London: Prentice Hall, 1980).

Foucault, Michel, "What is Enlightenment", in Michel Foucault, *Ethics: Subjectivity and Truth*, Vol. 1 of The Essential Works of Foucault, edited by Paul Rabinow (New York: The New Press, 1997).

Foucault, Michel, "What is Enlightenment", in Paul Rabinow (ed.), *The Foucault Reader* (London: Penguin, 1984).

Foucault, Michel, "Governmentality", in Michel Foucault, *Power, The Essential Works*, Vol. 3, edited by James D. Faubion, trans., Robert Hurley and others (London: Allen Lane, 2001).

Foucault, Michel, *Abnormal, Lectures at the College de France 1974–1975*, edited by Valerio Marchetti and Antonella Salomoni, translated by Graham Burchell (New York: Picador, 2003).

Franck, Thomas, "Who Killed Article 2 (4)? Or: Changing Norms Governing the Use of Force by States", *American Journal of International Law*, Vol. 64 (1970).

Freedman, Lawrence, "The Age of Liberal Wars", *Review of International Studies*, Vol. 31 (2005).

Fukuyama, Francis, *The End of History and the Last Man* (London: Penguin, 1993).

Francis Fukuyama, *State Building: Governance and World Order in the Twenty-First Century* (London: Profile Books, 2004).

Galtung, Johan, "Violence, Peace, and Peace Research", *Journal of Peace Research*, Vol. 6, No. 3 (1969), pp. 167–91.

Galtung, Johan, *Essays in Peace Research* (Copenhagen: Christian Ejlers, 1975).

Gheciu, Alexandra, "Civilising the Balkans, protecting Europe", in Jef Huysmans *et al, Politics of Protection* (London and New York: Routledge, 2006).

Giddens, Anthony, *The Constitution of Society* (Cambridge: Polity Press, 1984).

Giddens, Anthony, *The Nation-State and Violence* (Cambridge: Polity, 1985).

Giddens, Anthony, *The Consequences of Modernity* (Cambridge: Polity Press, 1990).

Giddens, Anthony, *Modernity and Self-identity: Self and Society in the Late Modern Age* (Cambridge: Polity Press, 1991).

Gilpin, Robert, *War and Change in World Politics* (Cambridge: Cambridge University Press, 1981).

Gilroy, Paul, *There Ain't No Black in the Union Jack* (London and New York: Routledge, 1987).

Gilroy, Paul, *After Empire: Melancholia or Convivial Culture* (London and New York: Routledge, 2004).

Glennon, M.J., "The New Interventionism: The Search for a Just International Law", *Foreign Affairs*, Vol. 78, No. 3 (1999).

Gray, John, "Pluralism and Toleration in Contemporary Political Philosophy", *Political Studies*, Vol. 48 (2000).

Gregory, Derek, *The Colonial Present* (Oxford: Blackwell, 2004).

Grotius, H., *The Law of War and Peace* (New York: Bobbs-Merrill, 1925).

Guberman, Ross M. (ed.), *Julia Kristeva Interviews* (New York: Columbia University Press, 1996).

Guess, Raymond, "Liberalism and Its Discontents", *Political Theory*, Vol. 30, No. 3 (2002).

Habermas, Jurgen, *Knowledge and Human Interests* (Boston: Beacon Press, 1972).

Habermas, Jurgen, *The Past as Future*, interviewed by Michael Haller, translated and edited by Max Pensky (Cambridge: Polity Press, 1994).

Habermas, Jurgen, "Interpreting the Fall of a Monument", *German Law Journal*, Vol. 4, No. 7, July 2003, p. 2; accessed at http://www.germanlawjournal.com.

Habermas, Jurgen, *The Philosophical Discourse of Modernity*, trans. Frederick Lawrence (Cambridge: Polity Press, 1987).

Habermas, Jurgen, *The Inclusion of the Other: Studies in Political Theory*, edited by Ciaran Cronin and Pablo de Greiff (Cambridge, Mass: MIT Press, 1998).

Habermas, "Kant's Idea of Perpetual Peace, with the Benefit of Two Hundred Years' Hindsight", in James Bohman and Matthias Lutz-Bachmann (eds), *Perpetual Peace: Essays on Kant's Cosmopolitan Ideal* (Cambridge, MA, and London: The MIT Press, 1997).

Habermas, Jurgen, "Three Normative Models of Democracy", in Seyla Benhabib (ed.) *Democracy and Difference* (Princeton, NJ: Princeton University Press, 1996).

Hall, Stuart "Introduction: Who Needs Identity", in Stuart Hall and Paul du Gay (eds), *Questions of Cultural Identity* (London and New York: Sage, 1996).

Hardt, Michael and Antonio Negri, *Empire* (Cambridge, MA, and London: Harvard University Press, 2000).

Hardt, Michael and Antonio Negri, *Multitude* (London: Hamish Hamilton, 2005).

Harriman, Ed, "Where Has all the Money Gone?", *London Review of Books*, Vol. 27, No. 13, 7 July 2005.

Hay, C. and D. Marsh (eds), *Demystifying Globalisation* (Basingstoke: Macmillan, 2000).

Hegel, G.W.F., *Elements of the Philosophy of Right*, trans. H.B. Nisbet (Cambridge: Cambridge University Press, 1991).

Held, David, *Democracy and the Global Order: From the Modern State to Cosmopolitan Governance* (Stanford, CA: Stanford University Press, 1995).

Held, David, *et al* (eds), *Global Transformations: Politics, Economics and Culture* (Cambridge: Polity Press, 1999).

Held, David, *Global Covenant: The Social Democratic Alternative to the Washington Consensus* (Cambridge: Polity Press, 2004).

Hersh, Seymour, *Chain of Command* (London: Penguin, 2004).

Higgins, Nicholas, *Understanding the Chiapas Rebellion: Modernist Visions and the Invisible Indian* (Austin, TX: University of Texas Press, 2004).

Hirst, Paul and Graham, Thompson, *Globalisation in Question* (Cambridge: Polity Press, 1999).

Hollis, Martin, *The Philosophy of Social Science: An Introduction* (Cambridge: Cambridge University Press, 1994).

Hollis, Martin and Steve Smith, *Explaining and Understanding International Relations* (Oxford: Clarendon Press, 1990).

Honig, Bonnie, "Difference, Dilemmas, and the Politics of Home", in Seyla Benhabib (ed.), *Democracy and Difference: Contesting Boundaries of the Political* (Princeton, NJ: Princeton University Press, 1996).

Howard, Michael, *War and the Liberal Conscience* (London: Temple Smith, 1978).

Huntington, Samuel P., *The Clash of Civilizations and the Remaking of World Order* (New York: Simon and Schuster, 1996).

Huysmans, Jef, "Discussing Sovereignty and Transnational Politics", in Neil Walker (ed.), *Sovereignty in Transition* (Oxford: Hart, 2003).

Huysmans, Jef, Andrew Dobson, and Raia Prokhovnik (eds) *The Politics of Protection* (London and New York: Routledge, 2006).

Inayatullah, Naeem and David Blaney, *International Relations and the Problem of Difference* (London and New York: Routledge, 2004).

Jabri, Vivienne, *Discourses on Violence* (Manchester: Manchester University Press, 1996).

Jabri, Vivienne, "Restyling the Subject of Responsibility in International Relations", *Millennium*, Vol. 27, No. 3 (1998).

Jabri, Vivienne, "Explorations of Difference in Normative International Relations", in Vivienne Jabri and Eleanor O'Gorman (eds) *Women, Culture and International Relations* (Boulder, CO, and London: Lynne Rienner, 1999).

Jabri, Vivienne, "Feminist Ethics and Hegemonic Global Politics", *Alternatives*, Vol. 29, No. 3 (2004).

Jabri, Vivienne, "Critical Thought and Political Agency in Time of War", *International Relations*, Vol. 19, No. 1 (2005), pp. 70–8.

Jabri, Vivienne, "War, Security and the Liberal State", *Security Dialogue*, Vol. 37, No. 1 (2006).

Jabri, Vivienne, "The limits of agency in times of emergency", in Jef Huysmans *et al, The Politics of Protection* (London and New York: Routledge, 2006).

Jabri, Vivienne, "Shock and Awe: Power and the Resistance of Art", *Millennium: Journal of International Studies*, Vol. 34, No. 3 (2006), pp. 819–39.

Jabri, Vivienne, "The Social, the International, and the Racial in Michel Foucault's Analytics of War and their Application to the Present", paper presented at the conference of the International Studies Association, San Diego, March 2006.

Jackson, Robert, "Sovereignty in World Politics: A Glance at the Conceptual and Historical Landscape", *Political Studies*, Vol. 47, No. 3 (1999).

Jackson, Robert, *Quasi-States: Sovereignty, International Relations and the Third World* (Cambridge: Cambridge University Press, 1990).

Joas, Hans, *War and Modernity* (Cambridge: Polity, 2003).

Kaldor, Mary, *New and Old Wars: Organised Violence in a Global Era* (Cambridge: Polity Press, 1999).

Kaldor, Mary, "Beyond Militarism, Arms Races, and Arms Control", in Craig Calhoun *et al* (eds), *Understanding September 11* (New York: The New Press, 2002).

Kaldor, Mary, *Global Civil Society: An Answer to War* (Cambridge: Polity Press, 2003).

Kampfner, John, *Blair's Wars* (London: Free Press, 2004).

Kant, Immanuel, *Political Writings*, edited by Hans Reiss, trans. H.B. Nisbet (Cambridge University Press, Cambridge, 1970).

John Keane, *Global Civil Society?* (Cambridge: Cambridge University Press, 2003).

Kelsen, Hans, *The Law of the United Nations* (New York: Praeger, 1950).

Koskenniemi, Martti, "The Lady Doth Protest Too Much: Kosovo and the Turn to Ethics in International Law", *Modern Law Review*, Vol. 65, No. 2 (2002).

Kristeva, Julia, *Powers of Horror* (New York: Columbia University Press, 1982).

Laclau, Ernesto, "Universalism, Particularism and the Question of Identity", in Ernesto Laclau, *Emancipation(s)* (London and New York: Verso, 1996).

Lawrence, Bruce (ed.) *Messages to the World: The Statements of Osama Bin Laden*, trans. James Howarth (London: Verso, 2005).

Leander, Anna, "Privatizing the Politics of Protection: Military Companies and the Definition of Security Concerns", in Jef Huysmans, *et al* (eds), *The Politics of Protection* (London and New York: Routledge, 2006).

Linklater, Andrew, *The Transformation of Political Community* (Cambridge: Polity Press, 1998).

Mahfouz, Naguib, *The Cairo Trilogy* (New York: Everyman's Library, 2001).

Mandaville, Peter, *Transnational Muslim Politics: Reimagining the Umma* (London and New York: Routledge, 2003).

Mann, Michael, *The Sources of Social Power*, Vol. II (Cambridge: Cambridge University Press, 1993).

Mann, Michael, *The Dark Side of Democracy: Explaining Ethnic Cleansing* (Cambridge: Cambridge University Press, 2005).

Marcuse, Herbert, *Negations: Essays in Critical Theory* (London: Free Association Books, 1988).

Marsh, David and Gerry Stoker (eds), *Theory and Methods in Political Science* (London and New York: Palgrave Macmillan, 2002).

McCarthy, Thomas, "Introduction", in Jurgen Habermas, *The Philosphical Discourse of Modernity*, trans. Frederick Lawrence (Cambridge: Polity Press, 1987).

Mesquita, B. Bueno de, *The War Trap* (New Haven, CT: Yale University Press, 1981).

Moravcsik, Andrew M., *Liberalism and International Relations Theory* (Centre for International Affairs, Harvard University, Working Paper No. 92-6, 1992).

Moravcsik, Andrew, M., "Taking Preferences Seriously: A Liberal Theory of International Politics", *International Organisation*, Vol. 51 (1997).

Mouffe, Chantal, "Democracy, Power, and the 'Political' ", in Seyla Benhabib (ed), *Democracy and Difference: Contesting the Boundaries of the Political* (Princeton, NJ: Princeton University Press, 1996).

Nardin, Terry (ed.) *The Ethics of War and Peace: Religious and Secular Perspectives* (Princeton, NJ: Princeton University Press, 1996).

Neumann, Iver B., *Uses of the Other: The "East" in European Identity Formation* (Manchester: Manchester University Press, 1999).

Nicholson, Michael, *Rationality and the Analysis of Conflict* (Cambridge: Cambridge University Press, 1992).

Nussbaum, Martha, "Patriotism and Cosmopolitanism", in M. Nussbaum (ed.), *For Love of Country: Debating the Limits of Patriotism* (Boston, Mass: Beacon Press, 1996).

Paris, Roland, "International Peacebuilding and the 'Mission Civilisatrice'", *Review of International Studies*, Vol. 28, No. 4 (2002).

Paris, Roland, *At War's End* (Cambridge: Cambridge University Press, 2004).

Pateman, Carol, *The Sexual Contract* (Cambridge: Polity Press, 1988).

Pick, Daniel, *War Machine: The Rationalisation of Slaughter in the Modern Age* (New Haven, CT, and London: Yale University Press, 1993).

Pufendorf, S. von, *The Law of Nature and Nations* (Oxford: Clarendon Press, 1934)

Rawls, John, *Political Liberalism* (New York, NY: Columbia University Press, 1993).

Raz, Joseph, The *Morality of Freedom* (Cambridge: Cambridge University Press, 1988).

Rengger, Nicholas, *International Relations, Political Theory and the Problem of Order* (London and New York: Routledge, 2000).

Reus-Smit, Christian, "Liberal Hierarchy and the License to Use Force", *Review of International Studies*, Vol. 31, Special Issue, December (2005).

Richmond, Oliver, *The Transformation of Peace* (London and New York: Palgrave, 2005).

Rose, Nicolas, *Powers of Freedom: Reframing Political Thought* (Cambridge: Cambridge University Press, 1999).

Roy, Olivier, *Globalised Islam: The Search for a New Ummah* (London: Hurst, 2004).

Said, Edward, *Orientalism: Western Conceptions of the Orient* (London: Penguin, 1978), p. 291.

Said, Edward, "Orientalism reconsidered", in Edward Said, *Reflections on Exile and Other Essays* (Cambridge, MA, and London: Harvard University Press, 2000).

Said, Edward, *Culture and Imperialism* (London, Chatto and Windus: 1993).

Said, Edward, *Reflections on Exile and Other Essays* (Cambridge, MA, and London: Harvard University Press, 2000).

Said, Edward, "The World, the Text, and the Critic", in Edward Said, *Power, Politics and Culture: Interviews with Edward Said*, edited by Gauri Viswanathan (London: Bloomsbury, 2004).

Said, Edward "In the Shadow of the West", in Said, *Power, Politics, and Culture, Interviews with Edward Said*, edited by Gauri Viswanathan (London: Bloomsbury, 2004).

Said, Edward, "The Arab-American War: The Politics of Information", in *The Politics of Dispossession* (London: Chatto and Windus, 1994).

Sands, Philippe, *Lawless World: America and the Making and Breaking of Global Rules* (London: Allen Lane, 2005).

Sassen, Saskia, *Globalisation and Its Discontents* (New York: The New Press, 1999).

Scarry, Elaine, *The Body in Pain: The Making and Unmaking of the World* (Oxford and New York: Oxford University Press, 1985).

Schmitt, Carl, *Political Theology*, trans. George Schwab (Cambridge, MA, and London: The MIT Press, 1985).

Schmitt, Carl, *The Concept of the Political*, trans. George Schwab (Chicago, IL: University of Chicago Press, 1996).

Shaw, Martin "Risk-transfer war, the militarism of small massacres and the historic legitimacy of war", *International Relations*, Vol. 17, No. 3 (2002).

Shaw, Martin, *War and Genocide* (Cambridge: Polity, 2003).

Shawcross, William, "It's No Time to Quit Iraq: We're Winning", *Sunday Times*, 21st May 2006.

Skinner, Quentin, *Liberty Before Liberalism* (Cambridge: Cambridge University Press, 1988).

Slater, David, *Geopolitics and the Postcolonial: Rethinking North-South Relations* (Oxford: Blackwell, 2004).

Slaughter, Anne-Marie, "International Law in a World of Liberal States", *European Journal of International Law*, Vol. 6 (1995).

Smith, Adam, *The Wealth of Nations* (New York: Modern Library, 1937).

Smith, Steve, "Singing Our World Into Existence: International Relations Theory and September 11th", *International Studies Quarterly*, Vol. 48, No. 3 (2004).

Sorel, Georges, *Reflections on Violence*, edited by Jeremy Jennings (Cambridge: Cambridge University Press, 1999).

Spivak, Gayatry Chakravorty, *A Critique of Postcolonial Reason: Toward a History of the Vanishing Present* (Cambridge, MA, and London: Harvard University Press, 1999).

Suganami, Hidemi, *On the Causes of War* (Oxford: Clarendon Press, 1996).

Sylvester, Christine, *Feminist Theory and International Relations in a Postmodern Era* (Cambridge: Cambridge University Press, 1994).

Tilly, Charles, *Coercion, Capital, and European States AD990–1990* (Oxford: Blackwell, 1990).

Tilly, Charles, "War Making and State Making as Organised Crime", in P.B. Evans, D. Rueschemeyer and T. Skocpol (eds), *Bringing the State Back In* (Cambridge: Cambridge University Press, 1985).

Toulmin, Stephen, *Cosmopolis: The Hidden Agenda of Modernity* (Chicago, Ill.: The University of Chicago Press, 1990).

Tsoukala, Anastassia, "Looking at Migrants as Enemies", in Didier Bigo and Elspeth Guild (eds), *Controlling Frontiers: Free Movement Into and Within Europe* (Ashgate Aldershot: 2005).

Vattel, E. de, *The Law of Nations* (New York: AMS Press, 1987),

Walker, Neil "Late Sovereignty in the European Union", in Neil Walker (ed.), *Sovereignty in Transition* (Oxford: Hart, 2003).

Walker, Neil "Sovereignty, International Security, and the Regulation of Armed Conflict: the Possibilities of Political Agency", in Jef Huysmans, Andrew Dobson, and Raia Prokhovnik (eds) *The Politics of Protection* (London and New York: Routledge, 2006).

Walker, R.B.J., *One World Many Worlds: Struggles for a Just World Peace* (Boulder, CO and London: Lynne Rienner and Zed, 1988).

Walker, R.B.J., *Inside/Outside: International Relations as Political Theory* (Cambridge: Cambridge University Press, 1993).

Walker, R.B.J., "International Relations and the Concept of the Political", in Ken Booth and Steve Smith (eds), *International Relations Theory Today* (Cambridge: Polity Press, 1995).

Walker, R.B.J., "Lines of Insecurity: International, Imperial, Exceptional", *Security Dialogue*, Vol. 37, No. 1 (2006).

Waltz, Kenneth, *Man, the State and War: A Theoretical Analysis* (New York: Columbia University Press, 1954).

Waltz, Kenneth, *Theory of International Politics* (Reading, MA: Addison-Wesley, 1979).

Waltz, Kenneth, "The Continuity of International Politics", Chapter 31 in Ken Booth and Tim Dunne (eds) *Worlds in Collision* (London: Palgrave, 2002).

Walzer, Michael, *Just and Unjust Wars: A Moral Argument with Historical Illustrations* (New York: Basic Books, 1977).

Weber, M., *Economy and Society*, Vol. 1 (Berkeley: University of California Press, 1978).

Wendt, Alexander, "On Constitution and Causation in International Relations", *Review of International Studies*, Vol. 24, special issue (1998), pp. 101–17.

Wheatcroft, Geoffrey, "They should come out as imperialist and proud of it", *The Guardian*, May 10, 2006.

Wheeler, Nicholas *Saving Strangers: Humanitarian Intervention in International Society* (Oxford: Oxford University Press, 2000).

Williams, Andrew, *Liberalism and War* (London and New York: Routledge, 2006).

Williams, Michael C., *The Realist Tradition and the Limits of International Relations* (Cambridge: Cambridge University Press, 2005).

Williams, Michael C. "What is the National Interest? The Neoconservative Challenge in IR Theory", *European Journal of International Relations*, Vol. 11, No. 3 (2005).

Williams, Raymond, *Culture and Materialism* (London and New York: Verso, 2005).

Zolo, Danilo, *Invoking Humanity: war, law, and global order* (London: Continuum, 2002),

Zizek, Slavoj, "A Leftist Plea for 'Eurocentrism'", *Critical Inquiry*, Summer (1998).

Index